ADVANCE PRAISE FOR 1ST AND FOREVER

"Football is all American. It always has been and always will be. Yet, nobody has their heads in the sand, starting with Bob Casciola. His lessons learned on all levels provide a gateway to lessons to be learned in the future on all levels. *1st and Forever* is both a feel good and feel enlightened read for football fans present and future."

—Chris Berman, ESPN

"The current concussion crisis that is plaguing football is a concern by all who love and appreciate the game. Concerned that the issue could prevent many young people from benefiting from the gridiron experience, Bob Casciola, one of football's greatest ambassadors, who played and served as a coach and an administrator, has skillfully penned for us *1st and Forever* answering the question as to why football must be preserved. Thanks Bob! This needed to be done."

—Vince Dooley, College Football Hall of Fame coach

"The deep-rooted affection that Bob Casciola has for the game of football resonates through the pages of *1st and Forever*. He reveals the inner satisfaction an individual can achieve while playing a sport as well as the gratification of being a part of a team that needs all performers acting in concert to accomplish success…. This book is not about blocking and tackling, it's about developing character and how a young man can grow and be a viable contributor to our society. All parents who have a son should read this book. Your understanding of the game of football and what it can do for young people will give you insights worthy of a deeper dialogue with your family."

—Bill Raftery, CBS Sports

"Bob Casciola's words resonate in these pages as football is under siege in this country. Great men have played this game, and if we're not careful an entire generation of greatness may never see the gridiron. Understanding how to protect the game but also grow the game is critical and his genuine approach here is heartwarming and effective."

—**Tim Brando,** Fox Sports

"Football could have no more authentic voice than Bob Casciola. "Coach Cas" has devoted his life to the game he loves. Now he has written a timely and important book on why football is so central to our culture. This is an important read for those engaged in the defense of America's favorite sport!"

—**Robert L. Ehrlich,** former governor of Maryland

"*1st and Forever* is just what the doctor ordered for football. A story about winners both on the field and off, this book can make anyone fall in love with the game and make diehards love it even more. Like me, Bob Casciola has spent a lifetime around the gridiron and no one is more qualified to paint a picture that casts football in the proper light to counter the shadows that have fallen across the hash marks. Sterling in its approach, convincing in its arguments, and timely in its message, *1st and Forever* etches a portrait of a game that has its best days still ahead of it."

—**Grant Teaff,** College Football Hall of Fame Coach and Executive Director Emeritus of the American Football Coaches Association

"Bob Casciola has captured football at its very core, what always has and continues to make this the most popular sport in America. I played the game, my brother played the game, and now both my sons play the game. So I've gotten to see the game through their eyes as well and I'm seeing the same thing, the same benefits and positive experiences, that I saw through my own. And, in that respect, what amazes me the most about football is the strategy of the game changes, the pace of the game changes, the Xs and Os of the game changes, but the experience of football never changes. What my sons are getting from the game is the same thing I got from it and, more than anything else, *1st and Forever* wondrously captures that spirit."

—**George Pyne,** former president of IMG and NASCAR

"Football teaches those involved life skills, the importance of hard work, and provides opportunities for the future. It unites people, teams, families, and towns. Football fans all come together from different walks of life to cheer for their team and a common purpose bigger then themselves. *1st and Forever* is about the game of football and its importance to America."

—**Jack Lengyel,** legendary coach of Marshall University & former Director of Athletics, U.S. Naval Academy

"Coach, teacher, promoter, and defender of the game of college football, Bob Casciola has a seasoned and wizened view of the game with which he has had a lifetime affiliation. He loves football and has seen countless kids benefit from the college game. He has a salient message that puts in measured perspective why we should all redouble our efforts to preserve and protect the game we love. Listen up."

—**Loran Smith,** University of Georgia Athletic Association

"Bob Casciola and Jon Land have done an exceptional job of portraying the many contributions that the game of football has made and will continue to make for the athletes who participate in the game. Bob's many experiences, insights, and profound successes throughout his career should bring encouragement and excitement to one and all who question the value and success of the sport on an individual level. This book is not only a tribute to a great sport but to all those whose lives have been touched by their own experiences. *1st and Forever* is a truly great read about football at its best!"

—**Larry Kentera,** ASU defensive coordinator 1967–79 and former head coach of Northern Arizona University

MAKING THE CASE FOR
THE FUTURE OF FOOTBALL

1ST
AND
FOREVER

FOREWORD BY ARCHIE MANNING | AFTERWORD BY BOBBY BOWDEN

BOB CASCIOLA WITH JON LAND

Post Hill
PRESS

A POST HILL PRESS BOOK
ISBN: 978-1-68261-538-6
ISBN (eBook): 978-1-68261-539-3

1st and Forever:
Making the Case for the Future of Football
© 2018 by Bob Casciola with Jon Land
All Rights Reserved

Cover art by Christian Bentulan

Post Hill Press
New York • Nashville
posthillpress.com

Published in the United States of America

FOR THE LOVE OF THE GAME

"The thing about football—
the important thing about football—
is that it is not just about football."

—Terry Pratchett,
#1 New York Times *bestselling author*

CONTENTS

FOREWORD

BY ARCHIE MANNING

"The Gold Medal is the highest and most prestigious award bestowed by the National Football Foundation. The award has been claimed by seven U.S. presidents, four U.S. generals, John Wayne, Jackie Robinson, John Glenn, and twenty-eight corporate CEOs. It has come to symbolize the game's unique ability to build leadership and instill the will to compete in America's young people which is critical to the future of our nation."

—Mike Tirico, *prior to the introduction of Archie Manning as the 2016 recipient of the National Football Foundation Gold Medal Award*

I cannot adequately express my appreciation to the National Football Foundation for this honor, and I'm not just talking about tonight. I'm talking about the opportunity you've given me to contribute to the development of the sport that has become a part of the fabric of my life, the legacy of our family, and untold others across the nation and increasingly around the globe.

When I think about all the things about football that I appreciate, it's the cherished friendships that top the list. More than gold or silver, football by any measure has enriched my life. It has truly been an honor to be part of this game. For all these years, I've lived by priorities that have also guided our household: faith, family, and football—in that order. Football is a game and despite what others say, it's not even an approximation of war. In our home, discussion of the game is incomplete without family. Obviously, that includes the efforts of our sons, and this year our oldest son Cooper's sixth grader, named Arch, will strap on a helmet and pads for the first time.

But when there's no DNA connection, no common ancestry, a football family is still made up of those people in your life who want you in theirs. Think of the offensive linemen who stand between the quarterback and being pounded to the turf, the trainer who ices a player down and wraps him up when all else seems to be falling apart. Think of the coaches, those dedicated, often underappreciated men, mostly guys who don't coach for money; they do it for the love of developing young boys into men. Often that high school coach has a bigger impact on a young man's life than anyone else in their lives. And the picture of family and football has to include a mother. Preparing a meal for her son before going out to play. I see her doling out sympathy after a defeat as naturally as a celebration hug. I see a snapshot of a jersey-wearing dad comforting a disappointed young man after missing a tackle, throwing an interception, or fumbling. I can hear the band, I can feel the rhythm of the cheerleaders' chants. I smile at booster club pizza parties and Gatorade victory baths.

You see, I grew up in a small town eighty miles from Oxford, Mississippi. I'd stroll down the street each autumn day catching leaves as they dropped from trees, imagining I was catching a football instead. I had no way to attend games, but I memorized the Ole Miss program, knowing every name, number, position, and hometown by heart. And Saturdays the radio immortalized the fortunes of my heroes like Jake Gibbs, Charlie Flowers, and others. Thousands of Mississippi kids dreamed of playing quarterback for Ole Miss and the legendary Johnny Vaught. And when all is said and done, my greatest thrill and honor in football was to be an Ole Miss quarterback.

Faith. Yes, in this sport we have to have faith. Whether on the field or off, we tackle and learn to overcome obstacles with faith. Often times, our faith is our only avenue to a sense of peace. It defines how we come to believe in each and every member of the team, the people who have our backs and do their part to move the chains and light up the scoreboard. Football is a great game. Yes, people get hurt, and it clearly challenges one's physical and mental courage. But in the process, it builds something that at every level teeters on the remarkable. It can be found in the determination of a third-string tackle aching for that chance, or kids choosing up on the playground or in a neighbor's backyard.

I understand that everything evolves, even our game. And like the changing seasons, everything goes in cycles, including how young people celebrate, how they want to dress different, be different. But it's still a game of blocking, tackling, competing, and getting up after you've fallen down and doing it all over again. That's called resilience. And no one can question the value of resilience in the ever-changing world around us. I'm a bit old-fashioned, but that's okay. I admire when opponents show respect for each other, including that well-deserved postgame handshake.

I've been chairman of the National Football Foundation for the past nine years. At times, I've been disheartened listening to the squawk of dissent and a growing chorus of harsh critics. I've been challenged, along with my counterparts, to help broker new bridges of understanding to grow the sport, bolster the disenchanted, and apply salve to the sport's bruised reputation. But I've also been encouraged by the monumental strides we've made to make this a safer game.

I can't say it any more clearly than this: football matters. Sometimes we apply the word "pressure" to football. I get it. Last-second decisions have to be made as 300-pound linemen begin their charge, refs stand whistle in mouth, TV cameras zoom in for millions of fans who expect each move as the clock ticks down. However, it didn't take much each week for me to remind my sons, and now my grandson, to focus on the fun. Celebrate the joy of playing, the camaraderie of team, knowing that every effort and everyone on that team matters. Now, at the end of the season, you hug your teammates and coaches goodbye and even put miles between you, but they're never far from your mind, always in your heart, and forever a connection to home.

So whether you stand on the sidelines, cheer from the stands, interact on a smartphone, or gather round the television for the national championship, football is America's game. It's up to us to be realistic, but by no means timid, as we imagine and build its future.

—From Archie Manning's acceptance speech upon receiving the National Football Foundation's Gold Medal Award at the Waldorf Astoria on December 6, 2016.

INTRODUCTION:

THE GOOD IN THE GAME

My lifelong love affair with the game of football began thanks to a combination of a bicycle and a radio. I must've been eight or nine years old, maybe even younger. I was riding a bike around the sidewalk in front of my house. It was right after the end of World War II, and the radio was blaring from the front porch while I made tracks over the pavement. My four brothers were listening to a football game with their friends, hooting and hollering as if they were in the stands. All of them were older than me, the nearest in age, Al, still eleven years my senior, so I was used to being solitary. Then again, I really wasn't alone, because there was the sound of the radio to keep me company.

I grew up in New Hyde Park on Long Island in New York. A working-class neighborhood where basketball hoops dotted the driveways and neighbors called each other by their first names, always ready with a smile or a helping hand. Back then, Notre Dame was the only college football team to have its games broadcast by a national radio network; in this case Mutual Radio, which meant the school's games could be heard all over the country. And as I was pedaling about, mostly in circles, I heard the play-by-play man blare the name of Notre Dame's famed quarterback, Angelo Bertelli, as he raced into the end zone for a touchdown.

Angelo Bertelli?

I didn't know anything about football in those days. But I was old enough to recognize an Italian name when I heard it, and that was enough to make me stop pedaling about and listen, enraptured and close enough to the radio to hear the occasional crackle of static. I'd found a hero in a fellow Italian whose name could be heard from coast to coast, thanks to the fact that he was a football player.

And if he could be a football player, I knew I could be a football player. I started out by playing catch and running routes with my brothers, especially Al. That prepared me for sandlot-style football, since we didn't have anything like Pop Warner in those days. I attended a Catholic grade school at the time, a pretty big kid for my age, though chubby. Every Saturday all the kids would gather at, ironically enough, Notre Dame Church because there was a field behind it that was perfect for football. And every Saturday the kids from my school would play the kids from the public school, and the one thing both teams had in common was that everybody wanted to play quarterback, just like Angelo Bertelli. On those Saturdays, playing in an *ad hoc* league that was anything but organized, I fell in love up close with the game I'd first fallen in love with through the radio.

Of course, back then I never imagined I'd be sharing my experiences with you in order to make a case for the future of football, why the sport matters now as much as it ever did, and why it needs to be saved.

Look, the game is in trouble. There's a lot of pressure extending all the way down to youth football, and a lot of parents don't want their kids to get involved in the sport. They see the risk of injury, especially concussions, to be too great. Who can blame them? There's been so much negative publicity about the long and even short-term effects of playing the game that kids are either not picking up a helmet or turning theirs in.

"Will marketers continue to want their brands associated with the game?" Marian Salzman wrote in the *Huffington Post* in March of 2015. "For now, many do—those audience numbers are hard to ignore—but a strong backlash is definitely brewing. To have a future, football will have to change. The game isn't inherently awful (full disclosure: I loved entertaining clients at the Arizona-Nevada college football game in the fall, so I might be a hypocrite as well as a skeptic). And I know that there are far more good people involved with the sport than there are bad. But American football needs a reinvention—of its brand, its transparency, and its standards for behavior and, most of all, safety."

And Terry O'Neill, founder and CEO of Practice Like Pros, a nonprofit for player safety that opposes full-contact practices during the off-season or at any time before high school, told *U.S. News and World Report* almost a year later to the day that, "if the [National Football] league stands behind this statement—understanding the correlation that's been established between head trauma and CTE, which is indisputable at this point—then there's only two conclusions: contact youth football must stop immediately and high school football has to cut off as much full contact as we can."

That article was entitled "Does Football Have a Future?"

I say it most definitely does, even though it has obstacles to overcome, confronting the sport with its greatest challenge since President Teddy Roosevelt threatened to ban football in the early 1900s unless changes were made.

"An intercollegiate conference, which would become the forerunner of the NCAA, approved radical rule changes for the 1906 season," the History Channel has reported on the subject. "They legalized the forward pass, abolished the dangerous mass formations, created a neutral zone between offense and defense, and doubled the first-down distance to ten yards, to be gained in three downs. The rule changes didn't eliminate football's dangers, but fatalities declined—to eleven per year in both 1906 and 1907—while injuries fell sharply. A spike in fatalities in 1909 led to another round of reforms that further eased restrictions on the forward pass and formed the foundation of the modern sport."

In other words, we've been here before. And then, just as now, steps were taken to preserve both the integrity and the spirit of the game. Football not only survived, it prospered from the changes basically forced upon it in 1906, emerging ultimately stronger than ever.

It has been said, in fact, that football is a measure of how far we have come as a country. At every level of competition, you see young men of varying backgrounds working together as a team, sharing a determination towards reaching a common goal. And in the process of reaching that goal having success, knowing failure, but most importantly having the opportunity to positively contribute.

We need to promote what I call "the good in the game," because there's so much of it; too much to squander and rob people of the experience that has helped build so many lives and usher so many young people on to great futures and careers. I'm not saying that everyone should play the game, but I feel they should have the opportunity, the chance, to do so.

I learned about all "the good in the game" because I was lucky enough to come into contact with the likes of men like Dutch Hafner, Bruce Gehrke, and Tom Cahill, along with Hall of Fame Princeton coaches Charlie Caldwell, Dick Colman, Dartmouth's Bob Blackman, and Connecticut's

John Toner, who became far more than just coaches to me in my most formative years. They were men who understood that playing football wasn't about the next four years of your life, it was about the next forty plus.

And that's why I decided to write this book, to promote all the good in this great game so other kids are given the same opportunities that I was. All sports can provide comparably great experiences, but football is different because there are so many people involved by nature. A college football team might boast a hundred players or more today, almost 10 times the size of a basketball squad or five times that of a soccer team. The result is exposure to more peers, more adults in the form of alums, fans, and coaches, and more opportunities to form the kind of life-changing experiences this book details as an example, again, of all the good that can come out of the game.

"The game has a wake-up effect," a terrific writer named Mark Edmundson chronicles of his experience playing football in his 2014 book *Why Football Matters*. "You find out fast that no matter who you are, you get rewarded for hard work.... When a boy is trying to grow up, football can be a force of education that works when no others can. The boy will listen to his coach and his teammates when he won't listen to anyone else. What he'll develop is what I began to develop on the rock-hard football practice field behind the stands at Hormel Stadium. He'll start to have an identity. He'll start to have *character*."

I think back to all the kids I recruited in Pennsylvania during my twenty plus years coaching, many of whose dads were coal miners and steel workers, and would be looking at a career in those mines or mills, too, if not for football. Some of them who you will meet in these pages have gone on to truly great things. I think back to the immigrants I coached for whom football became the essence of America, the very nature of the American Dream as their playing experience spring-boarded them to opportunities that never would've been there otherwise. You're going to get to know some of them in these pages, too. And, I suspect, their stories will leave quite an impression on you, in large part because of the impression football made on them.

In these pages, you're going to meet a cross section of people who run the gamut of the American tapestry itself, coming to exemplify what's best not just about the game, but also the country.

- **Tom Cahill**, the old-school coach who took over the storied Army program and ended up paving the way for a future two-time Super Bowl–winning coach's career.

- **Štas Maliszewski**, a Polish refugee who escaped Soviet domination to become one of the great defensive players in collegiate football.

- **Cosmo Iacavazzi**, who blazed a path from the coal mines of eastern Pennsylvania to become a record-setting College Football Hall of Fame running back.

- **Charlie and Pete Gogolak**, Hungarian refugees who ended up changing the game of football forever only because their upstate New York high school didn't have a soccer program.

- **Grant Teaff**, the coach of coaches who took the American Football Coaches Association to a whole new level toward the betterment of the game.

- **Jack Lengyel**, who took over the Marshall football program in the wake of a devastating tragedy and restored hope to an entire school, town, and nation.

- **Frank Cignetti**, an offensive genius whose lifetime in the game brought him home again, where he earned his ticket to the Hall of Fame.

- **Bob Hall**, who recovered from a near-crippling injury while playing for Brown University to be drafted by the Minnesota Vikings.

- **Paul Savidge**, a player nearly paralyzed on the football field whose injury inspired a long and distinguished career in medicine.

- **Murry Bowden**, a Texas cowboy who rode the ranges of Dartmouth College to football greatness, a Hall of Famer who later lent his skills to the construction of the College Football Hall of Fame in Atlanta.

- **Steve Jordan**, an All-American and six-time NFL All-Pro tight end who went on to parlay his greatest feats on the football field to even greater things off it.

- **Reggie Williams**, the linebacker many consider to be the finest in the storied history of the Cincinnati Bengals who was a finalist for the job of NFL commissioner after nearly losing his leg.

- **Mark Whipple**, a football lifer who has succeeded at every level, including a Super Bowl victory with the Pittsburgh Steelers, where he coached Ben Roethlisberger.

- **Don McPherson**, the legendary Hall of Fame Syracuse quarter-back who has turned his passions to waging a war on violence against women.

- **Bob Ehrlich**, who blazed a trail from the football fields of Gilman School and Princeton University to the Maryland governorship.

- **Chad Hennings**, who won three Super Bowls over his nine years with the Dallas Cowboys, after serving as a U.S. Air Force fighter pilot during Operation Desert Storm.

- **Dr. Tom Catena**, who went from the trenches playing for Brown University to being the only doctor for 400 square miles, and over 100,000 people, in the Sudan.

- **Dr. Augustus White**, a groundbreaking physician, "the Jackie Robin-son of orthopedics," who overcame the racism of the deep South to become a football player, war hero, and orthopedist of historic renown.

- **Danny Wuerffel**, a Heisman Trophy–winning quarterback who has given back far more than he ever took from the game.

- **Buff Donelli**, a coach who helped turn veterans of World War II into teachers and coaches after they played for him at Boston University.

- **William Campbell**, "the coach of Silicon Valley," for whom the Campbell Trophy is named in recognition of the example he set both on the field and off.

- **Steve Hatchell**, the president of the National Football Foundation who keeps the torch of the greatness that is football burning.

Their stories have one thing in common, the italicized word from Mark Edmundson's quote above: character. These are people of exceptional character who became who they are in large part because of their experience in and exposure to the game. They come from different backgrounds, different worlds, even different countries; in that sense encompassing what our country itself is all about. Brought together in life and in these pages thanks, again, to the game to which they have given as much as they received. They serve as shining examples of all that is good, not just in football but also America.

It's a lot more than wins and losses, in other words. It's the experience of the game itself that's just too important to shun or shed aside. Yes, we have work to do, issues we need to work on, and we'll address those in these pages, too.

"Nearly every man who has played ball and grown from it," Mark Edmundson wrote in his concluding chapter of *Why Football Matters*, "has, I'm sure, drawn on his former football-playing strength at one time or another. You got fired, you got divorced. Your child got sick and you have to stop your life as it is and begin living for the child. And when it happens (and it happens to almost everyone), you have no idea where you'll find the strength you need. You go home and you just look into your hands and you call on God or Jesus or your patron saint. And maybe that helps. But in my experience, nothing helps you to fight a battle like having fought one before and come out OK. Bad luck befalls you and you never know how you're going to deal with it, because it seems like nothing comparable has occurred before. But then you think back and you hear the old coaches and you remember what you achieved on the football field that maybe by rights you shouldn't have been on. Earlier you didn't know where you were going to get the strength, but now—now maybe you do."

So I'm writing this book to give back to football, because football has given so much to me. I've had no greater pleasure in my life than watching my grandson Will Twyman (pictured with me on the opening page of this chapter) play the game, earning first-team All-Ivy League, All-New England linebacker honors for Brown University both his junior and senior years. I want other grandfathers and grandsons to get that same opportunity, to experience not four years of a sport's effects, but forty plus instead. Because as far as football is concerned, we're at a kind of metaphorical first down in a game that deserves to last forever.

* * *

Remember how this introduction started with me riding around on my bicycle and hearing the name Angelo Bertelli over the Mutual Radio broadcast of Notre Dame football? When I got to Princeton to play football, our games were broadcast on radio out of Newark, New Jersey. One day, the new color man came down to the field to introduce himself to the players. I knew something was familiar about him even before he stuck out his hand and said, "Angelo Bertelli, nice to meet you."

The station had hired him to do the "color" for our games.

PART ONE:

THE CIRCLE OF FOOTBALL

"I obviously take a lot of pride in what I do on the football field, because that has the ability to influence a lot of people. That puts smiles on people's faces. That gives people a pep in their step on Monday morning when they go back to work."

—**Drew Brees,** *National Football Foundation Scholar Athlete, 2000*

CHAPTER 1

MY LIFE IN THE GAME—
"THIS KID HAS GOT SOME POSSIBILITIES"

I'd learn later that Angelo Bertelli had been recruited out of Springfield, Massachusetts. He'd become the first Notre Dame player to ever win the Heisman Trophy, even though Bertelli's career was interrupted by a stint in the Marine Corps, where he distinguished himself as much as he did on the gridiron.

When Bertelli entered Notre Dame in 1940, he was six feet, one inch tall and 173 pounds, a skinny but highly regarded tailback in the single-wing formation used by most college teams. When Coach Elmer Layden left to become commissioner of the National Football League, Notre Dame appointed Frank Leahy to replace him and Leahy immediately noticed Bertelli's passing talents, something he'd missed in his original scouting assessment when he'd been head coach at Boston College. As a sophomore, Bertelli, still a single-wing tailback, led the nation with a 56.9 percent passing average, completing seventy of 123 attempts.

In 1942, Leahy switched to a modified T formation, in which Bertelli would play under the center and take every snap. As he told his budding star, "Bert, you're the finest passer and the worst runner I've ever coached."

That summer, preparing for his new role, Bertelli said he took "a thousand snaps...maybe a million." Bertelli and the T formation were an immediate success. He passed for 1,039 yards and ten touchdowns. Celebrated sportswriter Grantland Rice referenced Bertelli as "the T formation magician."

During his senior year in 1943, the Marine Corps activated Bertelli after six games of Notre Dame's 10-game season. In the six games Bertelli started in, he threw 36 passes, completing 25 with 10 touchdowns. Bertelli's six-game 1943 performance was enough to win the Heisman Trophy, earning 648 votes. During Bertelli's three seasons, Notre Dame lost only three games. In 1943, Notre Dame won by a score of 43–5 on average. Bertelli's collegiate career earned him multiple awards. He was named to the 1942 and 1943 All-American teams. In the Heisman voting for America's outstanding college football player, Bertelli finished second in 1941 and sixth in 1942 before capturing the trophy in 1943. Though on active duty with the Marine Corps, the Boston Yanks selected Bertelli as their number one draft choice in 1944. Bertelli would eventually be inducted into the College Football Hall of Fame in 1972.

* * *

Like Angelo Bertelli, all four of my older brothers served in World War II. While I was chugging along through grade school, my brother Al was a tanker who landed at Normandy. Proceeding on with the Eighth Army, he was knocked out of three tanks and was awarded the Purple Heart. Upon returning, he married a gal from Mineola, New York, and decided I was going to be the first member of the family to go to college. To give me the best shot at that, he wanted me to go to high school in Mineola instead of the local high school. We used the home address of his wife's mother so I could enroll there in what was the closest thing I ever committed to a National Collegiate Athletic Association (NCAA) rules violation.

Mineola High was a fine school academically, but it also introduced me to organized football—a lot different, obviously, than the sandlot ball I was used to. I made the freshmen/junior varsity team, an accomplishment in itself. I didn't play much, but Jim Brown, the assistant who coached the JV, saw enough to see something in me.

"This kid has got some possibilities," he told the school's head coach and athletic director, Ken "Dutch" Hafner. "Give him a chance."

Hafner was a Springfield College graduate, going to school not far from where Angelo Bertelli had grown up. He listened to Coach Brown and put me in the starting lineup my sophomore year, where I remained for the next three seasons, never missing a game. During my senior season, he called me into his office and, in his gruff voice that sounded as if his words were strained through gravel, he asked me a question.

"How'd you like to go to Princeton?"

Hafner was born and raised in Lawrenceville, New Jersey, and had grown up in the shadows of Princeton University—just a few miles away. He'd fixated on finding a player who was right for the school through his entire coaching career up until that point, and he believed he'd finally found one in me. I was a good enough student and, he believed, a good enough football player for the school.

See, I was very lucky to have people like Dutch Hafner around me who were more than coaches, including Hafner's top assistant, Bruce Gehrke, a fellow Long Island guy from Floral Park. He'd been the last three-sport varsity athlete at Columbia and played in the famous game when Columbia upset Army in 1947. He was drafted by and played in the NFL for the New York Giants for a year. Eventually, Gehrke would go on to succeed Hafner as head coach. And in my time at Mineola High he had a great influence on me, not only on the field but also in the classroom.

I wasn't the only player Hafner, Gehrke, and the entire staff took a real interest in, just the only one earmarked for Princeton. And the idea of being the first in my family to not only attend college, but a college on that level, was magical in the same way hearing Angelo Bertelli's name over Mutual Radio had been, and just as impactful on my life.

Princeton saw the same qualities and potential in me that Coach Hafner had. But I was only seventeen years old and the school felt that perhaps I wasn't quite ready for either the academic or football rigors. So the Princeton coaches asked me if I'd consider going to prep school to hone my skills both in the classroom and on the field. So here I was, the first kid in my family to go to college, being asked to consider staying in high school an extra year.

What sealed the deal for me was the opportunity to play at not just any prep school, but the Manlius School, then a famed feeder to West Point with a great football program under the leadership of an ex-army officer from the Syracuse area named Tom Cahill. My brother drove me up there to visit the school, where I met the headmaster, athletic director, and Coach Cahill himself. I took an entrance exam and 10 minutes later the headmaster came out of his office after reviewing the test.

"You did very well," he told me, "and we're prepared to offer you a full scholarship."

I reported early to Manlius to take part in preseason football practice. There were 29 of us in all, many there in the hope of using Manlius as a springboard to a college football career. But early on I wasn't sure how long I'd be able to last. We were thrown to the lions in the form of two-a-day practices in the blistering heat, and after about the third day, I called home and spoke to my mother following the morning practice.

"Mom," I said, choking back tears, "there's no way I can make this team. They're so good. I have to come home."

"Bobby," she said, "you have to stay. You can't come home. You have to stay. So go back there and do better. You can!"

So back to practice I went and, sure enough, things started to fall in line, especially after the grueling two-a-day practices finally ended and we got into more football. All of us would be playing both ways, on offense as well as defense. But as a lineman on both sides of the ball, it was easy to get beat up each and every day.

Our entire schedule, all seven games, was primarily against college freshman teams. Stiff competition, to say the least, that we'd be hard-pressed to match. But we beat every team we played, some of them handily. Our record was 6-0 when the final game of our season arrived.

Against the plebes of West Point, Army's freshman team. A tall order, to say the least!

Our game was scheduled for Michie Stadium, cavernous and massive by any estimation, but especially to us Manlius kids. There was a road beyond the grandstand on our side of the field and a reservoir in view just beyond that. As we were warming up, the plebes made their dramatic entrance, over seventy of them, running single file down the Army sideline with a thunderous roar that sounded like a stampede, headed for the opposite end zone. An impressive sight for sure, but also an intimidating one.

Suddenly we all heard Coach Cahill's booming voice. "Look at the reservoir!" he shouted at us. "Look at the reservoir!"

He didn't want us any more intimidated than we already were by the spectacle of the Cadets' powerful appearance.

Minutes later, we gathered in an utterly silent locker room normally used by opponents of Army's nationally-ranked varsity team, at which point Coach Cahill uttered his famous pregame remarks.

"They got one thing in mind," he started, referring to the Army plebes we were about to take on. "They're primed and cocked to knock your jocks off. Gentlemen, the hay is in the barn. Let's go get 'em!"

So twenty-nine kids ran onto the field at Michie Stadium to take on the mighty Cadets. I can't tell you exactly what Coach Cahill meant by his oft-repeated "the hay is in the barn" phrase, but it became part of his legendary coaching career, adding to the mystique surrounding him that remains to this day. As for that day, we dominated the Army plebes and beat them 14–0, solidifying our undefeated season that ranked us as the best team in the Manlius School's storied history and sending me happily on my way to Princeton the following fall.

1953 UNDEFEATED MANLIUS SCHOOL FOOTBALL TEAM

John Andrusko
Joe Bonifacio
Bob Casciola
Paul Cambo
Dick Chester
Don Chirlin

Bill Creighton
Bruce Church
Don Clark
Jim Diblee
Bob Garn
Gene Grabosky
Steve Klein
Mo Knudsen
John Lawrence
Bob Misere
Neil McEachren
Ray Morey
Hal Northrup
Al O'Neil
Fred Pordum
Ralph Redling
Bob Renzi
Steven Robinson
Ed Ryan
Paul Stoecker
Bob Tallgren
Al Wertheimer
Dave Wheeler

* * *

I went straight from the Princeton playing field at Palmer Stadium to the sidelines in 1958. Dick Colman had been appointed Princeton's interim head coach my senior year in 1957 after Charlie Caldwell took sick with what turned out to be stomach cancer. Replacing a Hall of Fame head coach who'd been named national Coach of the Year in 1951, when Princeton was ranked sixth in the nation, was no easy chore, but Colman handled it seamlessly and with the kind of class that typified his character. We went up to play Brown in Providence, Rhode Island, when he called us all together to tell us that Charlie had passed away. After the season, Colman had the "interim" removed from his title and was named head coach, proceeding by necessity to move around several coaches on the staff. I was going into the army in January of 1959 the following year, so Colman said, "Why don't you coach for me in the fall before you go in?"

So my coaching career wasn't something I ever planned on; as a matter of fact, I'd been offered a job with a major bank in New York City. It just sort of happened, as a matter of convenience, but being back on the football field for the 1958 Princeton football season convinced me I never wanted to leave it. After I got out of the army, I called Coach Colman to see if my old job was still available and it was. He welcomed me back and, after three years coaching the freshmen, I moved up to the varsity level, where I coached the linebackers and defensive ends from 1961 through 1965.

But I was already starting to get antsy. While I was coming to the conclusion that being a football coach was what I wanted to do, I also realized I wouldn't be able to advance those ambitions coaching with a team that still relied on the old single-wing. I needed to learn, to master, the T formation to have a real opportunity to advance. I got the opportunity to do just that when the legendary Bob Blackman at Dartmouth called me regarding a spot that had opened up on his staff—coaching defensive ends and linebackers. Dartmouth had perfected the T under Blackman, who himself was a master of multiple formations that enabled him to win several Ivy League titles, including 1966, my first year there.

Three years later, I got a call from John Toner, then head coach for the University of Connecticut Huskies, who asked me to make the drive down to Storrs to meet with him. Normally, it's Dartmouth that's associated with snow, but I ended up stuck for two days when a blizzard struck Connecticut, giving me even more time to talk with John about what was to become my next move up the coaching ladder.

"Bob, they're going to make me the athletic director here," he told me. "I can't do that and coach football. So if you're willing to make the move, I'll put you in charge of the defense and make you head coach within a year."

I spent four years at Connecticut, highlighted by winning a Yankee Conference title in 1971. Coaching at the University of Connecticut, a state university, was a unique and rewarding experience—especially working with kids from the inner city. Led by a quality administrator and coach in Toner, our staff was composed of people with varying football backgrounds from high school experiences all the way to the college level. Men like Nick

Nicolau, Joe Giannelli, Bob Weiss, "Red" Kelin, Len Rivers, Tom Kopp, Andy Baylock, Tom Ryan, Joe Pascale, Roy Lawrence, Gary Blackney, and a young Chris Palmer, who went on to a successful career coaching in the NFL. All with personalities and talents that made them something special.

I might have stayed at Connecticut longer if the head coaching job hadn't opened up at Princeton after Dick Colman retired and his successor, Jake McCandless, stepped down. So I went home again in 1973, but I guess Thomas Wolfe was right in this case, since going home proved challenging at best. The school had let the program go a bit, at the same time Harvard, Yale, Penn, Dartmouth, and Brown had improved their teams considerably—Brown especially, because of a great friend of mine, John Anderson, with whom I'd run a football camp on Lake Winnipesaukee in New Hampshire for several years. We just couldn't compete the way we used to or needed to. In the wake of five less than stellar seasons, Princeton decided to move in a different direction. I got out of coaching and went into banking and investments with the First National State Bank, the largest bank in New Jersey. I did well and rose to become a senior vice president.

That's when I got a call from the owners of the New Jersey Nets, five guys who were all business. They'd offered my good friend Dave Gavitt, head basketball coach of the Providence Friars (who he'd taken to the Final Four in 1973 before going on to establish the Big East), the job of executive vice president and chief operating officer.

"Dave turned us down," one of the owners said, "so we asked him if he could recommend someone else. He told us he knew this guy, not a basketball guy, but give him two years, Dave said, and he'll know more than anybody."

I took the job in 1987 and ran the Nets for five years, when I got a call from the head of the National Football Foundation and College Football Hall of Fame, Bill Pearce.

"We're looking for a new executive director," Bill said. "You've been recommended to us, and we'd like very much to talk with you."

"Who recommended me?" I asked him.

"Jake Crouthamel."

Jake was a great player at Dartmouth who coached with me when I was in Hanover and took over as head coach after Bob Blackman left for Illinois. He then went on to be athletic director at Syracuse, rising to become one of the top ADs in the country.

The National Football Foundation offered me the job to run the entire operation, and I accepted the opportunity to go back to football, my true love. Years later, I attended a dinner in Providence, Rhode Island, where Dave Gavitt was being honored, and he couldn't resist turning the screws a bit.

"Bob, will you stand up?" he called to me when his time came to speak. "Some of you may know Bob Casciola. I want to introduce him tonight because for twenty-five years I listened to his Princeton bull, and it took two Dartmouth guys to get him his last two jobs."

I stayed at the National Football Foundation for fourteen years, during which time we moved the College Hall of Fame from its original location in Kings Mill, Ohio to South Bend, Indiana, home of Notre Dame, where the great Angelo Bertelli had stoked my interest in the game all those years before. What a wonderful opportunity it was for me to join an organization that is looked upon by all of football as the model of all that is "good" about the game.

An organization that today, under the leadership of its chairman, Archie Manning, and its president, Steve Hatchell, continues to grow the game with its 120 plus chapters across the country and its newly relocated and spectacular College Football Hall of Fame in Atlanta.

* * *

Over the years, by the way, I ended up becoming great friends with Angelo Bertelli of all people, and I remember this legendary Heisman Trophy winner telling me once, "Thank goodness Frank Leahy came along with the T formation. I could throw the damn ball, but I couldn't run a lick."

CHAPTER 2

TOM CAHILL— "MEN, THE HAY IS IN THE BARN"

I call the sport's ability to make a profound impact on the lives of those involved in it the "Circle of Football," kind of a play on the whole Circle of Life notion. Who, after all, could possibly have thought that I'd ever have the opportunity to befriend the man attached to the name that spurred my love for the game?

You just can't make stuff like that up.

Nor could you make up the career of Tom Cahill, which also encapsulates so much of the best of football. A few years after he led the team I played on at the Manlius School to an undefeated season, the personable Cahill left the school to take over as head coach of River Dell High

School in New Jersey, an already solid program he would eventually turn even more successful. For the 1958 season, Cahill elevated a player with a lineman's build and toughness to the position of quarterback. He was Cahill's kind of kid, full of fire and raw talent. Culled from a working-class background just as his coach had been and a rugged kid Cahill could relate to. Ever the disciplinarian, Cahill would often bristle at his quarterback's antics, but he was a winner and supremely coachable.

That quarterback's name was Bill Parcells.

In the superb biography *Parcells: A Football Life*, the book's coauthor, Nunyo Demasio, recounts an example of Tom Cahill's relationship with his young quarterback, an ironic precursor to Parcells' own Hall of Fame coaching career:

> As usual, Coach Cahill sent in the offensive play from the sideline. But this time, after assessing the defense's formation on third-and-goal, Bill ignored the coach's orders. His quarterback audible was executed poorly and River Dell failed to score. When Bill returned to the sideline, the coach beelined over to his quarterback. Aware of Bill's parents seated right behind the Golden Hawks' bench, Cahill wrapped his right arm around Bill's shoulders and redirected him so that the two faced the field.
>
> "Bill, the next time you make a call like that, your fat ass is going to be on the bench for the rest of your career, which fortunately isn't too much longer."
>
> "But, Coach, I saw something in the defense."
>
> Cahill snapped, "Dammit. When I tell you to run a play, you run it."

Several years later in 1966, Tom Cahill was named head coach of Army when the military academy's program was one of the nation's best. Desperately short of assistants, Cahill fielded any and all names to fill his staff, one of which, somewhat incredibly, was none other than Bill Parcells. Cahill was aware that the future legend had recently been fired from his job as defensive line coach at Wichita.

As told in *Parcells: A Football Life*:

> On hearing Parcells' name, Cahill reacted with silence. He knew firsthand that Parcells had been one of the best and smartest athletes in Bergen County, and his brother, Don, had graduated from West Point in 1965 after three seasons playing football for the Black Knights. But Cahill was also familiar with Parcells's hyper personality. The coach had flashbacks of the hotheaded forward who kicked basketballs when things didn't go his way, and the cocksure quarterback who occasionally ignored sideline instructions.
>
> After the brief pause, Cahill said, "Bill Parcells? Gee, I don't know. Why do you think I should hire him, Mickey?" Corcoran [who was then on Cahill's Army staff] responded incredulously to his fellow Irishman. "Why? Do you have to ask, Tom? Billy's one of us! He's a Jersey guy!"
>
> Cahill wasn't convinced, so he mulled things over for a few days while Corcoran continued to prod. Finally, he agreed to take a chance on his former quarterback, naming Parcells Army's new defensive line coach.

The rest, of course, is history. Parcells ended up going on to become head coach of Air Force and then, ultimately, to coach the New York Giants to two Super Bowl victories, earning his place in the NFL's Hall of Fame. But had Tom Cahill, he of the famed quote, "Men, the hay is in the barn," not offered Parcells the job that jump-started his career, none of that may have happened. Parcells might well have gone on to law school and taken all his considerable talents to the courtroom instead of the football field.

The Circle of Football again.

And Parcells kept the lessons he learned from his former high school coach close in his mind and his heart. Upon taking over the beleaguered New York Jets in 1998, "To jump-start Gang Green, Parcells focused on special teams, which contained mostly inexperienced players," Nunyo Demasio writes in *Parcells: A Football Life*. "The ex-Army coach had never forgotten what he'd learned in 1967 under Tom Cahill—that 'special teams' marks the quickest way to revitalize a struggling program."

But how did a high school coach from the likes of the Manlius School and New Jersey's River Dell High School end up taking over a program as storied as Army's, a national powerhouse at the time?

Well, following Parcells' senior season, Cahill's stellar reputation as a coach and disciplinarian earned him a job on head coach Paul Dietzel's staff at Army in 1959 as coach of the plebes, the team the Manlius School had beaten 14–0 in Michie Stadium my prep year. It was a great opportunity he relished for seven years, made even greater when Dietzel, who'd been an assistant under Army's famed head coach Red Blaik, jumped ship in 1966 to South Carolina before spring practice. Blaik, then athletic director, asked Cahill to run spring practice, even as interviews for Dietzel's position were underway. When these failed to yield a worthy candidate, Cahill was given the job.

"Three days before the annual spring game, Army tried a combat boot on Cinderella Cahill and suddenly shouted, 'It fits,'" *Sports Illustrated* reported on September 11, 1967. "A stunned Cahill had the job. He and his family moved into the big, handsome house that had been built for Colonel Red Blaik during his tenure at the Point, but the Cahills did not really settle in. It was not until fall, after Army started by beating Kansas State and Holy Cross, and then upset Penn State 11–0, that Tom came home and gave his wife Bonnie the word: 'Unpack.'"

The article went on to say that "Cahill, a quietly efficient man, amply demonstrated his skill. He moved several players to new positions, put three sophomores on offense, changed from an I to a pro-type T, and had Army throwing the ball. It was quite a switch from the ultra-conservative style of the Dietzel Cadets."

Meanwhile, Cahill faced an additional challenge in his debut season as Army's coach in the form of the first black football player to ever make the squad in tight end Gary Steele. A strapping and talented player with imposing size and speed, Steele presented Tom with a formidable weapon indeed and also what in lesser hands would've been a formidable problem.

Whenever Tom Cahill talked about Gary Steele, I never heard him once mention that he was black or any of the obvious hurdles accompanying that in a racially charged 1966 America; it just wasn't an issue for him. He'd talk about Steele's skill set, his work ethic, and how much having a tight end of his talent did for the offense he'd installed. Like Vince Lombardi, Cahill could talk football forever, but race never entered the discussion. Steele remembers his old coach this way.

* * *

Gary Steele met Tom Cahill for the first time when he, like me, played for the Manlius School against West Point's plebes, then coached by Cahill.

"He came up to me after the game," Colonel Steele recalls, "and said he looked forward to seeing me. In the years I played for him, I never heard him say a single thing about race. It was a tertiary issue as far as he was concerned. For Coach Cahill, it was about who the best player at each position was, nothing more. I was going to be a starter on the plebe team. But after that I was competing against those West Point upperclassmen. I didn't start out in the number one position on the depth chart. But by the first game I was."

How Steele got to the Manlius School, and then on to West Point, from Levittown, Pennsylvania, is a story in itself. He didn't play organized football until ninth grade, but he took to the game quickly, a natural. So much so that he was heavily recruited by none other than Penn State in the person of a young assistant named Joe Paterno and, by senior year, had pretty much made up his mind to become a Nittany Lion.

"Despite growing up in a military family, he had never dreamed of the academy," the *Baltimore Sun* wrote on December 5, 2008. "He delighted in watching a television series called *The West Point Story*. But none of the cadets looked like him."

"They wanted me at Penn State and I wanted to go there," Steele adds today. "I visited campus and had a meeting with Penn State's head coach, Rip Engle. We left his office and the walls that were literally lined with framed photos of Penn State's All-Americans through the years. The final frame was filled only by a question mark. Coach Engle pointed at it and said to me, 'Son, we think that could be you.'"

Then one day at school, an announcement over the PA summoned Gary to the principal's office at Woodrow Wilson High School.

"I wasn't a troublemaker so I'm wondering what it was I did. My heart was thumping when I stepped through the door. Waiting for me was Bill Shirofsky, an Army assistant football coach, who proceeded to tell me West

Point was interested in me. But he said that I couldn't get directly in, that I needed to do a year of academic prep."

Steele spent that year at the Manlius School and, while Penn State remained on his radar, Army's overtures proved impossible to resist. And he remembers one day in particular when he knew he'd made the right decision.

"Every Saturday, before each home game, we'd have the pregame team meal and then Coach Cahill would lead us to the part of campus known as Trophy Point, which featured a large obelisk memorializing the Civil War dead from both sides who'd attended West Point. The obelisk sits right next to a tall mast topped by an American flag. Turn one way and you look back across the Plain toward the parade grounds and cadet barracks. You look the other way down a hill and there's the Hudson River running toward Newburgh. During the Revolutionary War, this was where British ships came up the Hudson and made a sharp right turn. What a beautiful combination of history and beauty. And I think one of the things coach was doing was giving us a weekly lesson or reminder about the tradition of West Point and the academy's place in history. It was impossible not to be humbled and awestruck. And that was the thing about Coach Cahill. He wasn't a haranguer or a screamer. He was always low-key. He brought us up to Trophy Point and just let us kick at the leaves and get our heads right."

Army went 23-7 during Steele's career and he produced many big moments, from a game-winning catch against highly ranked Cal his senior year to a fifty-yard game-changer against Navy when he was a junior. He was picked to play in the East-West Shrine Game, a showcase for top prospects, and drafted by the Detroit Lions, his professional career waylaid only by the need to complete his obligated service.

After his brilliant playing career at Army ended, Steele went on to coach the plebes for three and a half years before building a distinguished career while serving the country, retiring as a decorated colonel. But the game remains close in his heart and in his mind.

"We live here in Carlisle, Pennsylvania, home of Dickinson College. We live across the street from the football stadium, and when I hear the sounds of the game, I can't resist walking around the corner to pay my three bucks and sit in the stands and watch the purest game in its purest form. This is Division III football. The stands aren't packed, but there's so much excitement and enthusiasm for a team that features a quarterback who's all of five foot nine. After the game ends, players always walk across the field and track to meet their parents. They play their hearts out and then come off the field to their mom and dad. In my mind, that's football at its best. Two thousand fans, just as rabid as Ohio State fans. Here you have guys playing football the way it was drawn up. These guys aren't going to the pros. They play because they love the game and that's enough."

It's a notion Colonel Steele has lived with much of his life, since the time his brother would pedal along on his bike with him while he ran the track to get in shape to play football for Coach Lou Sorrentino at Woodrow Wilson High.

"I think the game is still a great game," the colonel, whose son works for the Baltimore Ravens and his daughter for ESPN, says today. "Done well, done right, young men, and perhaps women, can have a great experience in football. It starts in two places: with the parents and the coaches. It can't be, it shouldn't be, 'Johnny's going to make it to the NFL.' Parents have to meter their expectations. One thing I think that applies to all sports is we can't let these kids believe they're better than they really are. Set the right expectations and the chances of a positive experience are raised considerably."

Today he likens his first experience at West Point, playing for the Manlius School against the plebes, to an episode of the old television show *The West Point Story*.

"I was awestruck. I remember watching that show as a kid and thinking, 'If only I could go there...' Well, I did and, by the way, we beat the plebes that day."

In June of 2017, Colonel Steele appeared at his beloved Manlius School (now Manlius Pebble Hill after merging with the Pebble Hill School in 1970) as the commencement speaker, offering the graduates three special life lessons learned from his own experiences both on the football field and as an officer in the U.S. Army:

- You are standing on the shoulders of people who went before you.

- How you deal with your failures defines your life.

- You know the right thing to do, so pick the "harder right" rather than the "easier wrong."

The colonel is also fond of a particular portion of the West Point Cadet prayer, memorized long ago:

"*Lord, make us to choose the harder right instead of the easier wrong, and never to be content with a half-truth when the whole truth can be won.*"

And what does that mean to him?

"In everyone's life, there are going to be stormy seas, and there is going to be fog," he told Syracuse.com during his visit to the former Manlius School, where he laid the foundation for the great things in his life to come. "Over the years, those words have been a beacon to keep me from crashing into the rocks."

* * *

Tom Cahill didn't just make the most of the opportunity to coach Army; he seized it and turned the program around. He led the Black Knights to an 8-2 record his first year out of the box and was named National Coach of the Year. It was the perfect situation for him, another one of those strokes of fortune you can't make up. Sure, circumstance had created the opportunity, but Cahill's work ethic had prepared him for it. He became a national figure, pictured in highlight reels and in major newspapers across the country. A sudden celebrity who still closed every pregame speech with, "Men, the hay is in the barn."

Here's how *Sports Illustrated* characterized the stellar first two seasons under my former coach from the Manlius School on September 9, 1968:

> *Coach Tom Cahill was sitting on a table in the drab Army dressing room in Philadelphia's John F. Kennedy Stadium one afternoon early last December. His team had just lost to Navy and somber Army officers were filing by to pay their respects. Cahill, puffing leisurely on a cigarette and with a half-smile on his rugged face, hardly looked like a coach whose team had been beaten in what Army and Navy brass rank as the only game. His response to one well-meaning consoler must have shaken the granite of West Point. "It's not the end of the world," said Cahill matter-of-factly. "It's just another football game."*

Navy just another football game? It may be heresy but that's the attitude that prevails at West Point these days, and it has won Army a lot of football games in the past two years. The man responsible is, of course, Cahill, the obscure former plebe coach who in 1966 was hauled forth from a backroom and brought, blinking, into the bright lights to take over as head coach because nobody else was handy at the time. A few months later he was [national] Coach of the Year and in a position to say that beating Navy could no longer be the sole goal of an Army football season.

Not that beating Navy doesn't mean a lot to Cahill and his team. Failure to defeat the underdog Middies last year gave Army an 8-2 season instead of 9-1, and the loss was a nuisance because people are beginning to take Army seriously. Once again, they are expecting the Cadets to do well—against everybody. After several years of dull, stodgy football, the Army team is stimulating. Its offense, which operates from a wing T, is designed for springing players loose for long gains. Nor do the Cadets hesitate to throw the ball. In fact, Army passed 229 times in 1967, 50% more than it did in the last pre-Cahill year, 1965. On defense, Army players swarm the ball carrier and keep coming at him until their quarry is pinned down.

Cahill's style and his calm approach have paid off. The Cadets have had two 8-2 seasons—and an even split with Navy— since Cahill took over, and last year they were set to go to the Sugar Bowl when the Pentagon inexplicably ruled that while other service academies might send teams to bowl games, Army could not because "it would tend to emphasize football to an extent not consistent with the mission of the academy, which is to produce Army officers."

I can't tell you how many games Tom Cahill coached for the plebes, but he coached 81 at Army, compiling a trio of stellar seasons before the Vietnam War drained the school of much of its football talent and left the team unable to compete effectively against the stiff competition still on its schedule. He left Army after the 1973 season but returned in 1984 as the color analyst doing the team's games on radio. He died in 1992 a day before he was scheduled to broadcast the game against Wake Forest.

Playing for Tom Cahill at the Manlius School had a profound effect on me. He was more than just a coach; he was a mentor and role model, exemplifying everything that's great about the game of football right down to earning the opportunity to coach one of the country's most storied programs because he was ready when that opportunity came. He didn't chase success as much as he provided it for others. And whether he was standing on the sidelines of the Manlius School, River Dell High School, or West Point, he coached the same way and left everyone who ever played for him better for the experience. He built teams and in doing so, he built men. He touched lives, changed lives, not just mine or Bill Parcells' but plenty more, probably more than anyone can count.

"He speaks our language," Townsend Clarke, captain of the 1966 8-2 team, once said of Cahill.

Clarke, who'd previously been voted "Best All-Around Athlete" at the Manlius School in 1963 and was called by Cahill's predecessor Paul Dietzel, "the best defender he has ever coached," according to InsideArmySports. com, starred during Cahill's first two seasons. He was named All-American and All-East his senior season while earning the reputation for being one of the storied program's finest linebackers ever. He also played basketball for Army and joined Gary Steele in the Army Sports Hall of Fame in in 2016.

Clarke followed up his final tour in Vietnam by attending law school at Harvard, where he made an immediate impression. On the very first day of classes that year, Professor Fred Sturdivant remembers him as the first student he called on.

"The minute I said, 'Mr. Clarke, will you begin please,' the young man jumped to his feet, snapped to, and barked, 'Sir, yes, sir!'" he recalls in Anita Raaghavan's book, *The Billionaire's Apprentice*. "It scared the hell out of me. All the other students sat there traumatized, thinking, *is this what I am supposed to do?*"

Clarke, who has gone on to a stellar career in business, remains effusive in his praise of Tom Cahill, as well as his experience at Army as a whole.

As does Rollie Stichweh. "Tom was an outstanding coach and a wonderful human being. He was my primary recruiting contact, my Plebe Coach, and then, after my tour in Vietnam, I returned to West Point and was his QB Coach when he became Head Coach, joining Bill Parcells and Al Groh as an assistant on the staff."

Rollie was the epitome of an Army athlete and for many years was the leading passing and running quarterback in Army football history, thanks to his stellar career from 1962 through 1964. No less an authority than Darrell Royal, Hall of Fame coach of number one rated Texas in 1964, called him "the best back in the country." Rollie's career was further highlighted by beating the vaunted Navy team led by Roger Staubach in 1964.

And his accolades included more than an election to the Army Sports Hall of Fame. Rollie was also twice decorated for valor in Vietnam as Captain in the elite 173rd Airborne Brigade. Once out of the service, he rose to become a managing director at a major consulting firm. And over the years he's continued his extraordinary service to West Point as a major booster of both Army football and athletics in general.

George Madison, a former eight-term member of the New York assembly and an ardent supporter of the Academy and its sports teams, was also a great admirer of Coach Cahill.

"Cahill was neither flashy nor did he arrive at West Point accompanied by great fanfare, bearing an impressive pedigree," Madison recalls, a friend of the esteemed coach who's nurtured a fifty-year relationship with West Point. "Perhaps that is why he often is omitted from the pantheon of West Point football. I think it is a mistake, however, to underestimate the contribution of this humble, unassuming man who took the coaching reins and compiled an impressive record during a transitional time in American history. His teams reflected his personal hierarchy of preparedness, nobility, and sportsmanship."

Madison concludes, noting Grantland Rice's timely poem, *"for when the one great scorer comes to mark against your name, he writes not if you won or lost, but how you played the game."*

Tom Cahill would have been pleased to be judged by that standard.

A few years ago, we held a reunion for that Manlius School team that went undefeated in 1953. Tom wasn't there, of course, but his kids were, and I can't tell you how many times his famed moniker, "and remember those guys in that other locker room are primed and cocked to knock your jocks off," echoed through the crowd.

And you know what, men? That hay is still in the barn.

CHAPTER 3

ŚTAS MALISZEWSKI— ON THE ROAD FROM THERE TO HERE

Nobody played football in displaced person camps in Germany after World War II, so Stanisław "Śtas" Maliszewski wasn't introduced to the game until his family immigrated to America. They had fled what is now Belarus to avoid the Bolsheviks, who had been responsible for the death of his mother's family prior to the war, opting for forced labor instead of risking the same fate in the latter part of 1944.

"I was just a few months old when we left," Śtas writes in an autobiographical work entitled *On the Road from There to Here: My Journey from the Old Country to Princeton...and Back.* "Traveling in a horse-drawn cart with all our possessions, we joined a long line of other Poles moving west.

We got about 20 miles before a fighter plane, presumably Russian, strafed us. People jumped into ditches as bullets ripped through the column. Bodies lay scattered along the road. Our horse was killed, so my parents abandoned the cart and took only what they could carry. Carrying me, and with my brother in tow, they walked hundreds of miles to Płock, Poland, and boarded a train for Germany."

Sometime in the following year once they reached Germany, in a forest outside one of those displaced persons camps, Štas' father happened upon a Russian refugee hiding in the woods and offered him shelter. They kept him and his family hidden from the British, out of fear they'd be put in boxcars and sent back to the Soviet Union, which because of the Yalta Agreement was the practice at the time right after the war ended. That family lived in a camp comprised primarily of Poles, protected by Štas' family. They were Baptists and in the United States, Baptists were very aggressive in resettling their religious brethren. In this case, the World Council of Churches in New York found them a Baptist church to sponsor their entry into the United States.

Years later, the refugee Štas' father had found hiding in the woods and rescued went to that same World Council of Churches to petition for the Maliszewskis to be similarly sponsored. The council found a Presbyterian church in Davenport, Iowa to fund the family's travel, as well as arrange for employment and housing. Being Catholic and after facing so much oppression, the family feared the Presbyterians would send them back once the truth was uncovered. But thanks to the warmhearted people of Davenport, that never happened.

Štas was six at the time and became a solid student, good enough in both academics and football to ultimately win admission to the Catholic high school Assumption that until that year had been St. Ambrose Academy. His goal, like all Assumption players, was to go to Notre Dame, and the school aggressively recruited him. But at the time Štas' mother was working as a domestic for a family that had a son who was attending Princeton, James Leach, who would later go on to become a renowned congressman from Iowa for thirty years. Jim Leach engaged Štas in conversations regarding the possibility of attending Princeton instead.

"Have you ever thought about going to Princeton?" the future congressman asked him.

"Jim," Śtas had responded curtly, "I never thought about going to Princeton."

But Jim brought some Princeton alums with him, exposing Śtas to the Ivy League for the first time and impressing him enough to give the school a serious look.

"The first time I was introduced to football was a high school game in Davenport where Bob Leach, Jim's brother, was playing," Śtas recalls today. "In those days, all the seating was reserved and we were right on the fifty-yard line, the perfect way to see football up close and personal."

So this six foot, two inches tall, 220-pound Polish refugee who spoke no English until he got to America arrived in the Ivy League. In the mid-1960s, players went both ways, offense and defense, and Śtas excelled on either side of the ball. He played guard in the old single wing, responsible for leading all the reverses, one of our key plays. On defense Śtas played linebacker, where his aggressiveness shined through. If you had the ball, if you were there long enough, he was going to find you! He was a dominating football player who could run like a deer and had a nasty streak to him, rooted in that aggressiveness.

But in his entire career he never took a single cheap shot or earned even one unsportsmanlike penalty. He was a model of how to play the game right, and the game treated him very well in return. Śtas played on the Princeton team that went undefeated in 1964, won seventeen out of eighteen games through his final two seasons, made first-team All-American his junior and senior years, and senior year was named a consensus All-American, one of only two consensus All-Americans from the Ivy League, the other being Ed Marinaro. He would later go on to sign with the Baltimore Colts.

After his football career concluded, Śtas enrolled at Harvard Business School and then continued on to an extremely successful career in business, far from that refugee camp in Germany. Those strangers in Davenport had given Śtas a chance, and football helped him make the most of it.

So what does he think about the state of the game today?

"The emulation of the game is too much on the pros," he said recently. "Trying to rip somebody's head off, that's a problem! Because that's not the game, and yet there are people who think that is the game. It's better at the collegiate level, where the basic element of football remains the same: our best guys against your best guys. If you really think about it, stepping back, football is a tug of war. One side's trying to push, or pull, the other side across the field. That's the way the game works, a back and forth struggle. It's all about territory. You're trying to move the ball and the other team is trying to stop you. It's that basic. But instead of learning how to play the game right, why are kids today trying to emulate people who are playing the game like thugs?

"I've spoken with people who are fed up enough to think radically: take the helmets off, they say. And there's a logic to that. Because if you think about it, as you watch the pros, the so-called role models, play, the severity of the injury inflicted is directly proportional to the level of protection the player is wearing. The more the player feels secure, the more he'll deliver harder blows. Here's my question to young people who emulate this kind of play: what is it you don't understand about hitting your head against the wall? You feel it and go, 'ouch!' But the helmet makes it so, on impact, you don't necessarily feel the 'ouch,' so you end up whacking opposing players even harder."

* * *

Football without helmets?

As crazy as that sounds to football purists, it represents a rising school of thought among those with an ardent desire to both preserve the game in some form and those with an equally ardent desire to see football changed so much that it barely resembles the game we know today.

"As concerns over player safety mount, the national governing body for youth and high school football is considering a version of the game that could look radically different from what football fans might expect," reports a February 2017 article on NPR entitled "Big Rule Changes Could Make Youth Football Games a Whole Lot Smaller." Colin Dwyer writes, "It's a leaner, less contact-inclined game, focused on fostering well-rounded athletes and cutting down on the kinds of bone-rattling, open-field hits that can leave parents cringing in the bleachers. It is also, for now, just a glimmer in the eyes of its creators at USA Football: The organization will be introducing new rules in a pilot run at select youth football programs across the country for the fall season."

The article goes on to provide "a breakdown of what players and parents can expect from the modified game," according to USA Football communications manager Tom Yelich:

- A smaller playing field, which dramatically shrinks the 100-yard field to a length of 40 yards. The smaller size allows a typical field to be split in half, so that two separate games can be played on the same surface at once.

- Fewer players on each side. In a typical game, eleven players for each team would be on the field at once; in the modified version USA Football plans to audition, that number will be reduced to seven—though it hasn't ruled out the possibility of anywhere from six to nine.

- There will be no special teams. In other words, that means no special teams in a bid to cut down on the punishing open-field hits those plays often involve.

- Players at the line of scrimmage cannot use a "three-point stance"—a body position that allows for great leverage and more power off the line.

- Players must rotate positions, rather than specialize in just one.

- Coaches must ensure players of equal size are matched up against each other.

Look, I'm for anything that keeps people involved in the game, and if it takes drastic changes to the rules like the above to keep kids involved and playing, then we need to give those changes serious consideration. Because even though not all the kids will go on to play beyond youth football, some will. And rule changes like this could conceivably relieve the pressures on parents, giving their children a chance to play the game and, most importantly, get a feel for the game. I'm all for anything that allows kids to experience throwing, kicking, and running without the damaging contact, because the fundamental aspects are all still there. Football would still be a team sport, and what makes the game so wonderful is the experience of playing a team game. That's the experience we all want kids to take from their initial years of exposure to the sport. And we want that experience to be positive for both players and coaches, no matter what it takes. It comes down to limiting the game a bit, without reinventing it entirely.

In contrast, we have a terrific youth football program in the Scottsdale, Arizona area where I now live that I think could serve as a nationwide model, without taking the more extreme measures advocated by USA Football. I'll let the content from the "Mission and Safety" link on their website speak for itself.

CAVE CREEK YOUTH FOOTBALL

MISSION

Cave Creek Football (CCF) is a community based, youth football organization that instills the Cave Creek Falcon culture prior to attending High School in the local community. Players will develop a direct influence from their local High School Coaches including alignment of Techniques, Terminology, Formations and Skill Sets that they can expect to see at the High School Level. Opportunities are available through Camps and Clinics providing direct interaction and name recognition between these players and the High School Coaches. This alignment is becoming commonplace among club teams in the American Youth Football (AYF) league.

SAFETY

CCF incorporates "Heads Up" tackling techniques and all coaches are USA Football certified. We encourage you to educate yourselves and your athletes with additional information from USA Football "Heads-Up."

A brochure detailing the program adds more about the USA Football "Heads Up Football" training program and the league's emphasis on player safety: "This program stresses player health and safety in practices and games. We also require at least two Team Staff members to be Red Cross CPR certified and have certified medical staff at all games."

Cave Creek offers programs for kids nine to thirteen years old and includes flag football as well as tackle. But to me, and I think Stas too, which game you're playing isn't as important as how safely you're playing it. So the idea of having coaches certified by USA Football, the very organization otherwise contemplating far more radical changes in the game, is a great step toward prioritizing and maximizing player safety.

* * *

J. Scott Brown, the league's deputy commissioner, enthusiastically agrees, stressing that Cave Creek Youth Football is a community-based system as opposed to a club. There are no cuts, and the program strives to keep its registration and equipment fees as low as possible, offering scholarships to players who otherwise would still be unable to afford the cost. The program maintains an active relationship with the local high school, whose coaches regularly run clinics for all kids playing in the league. Cave Creek plays strictly in the fall and encourages participants to participate in other sports as well.

"I've seen plenty of great kids start in our program and then go on to play club for a couple years, and suddenly they're burned out," Brown says. "I see them around and ask why they aren't playing, as if they were hurt. But, normally, they quit because it just wasn't fun anymore. There's too much travel, too much practice time year-round, and they don't get to see their friends. Hey, they've got plenty of time to get a job when they're older. Playing football shouldn't feel like a job, especially for young kids.

"It's a shame right now that there's so much bad publicity out there. The game is part of the American fabric and culture. It's part of our nation, part of growing up. *Friday Night Lights* for high schools, Saturday is game day for colleges, Sundays for the pros. We want our program to be the start of that, so we emphasize going out there and enjoying the game. It's not that we think our players are all going to be great, but we want them to get that experience, to understand the game, to appreciate what it's like to be a student-athlete. We're not just out there to throw our players onto the field on a Saturday morning, and then we're done. We stress the importance of the classroom, help make our players solid community members. We want to think we've given them a base to grow into good citizens. That rounds out the whole experience of playing the game."

For those thinking about starting a league, Brown offers some advice.

"First, be honest with the kids and the parents. We were that new group when we first started, and we knew we'd be playing against experienced coaches and experienced teams. We were starting at zero and needed to temper expectations. We may not win, we may not score much, but we were going to have fun and expose our players to this great game. Second thing, you have to have structure. You need to have good people on a working board to build a program like we've done with Cave Creek. Have guidelines in place for coaches and follow up to make sure they get the proper training, keep getting it, and be recertified on a yearly basis. As director, everything you do is about protecting kids, creating the safest environment possible. Third thing is you have to be financially responsible, as well as viable. It takes a lot of money to get started in anything, and running a youth football program is like running a small business. You have to be able to tell that parent where every dollar goes and why we need them to help with the fundraising so we can run the program on the high level we feel is a necessity. When you think of football, you think fall. But we have to do so much ahead of time. Online registration starts in March and goes through May, with in-person registration too. We're buying equipment, recertifying helmets, making sure all the insurance is paid, booking field rentals—it never really stops. So much money gets spent before the kids get on the field, but it has to be to ensure their experience is a positive one. Then those same kids become the best ambassadors for the game you can possibly have."

* * *

Stas, similarly, is up front about his thoughts on the game today.

"There are two things I think players need to do better that would go a long way toward turning the negatives of the game into positives," he says. "The first is to restore the sense of pride and privilege in playing for your school. That was important to me in everything I was involved in, not just football. Assumption was a very small school, comprised of maybe 500 students total. Davenport High averaged 1,200 in a single class *alone*, nearly ten times our size. We played them every year and didn't beat them very often, but it meant so much just to represent our school in trying, like David versus Goliath!

"The other thing, when you're lucky enough to be around coaches who stress teamwork and camaraderie, is that you learn to keep your composure under pressure. That to me is the most important life lesson I took from the game, and there's no reason why today's players can't learn the same thing. You can't learn it in the classroom—did anyone ever take your pencil away or tear up your paper while you were taking an exam? Of course not! Football is more like life; it's not just how well you can play, because there's somebody else on the other side of the ball trying their best to stop you. On occasion students would ask me prior to a game whether we were going to win. My reply to them was very simple: we practiced hard this week, and you don't have to practice to lose!"

Stas is fond of recalling an interview from the well-regarded documentary film *Harvard Beats Yale 29–29*, released on the fortieth anniversary of the now famous game played in 1968. The interview features a player speaking passionately about how much he wanted to hurt a player on the other side, how that was his first priority. What he doesn't mention is the fact that he ended up getting penalized at a crucial juncture that may well have kept his team from winning.

"Now," Stas elaborates, "the coaches we had were culled from the Greatest Generation. Ray Ambrose, for example, who came to Assumption from the 101st Airborne, D-Day, and his experience as a POW. Let me tell you, after you've been through all that, football is put into perspective, and when a man like Coach Ambrose spoke, we listened. I missed playing my sophomore year because of a broken leg I suffered in baseball. So I came to practice junior year determined to win the job of starting fullback.

"'You want to be where the action is?' Coach Ambrose asked.

"'Sure,' I said. 'That's why I'm going out for fullback.'

"He just looked at me and smiled. And I didn't figure out why until we went up the river to play Clinton High. We weren't very good at the time, and they were beating us up pretty badly. So I'm standing next to Coach on the sidelines while Clinton's driving down the field, and I pestered him, 'Put me in. Let me play defense.' He smiled at me, sent me in to play linebacker and, boy, was I lost. Even though we scrimmaged hard, everything was happening so fast, and that's the biggest difference as you grow into the game, because if you keep at it, the speed of the game slows down, almost like everything's happening in slow motion. That's the transition that changed football for me, learning how to slow the game down."

Śtas played at a level that earned him first-team honors on the All-Ivy Silver Anniversary Team in 1981 as a linebacker. I noted earlier that he was also a very aggressive and dominating player. Does he agree?

"Absolutely...I always felt that when we played, the ball was neutral. It was just as much my ball as your ball, and I was going to go get it. Defensively, many players think the most important thing would be to guess where the ball carrier is going. My approach was to determine what I was going to let that ball carrier do; I have the advantage because all I have to do is get in the way. The ball carrier has a problem because I'm in the way. It's really a mindset."

To say the least. A 1965 *Sports Illustrated* story described Maliszewski as "a sensitive, deeply religious young man who, Princeton coaches say, gets nasty only when he removes his two front teeth before a game, and then he is about the nastiest thing ever to draw a pro scout to a Princeton football game."

Uh-uh, Śtas says, taking issue with that quote. "Nasty is someone who wants to hurt people. Walking on the Princeton campus one day, somebody asked me, 'Do you like getting hit?' I responded, 'No! I like hitting people.' The real line for me is the line between playing hard and being nasty. A nasty player is somebody who wants to hurt somebody else. That has no place in life and no place in athletics. Did I hit some guys hard? Damn right I did, but not to hurt them. That was the last thing in my mind."

Academically at Princeton, he majored in philosophy. His senior thesis was titled "The Existence of God in Hume and Kant." And for Śtas, and so many other football players I've been around over the years, the hard-earned lessons learned on the field are never lost; they're applied, instead, to life after they hang up their cleats.

As Śtas puts it, "The harder you work, the more you're going to be able to achieve your goals. You hear people saying all the time, 'I want to win.' But that's not enough, because the other team wants to win too. Hell, I want to fly like a bird. We can want all kinds of stuff. In football, anyway, you accomplish your goals by making yourself faster, by grasping the game, by not losing your composure. Let's not kid ourselves; in games like this, when teams are evenly matched, sometimes things just go your way or not. Back to the business about tug of war, in order for me to advance a yard, the other team has to lose a yard. So it's a zero-sum event that's happening. That's why coaches, after a loss, often say, 'If we had done this, then...' Well, sure, but the other team would have done something different too—the opponent doesn't stand still. And that's not limited to football; it happens in life.

"Football helps teach you how to react. How to stay a step ahead of the other guy, no matter where he goes."

But that's not the end of the story. The dedication and perseverance Śtas took away from the game extended to a happy resolution to his war-torn past.

"In the last ten years my wife, Julia, and I have made six trips back to where my mother's family had lived and where I was born," Śtas writes in *On the Road from There to Here*. "I didn't know if any of her relatives were still alive. Happily, we discovered them in Poland, Belarus, Ukraine, and Russia. In spite of the horrors inflicted upon them, they had found ways to maintain their identity, even in a communist state. We hold a reunion whenever we visit Belarus. Many of the Tatur clan are university professors, no less. They have a website dedicated to the family and an impressive book that chronicles our history. We placed a headstone at the local cemetery for my mother's brother, Roman. As far as we know, it's the only headstone in Belarus written in Polish, English, and Russian."

CHAPTER 4

COSMO IACAVAZZI–
FROM THE COAL MINES TO THE GRIDIRON

The first time Cosmo Iacavazzi scored a touchdown against Yale in the Yale Bowl, playing for Princeton in the same era as Śtas Maliszewski, he threw the ball up into the stands beyond the end zone.

"Son," the referee told him, "if you do that again, I'll have to give you a penalty."

"Sir," Cosmo responded, "if I can do that again, you can go right ahead."

Cosmo indeed did it again for us in that game, in which we crushed Yale to claim an undefeated 9-0 season.

We recruited Cosmo out of Scranton, Pennsylvania, in one of the most heated recruiting battles of my career, because he was as great a player as we ever pursued. He could have gone to Penn State, West Point, or pretty much anywhere else. But thanks to his father, the owner of a trucking company, Cosmo had come to value getting an education as much as he did the football showcase. He was third in his class at West Scranton High and wanted to be an aeronautical engineer, so he ended up narrowing his choices to a pair of Ivy League schools, Princeton and Cornell. It was the longest recruiting experience of my life, meeting him and watching him play a high school championship game in November, four months ahead of his eventual decision. Ultimately, Princeton's aeronautical engineering facilities proved too impressive to turn down.

He came to us as a T-formation fullback, a formation in which the tailback garners the primary running responsibility. Cosmo was a punishing runner and occasional blocker. At five foot, ten inches tall, and 185 pounds, he was built like a block of granite, and we made him the featured back in the single wing from the first day he arrived as a freshman. In those days, freshmen weren't allowed to play varsity, so he didn't claim his starting job at fullback and linebacker until his sophomore year, eventually making All-American. Because of his offensive talents, he enabled us to create new formations within the single wing, such as placing him behind the tailback in the I-formation to give him a chance to run option plays as the primary runner and incorporate a whole new passing game into our system.

"That was my approach to the game, the way I learned it," Cosmo recalls today. "Pennsylvania football is a hard-hitting game. You win games by out-hitting the other team. When someone was coming after me, if I couldn't get away from him, I wanted to hit him as hard as he wanted to hit me, with the reverse being true when I played defense. But I'm talking about good, solid hits. Lower your shoulder, drive into him and drive him back as opposed to going for the head to injure him, which I've seen all too often as the game has developed. I'm not trying to hurt the guy; I'm trying to stop him. Cheap shots never entered the picture. Bad football is hitting a guy high and hard when he's unprotected, with the intention to injure him. Aggressive football is hitting him low and hard enough to drive him out of bounds. That's a subtle but crucial distinction."

We used to hold the first few weeks of preseason practice at a camp in Blairstown, New Jersey. Cosmo made the team as a sophomore while we were there, and then we moved the team to our home in Palmer Stadium. There's a practice field beyond the end zone where the freshmen played their games, and that's where we practiced. Prior to our first game, we scrimmaged Lehigh and got our first look at what Cosmo could do against real competition. He broke off a couple of big runs and pretty much dominated both sides of the ball whenever he was on the field. Let me tell you, he was something to watch!

As it turned out, watching the scrimmage from the sideline that day was Princeton's president Robert F. Goheen, standing with the dean of students, Bill Lippincott. Goheen, the son of a minister, was an alumnus and classics major who'd taught at the university prior to being named president in 1957.

After watching Cosmo run, he turned to Bill Lippincott and said, "Who is that?"

"That's the player everyone's so excited about," Lippincott told him.

"What's his name?"

"Icavacki," the dean replied, managing to mangle Cosmo's last name.

Goheen, having spent time in the Far East with his family, responded, "Is that Japanese? Asian?"

Whatever it was, there's now a street named after him in his hometown of Scranton called "Cosmo Iacavazzi Way," and a statue of him stands outside the West Scranton stadium where he played his high school games. No one seems to have a problem pronouncing his name anymore.

We built our offense around "Cos," as we called him, because he could do things with the ball we'd never seen before and, equally important, he was an incredible leader. I can remember him bringing the team together at the end of practice to run plays against defenders holding shields. He also never did anything without running forty yards down field in a sprint. And before you knew it, the whole team was joining him, needing no prodding from Cos or the coaches. If it was good enough for him, it was good enough for them.

"I played by one simple rule," he recalls. "Try to better your best to help your team win. Playing football is all about living in the moment. In high school, we used to practice on a field that was all rocks, gravel, and glass. When it rained, mud would run down your socks; you were cold and wet and uncomfortable, but you still went out there and did your job. Whenever I stepped on the field, it was all about making every play, and making every moment count. I didn't do the things I did, like those forty-yard sprints when running plays, to impress anyone. I did them to get myself ready, so I'd be prepared in a game. Every time I stepped onto the field, I brought focus and intensity. I was captain of my high school team senior year. And one of the things our coach made us do after every practice was get ourselves into four or five lines and run sprints up and down the field. After practice, I did the same thing at Princeton, and by the end of the season, the whole team was running those forty-yard sprints with me. That's how I tried to play the game, leading by example."

Cosmo, who played one season for the New York Jets, later applied his drive and charisma to a variety of pursuits, including engineering, working in finance on Wall Street, starting a cable television company, running a property management company, and serving as mayor of Hillsborough, New Jersey. Recalling that while at Princeton he worked from 7:00 a.m. straight through to 2:00 a.m. more days than not to keep up with his classwork, he firmly believes that football paved the way for his later success.

"I learned some incredible lessons from football, and they were imprinted on me early."

But there are plenty of lessons from today's game Cosmo doesn't keep nearly as close to his heart.

"I'm a little concerned, a little frustrated. The basic game is still there, still great. But it's not worth losing a life or risk becoming a babbling idiot. So I'm all for prioritizing the safety of the game. These guys are so much bigger and stronger than we were, it figures they can hit so much harder. That's a symptom of the problem, but not the real root. I think money is too much a part of the game—*that's* the real root. The game of football is dominated by the NFL, and the NFL is in it for the money—I'm not knocking that on its own, because that's the way it is. What I am knocking is that it could be said the NFL is all about protecting the brand, not as much protecting 'the game.' The game, to an extent, is being sidelined in favor of the brand—hot dogging, hard hit highlights, that kind of thing. Turn on highlight shows and watch how they focus the big hits that hurt people. So kids watching see that and then they're trying for the big hit too, emulating their heroes. Still and all, more focus needs to be placed on protecting the game by doing a better job of protecting the players, and that goes for the collegiate level too. In several states, the highest paid employee is the state school's head football coach. And he's paid to win. That's the antithesis of how I learned to play the game and how I believe the college game should still be played today."

And yet the college football brand remains iconic, to say the least.

"The already intense interest in college football continues to grow," National Football Foundation president and CEO Steve Hatchell said in a 2015 report entitled "College Football Ratings and Attendance Remain Strong" compiled by the NFF. "Embracing ever changing technology, the leaders of our sport have done a spectacular job in ensuring that the fan experience not only keeps pace but sets the standard in innovation. We are grateful to the conferences, bowl games, and the media for their creativity and commitment in delivering a first-class product that allows fans to experience the game in every imaginable way."

"The game has benefited enormously from the commitment of every major media sports outlet," the report continues, "including the American Sports Network, Big Ten Network, BYUtv, CBS, CBS Sports Network, ESPN, ESPN Classic, ESPN on ABC, ESPN2, ESPN3, ESPNews, ESPNU, FOX Sports, FOX Sports 1, FOX Sports 2, FOX College Sports, FOX Sports Net, the Longhorn Network, NBC, NBC Sports Network, Pac-12 Networks, Root Sports, SEC Network, and multiple regional and local outlets. Throughout the regular and bowl seasons, these outlets continue to capitalize on college football's ever-increasing popularity to produce an increasingly dynamic product that engages fans on new levels."

The report concludes that "the overall attendance for NCAA football games across all three divisions drew 49,057,966 fans at home games, neutral-site games, and postseason games in 2015."

And the growth in college football attendance over the last few years is equally impressive. The numbers showed yet more incremental improvements for the 2016 and 2017 seasons, indicative of a sport that is thriving now but may find the trend lines reversing if the direst of predictions on the future of football come to pass.

Just as Cosmo Iacavazzi intimated, the incredible popularity of both professional and college football helps explain both the problems facing the game and the difficulties in correcting them at the same time, since money has become the ultimate driving force. But that doesn't diminish Cosmo's affection for, commitment to, and belief in the game. Not at all!

"The relationship experiences that come from all of that is what I've always loved and respected about football," he told *Town Topics*, Princeton's weekly community newspaper, a while back. "You share such a range of intense emotions, sadness, gladness, pain, and suffering with your team-mates and your coaches. You know your opponents did the same thing so you respect that in them."

He expounds on that today, stressing the life lessons football taught him that he wouldn't trade for anything and his desire to see today's youth continue to have the same opportunities on the field that he had.

"Basic premise: you've got to be innately competitive. My coaches or-ganized the game. They laid out the steps by which you got better, succeed, win. In any environment—football, business, on any stage you're on—you have to ask yourself what goal are you trying to accomplish and how do you get there, step by step incrementally. Whether it be in football or life, when you get knocked on your ass, you don't quit, you get up. You go back to what you're taught. I worked in New York for a big brokerage firm—all those rules applied as much to that part of my life as the part of my life centered around football."

* * *

Ironically, Cosmo played for the same legendary high school football coach Sam Donato as Frank Kush. Thanks in large part to football, not only did Kush overcome his impoverished upbringing, he also went on to achieve great things in the game. Indeed, it takes a special coach and person to build a college football program into a national power, but that's exactly what Kush did at Arizona State University.

Born to Polish immigrants, Frank was the fifth of thirteen children and shared a bed with five of his brothers in the working-class coal town of Windber, Pennsylvania. Football became his ticket out of both poverty and the back-breaking mines in carving out his own slice of the American Dream that came to so define the game in the post-World War II era. An undersized lineman who fought his way onto the Michigan State roster, he ultimately helped lead the 1951 Spartan team to the national title.

It was as a coach, though, where Frank Kush truly distinguished him-self. In 1958, at the tender age of 28, Kush took over the Arizona State program and built it into a national powerhouse, amassing 231 victories over his 22-year career that included two undefeated seasons in 1970 and 1975 respectively, in addition to being named National Coach of the Year in 1973.

But, regrettably, that's not the only thing Kush is known for. His dominant tenure at ASU came to a controversial end when his legendarily hard-nosed approach to coaching resulted in allegations of physical and mental abuse by a player who later went on to sue the school. While those allegations were never proven, they cast a long shadow over Kush's legacy. His approach to the game derived from the fact that he had come from nothing and knew football had provided his ticket out. That fostered a relentless intensity in Frank, spurring him to instill in others the same mindset that had allowed him to escape the coal mines of Western Pennsylvania.

"It's been a consistent message from all the people who have called me with their condolences that it wasn't so much about the football, it was about what he did for them and how much better in life they are," his son Danny told *Arizona Central* in the wake of Frank's June, 2017 death. "He was like a father figure and mentor."

"If you talk to his players they'll tell you they were boys when they came here and they left as men," added Rocky Harris, chief of operating officer for Sun Devil Athletics, for the same article. "The reason for that is he spent most of his time coaching them as people and trying to make them better and stronger people, and with that you win football games."

Kush's career went on to have a second act when he served as head coach in both the Canadian Football League for the Hamilton Tiger and in the NFL for the Baltimore Colts. But it's Arizona State he's most remembered, and celebrated, for. While his style was a far cry from the rules and regulations put in place to make the game safer today, what he brought to it directly reflects his fervent belief that character was far more important to a team's success than a mastery of Xs and Os. In that respect, Frank represents the last vestiges of a by-gone era that cannot properly be judged by contemporary standards. Time may have passed him by, but not what drove him to make his players into the best they could be on the field and off it. And, since his induction into the College Hall of Fame in 1995, he's been joined in the Hall by no less than six of those players.

"Frank Kush," says Cosmo Iacavazzi, "came from a tough background and played tough football. Frank, in his own indomitable way, with his own distinctive style, used football to take boys and turn them into men of stature, performance and accomplishment both on and off the field."

And that field today is named "Frank Kush Field at Arizona State Stadium."

* * *

"Much of my success in life, directly and indirectly," Cosmo continues, "is owed to football, the lessons I took from the game. Preparation, sacrifice, study—being part of a bigger picture, a cog in the machine. In chasing success on or off the field, you prepare for something, you become part of the team, and then you practice until you get it right. Of course, there is one glaring exception: life offers no referees or out of bounds lines to make sure you play by the rules. Life doesn't have that. There are people who will skirt the rules—lie, cheat, and steal—and no penalty flags go flying. But the secret to success that the game helps you master is how you work with people. Set the goal and then figure out how to attain the goal. And if your best wasn't good enough, you push even harder to be better, the perpetual question to ask yourself being how much did I improve on my best if my best wasn't good enough. That was yesterday. Today I'll work on making my best better.

"The indelible lessons I learned playing football were imprinted on me early. My high school coach, Sam Donato, had the greatest influence on me other than my family members. Sam taught me that you give your best effort all the time no matter what you are doing, so that's what I did. I've never been that big or fast so I thought I'd just give it my best effort, and that was my edge. I was taught a framework to create success, and that has stayed with me ever since."

CHAPTER 5

THE GOGOLAKS—
KICKING THEIR WAY INTO HISTORY

"Can you imagine getting up at 3:00 a.m. and leaving your home and basically not going back for thirty-three years?"

Charlie Gogolak posed that rhetorical question in the National Football Foundation speaking program celebrating his being honored in 2015 for his Outstanding Contribution to Amateur Football—an apt description of what it was like fleeing Hungary in the wake of Soviet dominance and oppression. He, his parents, and older brother Peter had made it across the border into Austria just days after the Hungarian Revolution had failed. His father was a dentist and they took refuge with, of all things, the family of one of Dr. John Gogolak's patients.

"It was a horrible experience," Charlie, who was just twelve years old at the time, says.

After traveling by train from Budapest to near the border, they hiked the last twenty miles in freezing temperatures to freedom, the first step in a perilous journey that would end happily in the United States. The family's new life started at a converted military barracks at Camp Kilmer in New Jersey before ultimately settling in upstate New York, specifically a small city on the St. Lawrence River along the Canada-U.S. border called Ogdensburg. It was there that the Gogolak brothers, both soccer players back in their native country, went to high school at the Ogdensburg Free Academy.

There was a problem, though. The school had no soccer program! So Pete and Charlie opted for what was the next best thing, a reasonable facsimile in their minds: football. As kickers, of course.

"I lined up at a forty-five degree angle as I would kick a soccer ball with my instep," Pete says, recalling the first time he prepared to kick in practice. "And the holder looked up with a very frightening expression, saying, 'Gogolak! The goalposts are straight ahead. You are not supposed to kick the ball into the stands. But even more importantly I think you are going to kick me in the face or you are going to kick me in the ass.'"

Charlie, on the other hand, was saved from a similar spectacle by the fact that he only punted in high school. Pete, the elder of the two, graduated a few years ahead of him and went on to Cornell, in large part because they made him an offer he couldn't refuse.

"I couldn't afford not getting financial aid," he says. "I spent a weekend at Cornell, and I just loved the school, fraternity life, and everything else and they gave me some financial aid. They gave me a job. I was washing dishes in the fraternity house."

When he was ready to follow his brother into the college ranks, Charlie penned a bunch of letters he sent out to prospective schools, not letting the fact that none of them had recruited him discourage his efforts. The letter read something to the effect of, "Dear Sirs: My name is Charles Gogolak. You may know of my brother, a soccer-style kicker at Cornell, and I'm interested in your school."

Among the few schools that responded was Princeton, in spite of the fact that no one on our staff had any experience with a soccer-style kicker.

Our freshman coach, Walter "Pep" McCarthy, made the drive north to pay Charlie a visit.

"It was the coldest place I've ever been in my frigging life," he reported upon returning.

"What about the kid?" head coach Dick Colman asked him.

"He's not very big, but he's very smart."

We took a shot on Charlie, having no idea how much he was destined to change not only our team but the game of football forever. In those days, having a kicker who could kick forty, even thirty-five-yard field goals, was a rarity. But Charlie regularly split the uprights from fifty and beyond, so it wasn't long before we realized we had something very, very special.

"We had a fantastic team," he recalls of the squad that included Štas Maliszewski and Cosmo Iacavazzi, "and a coach, Dick Colman, who really believed in the value of the field goal. My college career just skyrocketed. It was kind of the perfect storm. I had a single-wing center, Kit Mill, who could snap the ball so the laces faced forward when they hit the holder's hand. The holder, Bob Bedell, was absolutely fabulous and was a nurturing kind of guy, really increasing my confidence. We had a single-wing offense that was in the opponent's territory a lot, so I always got a lot of attempts."

And he made almost all of them, including going six for six with a 52 yarder in our 1965 opening game that season against Rutgers.

"What are your thoughts on today's game?" a reporter asked the Rutgers coach at the time, Dr. John Bateman.

A frustrated Bateman replied, "We got beat by a frigging Hungarian refugee."

Princeton's competition didn't take their new threat lightly, searching far and wide in a desperate attempt to negate the advantage Charlie provided.

"I remember we went up to Cornell in 1965, when we were on a thirteen-game winning streak. I went out to try the first field goal, and Cornell had two defensive backs standing on the shoulders of two defensive tackles, positioned to block the kick. Well, we weren't about to take that lying down, so Coach Colman petitioned the NCAA to change the rule by making that a penalty. The following Monday, the NCAA came down with the rule that, in order to start a football play, you have to have two limbs on the ground. That took care of that."

But not everything. At Yale, when Pete kicked off one game, the referee called a penalty on him for being offside. The opposing head coach, Yale's John Pont, had alerted the ref to the fact that, by nature, a soccer-style kicker's plant foot was several inches ahead of his kicking foot, and also past the forty-yard line. If that interpretation of the rule stood, it would mean that soccer-style kickers wouldn't be able to kick off but, once again, saner heads prevailed and the rule ultimately stipulated that he wasn't, in fact, offside.

Not to be denied, our rivals continued to search for a way to stop Charlie's dominance. Dartmouth went so far as having two linemen lie down next to each other on the field instead of taking their place on the line. Since they were technically on defense, they couldn't be penalized for an illegal formation, and they did indeed have at least two limbs on the ground. A safety would then try to time the snap of the ball to use the supine players as a springboard to leap over the line and block the kick as it climbed. Because this was the final game of the year, the rule wasn't changed until the following season, when it was written you couldn't vault the line.

Charlie became the first kicker ever taken in the first round by an NFL team, in 1966 by the Washington Redskins. But Charlie informed the Redskins owner, Edward Bennett Williams, that he intended to go to law school.

"Sign with us," Williams promised, "and I'll pay your way."

Charlie did sign with them for 150,000 dollars and started kicking for the Redskins in preseason. I was his position coach at Princeton but was under strict orders not to coach him at all. Head coach Dick Colman was paranoid about doing anything that might hurt Charlie's rhythm or, worse, get him hurt. To that point, Charlie's senior year Dick ordered him to run off the field as soon as he kicked off. He was too small to tackle anyone anyway, the logic went, so why risk the crunching block that would almost surely result from his already having been targeted? Besides, most of Charlie's kickoffs went into the end zone and we could cover with only 10 men.

Well, Edward Bennett Williams had hired Otto Graham to coach the Redskins not long before training camp, and the first time Charlie kicked off in a preseason game, he ran off the field just as he had at Princeton. Graham turned to his right and saw him standing there.

"What the hell are you doing here?" he barked.

"I always do that after I kick off," Charlie told him.

"Are you crazy? Don't you ever do that again! We're only covering with ten people!"

That's why, to this day, Charlie will jokingly tell you that Dick Colman was smarter than Otto Graham. But, to Graham's credit, he learned the value of the weapon he had soon enough.

"We were playing the Cowboys on the road in the Cotton Bowl," Charlie recalls. "It was early November and the game was nationally televised. Our great quarterback, Sonny Jurgensen, had driven the ball to the Cowboys' thirty and normally would have gone for the touchdown, since field goals were hardly a sure thing back then. That was Graham's first thought during a timeout, but Sonny said, 'Hey, you've got a great kicker. You're paying him a lot of money. Why not let him kick the winning field goal?' So he protected the ball and ran the clock down to ten seconds. I came in, kicked the field goal, and the team carried me off the field on their shoulders. That's the moment I knew I could produce under pressure at the pro level."

"Before the advent of the Gogolaks, kicking had been an inexact science for the pros, to say the least," Larry Felser wrote in the *Buffalo News* on September 5, 2004, as to the lasting and profound influence Charlie and his brother Pete had on the game. "Full-time players such as Cookie Gilchrist and Mack Yoho did the kicking off and field-goal attempts. They wore a flat-toed shoe on their kicking foot so that they could slip into their added role. A kicker who was successful half the time on field goals was considered a major asset...In the 1966 NFL draft, the Washington Redskins took Charlie in the first round. Straight-ahead kicking was on a path to doom. Everyone, it seemed, had to have a sidewinder. It wasn't just the length of field goals. It was the accuracy and the longer kickoffs which produced inferior field position for the opposition."

Charlie was still kicking for the Redskins when the team hired Vince Lombardi to replace Graham in 1968.

"Lombardi had a way about him. He knew about psychology. One time we were walking back from lunch at Dickinson College, where they held preseason camp, and he says to me, 'You know, Charlie, I can't yell at these guys the same way I yelled at Paul Hornung and Jim Taylor. Hornung and Taylor would just get mad. Taylor would come over to me and growl and when he went back onto the field he'd knock somebody on his ass. But if

I did the same thing here, I'm afraid the players would figure they weren't any good and that I hated them. I knew if I knocked those guys in Green Bay down, they'd get right back up. I'm not sure of that here, so I've got to go easier.'

"I've always wondered why Lombardi said that to me. Maybe because I was the kicker. Maybe I just happened to be the one walking back with him from lunch."

Like many football experts, Charlie feels Lombardi would be every bit the coach today he was then, because what's good about the game, its most important aspects, have not changed. After all, so many Lombardi-era Packers have spoken of their coach as the master lesson teacher not only about football but all sorts of positive things that define so much of what the game is truly about—effort, training, discipline, teamwork, grit. The list goes on.

"The lessons you learn playing football would be very difficult to learn doing anything else. I remember the Redskins had a kicker decal on every single locker, as a signal that reminded the players that kickers might be off on an island somewhere else in practice, but we were still part of the team. Everyone had a job to do, everyone had a responsibility to stick to the details. Master those details, everybody does their job, and the team will be successful. Every play has so many working parts. You do your part to make the play successful wherever you're aligned. My being able to get a kick off before it's blocked means the center has to do his job, the holder has to do his job, and the blockers have to do their jobs. Every play is a perfect microcosm of corporate structure. You learn very early on in football that attention to even the smallest detail is vital for the success of the team, just like it is in business. But the origins of learning that for me were on the football field. So it's a shame some kids aren't getting the opportunity to learn those kind of things."

A friend once asked Charlie if he ever had any idea that what he was doing would generate so much talk to this day.

"I told him no. I was just trying to be as good as I could and stay healthy. I had no clue it was going to have a lasting impact. I had no notion I was going to be an innovator."

Speaking of a lasting impact, a plaque hangs in the local town hall where Charlie and Pete grew up, a magical sight that greeted them upon their first return to Hungary in 1989. But their legacy extended far beyond that.

"They play football over there now, they've got a league modeled after the NFL," he beams. "It's called the Hungarian Federation of American Football [MAFSZ] and was started back in 2005."

The league currently has 23 teams competing across three tiers, up from a total of only four teams when it first got started. The most recent champions were the Miskolc Steelers, but the Budapest Wolves have won the most titles with six, making them the New England Patriots of MAFSZ.

Recently, Alan Pergament, a reporter for the *Buffalo News*, was watching the credit scroll of the hit NBC television show *This Is Us* and noticed the name "Charles Gogolak" included.

"When my brother attended Princeton University in the 1960s," Pergament wrote in his March 3, 2017, story, "I remember the cheer, 'Go, go, Gogolak,' when soccer-style kicker Charlie Gogolak came on the field during college football games. Some Buffalonians said it, too, when Charlie's older brother Pete kicked for the Bills when they won two American Football League titles. Once I confirmed Charles was Charlie's son, I decided I had to 'go, go, see Gogolak' on my recent California trip. We met at a Los Angeles restaurant to discuss the influence his father and uncle had on college and professional football and the road Charles took to 'This is Us.' Not even 'This is Us' writer-creator Dan Fogelman might have imagined the football part of the story."

But Charles isn't the only Gogolak who's made an impact with a camera. Another son, Steven, produced a brilliant 74-minute film called *Ticket to Freedom* as a college senior.

"We went to Hungary last March and shot hours of footage," Charlie says, the emotion crackling through his voice. "Steven interviewed me and Peter where we had grown up and from where we had ultimately fled. We've shown *Ticket to Freedom* at schools, clubs, organizations, and, let me tell you, there's not a dry eye in the house when the lights go back up."

Speaking of dry eyes, there weren't many of them in FedEx Stadium on October 16, 2016, when the Redskins honored both Pete and Charlie.

"We didn't know we were being honored," Charlie recalls. "We thought we were going to be celebrating various events on the anniversary of the Hungarian Revolution at the embassy. Then a car picks us up and takes us to the stadium instead."

The halftime ceremony was presided over by Hungarian minister of national development Dr. Miklós Seszták. Also in attendance were Hungarian ambassador Dr. Réka Szemerkényi, chief advisor to the prime minister of Hungary Dr. Jenő Megyesy, and chairman of the Foreign Affairs Committee of the Hungarian National Assembly Zsolt Németh, who presented the Gogolak brothers with a gift on behalf of the government of Hungary. A special Redskins jersey was given to Charlie and the official game day football to Pete.

"I don't think Peter and I had any idea what we had started, or that toe kickers would disappear forever," Charlie says. "Would it have happened anyway? I guess we'll never know."

One thing we do know is that in 2009, the Gogolak brothers were featured in one of those classic NFL Films documentary productions made by the legendary Steve Sabol. It was titled "Top Ten Things that Changed the Game."

PART TWO:

THE GOOD IN THE GAME

"Football is like life—it requires perseverance, self-denial, hard work, sacrifice, dedication, and respect for authority."

—Vince Lombardi

CHAPTER 6

GRANT TEAFF—THE COACH OF COACHES

*"I feel very honored to be asked to add my 'thanks' to the
many you will receive regarding your 'incomparable' career
as executive director of the American Football Coaches Association. You have improved the game in every conceivable
way but most importantly you have elevated and given more
'meaning' and 'purpose' to the title 'coach.' So, thank you,
Coach Teaff, thank you!"*

—*A note from Bob Casciola on Grant Teaff's retirement as head
of the American Football Coaches Association*

Have you ever heard of Angelo State University? It's a small school in Texas where Grant Teaff coached from 1969 to 1971, attaining a 19-11 record and finishing a respectable third twice in the Lone Star Conference. Prior to that he'd compiled a 23-35-2 record for the McMurry University Indians from 1960 to 1965. He'd played for both schools, so the stints made for nice fits and a fine career starter.

Grant Teaff never played for Baylor, but that didn't stop him from taking over a program wallowing in mediocrity and downright failure. He wasn't the first name on Baylor's preferred list, but the program's status, coupled with its harsh competition in the Southwest Athletic Conference that included Texas A&M, SMU, and mighty Texas kept the school from being the first name on any big-time candidate's list. So Baylor went with Teaff, who'd developed a reputation for getting along with people and being a true motivator during his time coaching smaller college programs. On the surface, that didn't make him the ideal prospect for turning Baylor football around, but that's exactly what he did. Big time.

Grant has written several books, most recently one entitled *Beyond the Game*, about which a recent review left on Amazon said, "Required reading for any athletics coach. With the continued societal breakdowns of family, education, morals, and values, the last line of defense for many athletes is the quality of coaches whose paths they cross. Outside of wins and losses, coaches make a tremendous impact on the character traits of today's players—and are often the father figure for far too many young athletes. GREAT book from Coach Grant Teaff."

And that's the way people refer to him—as "Coach," the same way you might address a doctor or officer in the military by their title, and rightfully so. For starters, he turned the Baylor program completely around. The team had been 7-43-1 in the five seasons preceding Teaff's arrival. But he quickly transformed Baylor into a competitive program, and in 1974 the team won eight games and captured the Southwest Conference title for the first time since 1924. Along the way, they defeated the mighty Texas Longhorns 34–24, after rallying from a 24–7 halftime deficit. It was Baylor's first victory over Texas in seventeen years. That season in general, and the win over Texas in particular, are commonly referred to as the "Miracle on the Brazos," named after the Brazos River near the Baylor campus.

Teaff remained Baylor's coach until 1992, winning the Southwest Conference title again in 1980. His teams won the Peach Bowl in 1979, the Liberty Bowl in '85, the Bluebonnet Bowl in '86, and the John Hancock Bowl in 1992 in his final game as coach. His Baylor teams were notable for success against the University of Texas, finishing with a 10-11 record against Texas, including a 38–14 upset win over the Longhorns in 1978. By comparison, in the fifteen seasons preceding Teaff's arrival, and the fifteen years following his departure, Baylor had a 1-29 record against the Longhorns.

Coach Teaff won 170 football games at Baylor, including those two Southwest Conference championships, and he coached in twenty postseason bowls and all-star games overall. He was named Coach of the Year six times in the Southwest Conference and received National Coach of the Year awards from the American Football Coaches Association and the Football Writers' Association.

"Coach Teaff to me is someone who exemplified what college football is all about," Mike Singletary, a ten-time All-Pro and two-time NFL Defensive Player of the Year, said on the occasion of being inducted into the College Football Hall of Fame in 1995. (He was later inducted into the NFL Hall of Fame as well in 1998.) "I came out of high school not very highly recruited. All I had at that time was a dream, a dream to go forth and make a difference. And there I met such a man to help me direct that dream."

Singletary's comments notwithstanding, the real Miracle on the Brazos, though, may well have been what Grant Teaff went on to do after his coaching career concluded. Taking the helm of the American Football Coaches Association, he became a model for everything that's good about the game that grew in both popularity and notoriety during his 22-year tenure there. And in achieving that he became one of the top leaders of college football.

"When I took over the AFCA," he recalls today, "we had three employees working out of two rooms in an Orlando, Florida strip mall. Being from Texas, and keenly aware of the hotbed of football culture down there, the first thing I did was establish a true national headquarters in Waco. And in my 22 years running the organization, I had the opportunity to work with hundreds of young coaches, helping to ingrain in them the need to keep the game fun, safe, and a true positive experience. The game itself is one of the great teachers of young people. It has the capacity to instill great lessons but, first and foremost, you need to have coaches who are educated on how to use the game to teach those lessons."

Teaff speaks passionately about the game because of all it meant to him. He's dedicated his life to improving football so thousands and thousands of others will be afforded the opportunity to enjoy the same experience he had. In 2002, the *Sporting News* ranked Teaff as one of the most powerful administrators of college athletics. In December 2004, Teaff was named one of the most influential people in college sports by Street & Smith's *SportsBusiness Journal*.

"We've faced challenges like this before," he notes, recalling the era of President Teddy Roosevelt, a football player himself. "In 1906, football was a very violent and brutal game. So Teddy Roosevelt called together coaches from the eastern part of the U.S., where the power of the game was centered, and told them, very simply, 'Fix it, or I'm going to ban it.' Out of that, the American Football Coaches of America was formed, and a few years later, the NCAA came along. Rules were needed then not only for how to play the game safely, but also regarding guidelines for eligibility. So the sport, in a few short years, had managed to go from near extinction to a thriving network of teams and burgeoning leagues that would form the basis for the game today."

Speaking of today, Teaff sees the challenges we're facing as much the same now as then, but he is adamant about the need to not just save the game but improve it so it may continue to grow and thrive.

"First of all, the game is a contact sport. You have to become a mentally tough person. Football was so important in my life for my development. It shaped my character in a profound way. I grew up in a family that taught me values and a work ethic. When I played the game, I learned a lot about myself I didn't like, and I was able to change it. After my parents, my football coaches had the biggest effect on my life. During that period of time I was playing high school football, I decided this is what I wanted to do: coach football and have the same effect on kids my coaches had had on me. Consider just one of the lessons football taught me: the ability of an individual to come to grips with the fact that there's going to be defeats in life and you have to find a way to overcome those defeats—that's one of the primary components of success in whatever you do. The best way to relieve the sting of failure is to work to correct those things you need to improve on.

"But the importance of football goes deeper than that. Basically, we're a society here in America in which there are 26 million fatherless kids, meaning they lack the kind of traditional male role models that make a huge difference in the lives of kids. That's where football coaches come in. We have the responsibility to teach kids beyond the game," Teaff elaborates, referring to his own terrific book by that name. "*Beyond the Game* itself analyzes how America found itself in this position, how so many young people ended up with values that are skewed. The ones we're able to draw into football, we can teach them the true values that they otherwise might never experience. And they can begin to take those values to heart and turn them into positive experiences."

Teaff relates an especially pertinent example from his own life.

"My high school coach, Coach Keyser, was my math teacher too. He was nicknamed Mule for his big, long face. But he was also a true Renaissance man. He flew airplanes, climbed mountains, taught, coached, wrote poetry. One day he gave us a test that had ten questions, and there was one that totally baffled me. I just couldn't figure out the answer, so I gave up and turned in my paper. He just glared at me and, after class, pointed for me to come up to his desk."

"'Grant,' he said, 'you didn't answer one of the questions.'

"'I couldn't' was all I could think to say.

"Coach Keyser gave me that look again. 'You handed in the paper when there were still ten minutes left of class. That means you quit. Your greatest asset isn't your athletic skills, it's your mind. And until you learn how to control that, you'll never reach your goals.'

"That incident changed the entire way I looked at school, football, and life. The one thing I can control, that all of us can control, is our minds. If I can control my mind, I can control myself and my actions. And, over the years, that led me to develop four of what I call controls, keys to success, because anybody who uses and accepts them becomes the controller of their own lives:

1. A positive attitude and approach to life
2. A total effort to anything I commit myself to
3. Self-control and self-discipline
4. Caring for others

"It comes down to the old adage, mind over matter; if you don't mind it won't matter. If you don't care about your players, you're not going to be able to teach them the way they need to be taught. You fall short, the way

I did when I handed that test in when there were still ten minutes left in class. I learned all that from football.

"The problem is that fewer young people are getting to experience that. A lot of parents don't want their kids taking the risk of playing. They're concerned, and rightfully so. There's no question that fear of concussions specifically has been a deterrent to participation in the game. But there's another side to that," Teaff stresses.

There is indeed. Take this September 2011 article by Dale Robertson in the *Houston Chronicle*, entitled "Youth Football Less Dangerous Than Thought," in which the points raised remain as relevant today:

> At a time when hypersensitivity to the dangers of the game—especially concussions—has never been more acute, is something wrong with this picture?
>
> "Actually, little league football is pretty good," suggests Dr. Gary Brock, who specializes in pediatric surgery. "It's not the safest place a kid can be, but it's not the most dangerous either. A lot of parents have that impression, but in the young age groups, pre-puberty, we don't see it at the clinical level."
>
> Children all around the Houston area started their seasons over the Labor Day weekend. The Greater Houston Youth Football League (GHYFL) alone has nearly a thousand players, ages 5 through 12, divided among its eight associations. Yet ironically, it's those little girls waving pompons on the sidelines who, Brock believes, are on the most precarious path.
>
> "We see more catastrophic injuries among cheerleaders than among any group of athletes," Brock said. "The risk per hour of activity is seven times greater than with other participatory sports. It cracks me up when parents tell me they won't let their sons play football but then push their daughters into cheerleading."
>
> The raw data indicates 3.5 million kids each year are injured playing sports, and almost two out of five traumatic brain injuries among children are associated with athletics or recreational activity. But Brock says the total is actually small compared to the overall number of participants. And while football may

send more boys to the doctor's office and soccer more girls, the statistics are skewed significantly because so many are playing those sports.

The article goes on to say that:

Doctors Brock, Derman, and Lowe routinely see children who have suffered head trauma from sports other than football. Lacrosse, for one, can be dangerous for beginners because they're clumsy and haven't yet learned how to deftly wield their sticks. Also, girls who play soccer tend to be concussion-prone because of collisions and headers.

With baseball now requiring a nearly year-around commitment, Brock said repetitive stress injuries to shoulders and elbows have practically become an epidemic. Ironically, the kids with the best mechanics end up doing the most damage because they throw so hard, literally overpowering underdeveloped bones.

Brock, speaking from experience after 20 years in childhood orthopedics, believes the backyard jungle gym or monkey bars are markedly more dangerous than the football field.

"I tell parents that it's safer to send their children to Pop Warner (football)," he said, "than to the playground."

Grant Teaff took all these principles one step further with the work he did while running the American Football Coaches Association, the importance of which he details in his most recent book, *Beyond the Game.*

"Coaching is a special profession. To be truly successful, a coach must exhibit leadership with his staff, with his players, and with his community. In addition to handling the technical aspects of football, a coach has a number of other core responsibilities, including teaching values, developing a sound work ethic with colleagues and athletes, and emphasizing to the players the benefits of receiving an education. The coach has an opportunity to teach meaningful life lessons through the game of football."

When Teaff took over the AFCA in 1994, he set forth twenty major goals to establish a championship organization and achieved every one of them, a process he expounds on even further today.

"We need coaches entering the game at all levels willing to become what they're capable of becoming. If you're gonna preach a sermon, you better dang well practice what you're preaching. One thing: adults, when we talk, we need to live what we talk about. The game of football itself can be a great teacher. Those who play the game know the value of it and have to learn how to articulate that. You have to know that you're responsible for the young person, so it behooves every coach to be involved in the safety of the game.

"In all honesty I think it's going to take a lot of work, a lot of effort to keep the game going. The way our society is today, with so many distractions and other interests. When I was growing up, there wasn't much else to do, and football put you in the heartbeat of your community and school. But it's hard work and sometimes it's painful. My simple thought is that this game is so important to our country, has been and will be, thanks to the way it trains and prepares future leaders. Football draws people together and, more than anything, teaches them they can overcome obstacles because they did that on the field."

In *Beyond the Game*, he lays out the four primary qualities he believes coaches must possess:

- *Commitment—Faithfully adhering to a set of basic precepts (persistence with a purpose).*
- *Compassion—The emotional capacities of empathy and sympathy, particularly for the suffering of others.*
- *Leadership—The ability to influence the behavior and actions of others to achieve an intended purpose.*
- *Perseverance—A demonstrable work ethic characterized by a high level of industriousness and a desire to see the job through to its completion.*

"As a coach," he relates in the book, "it's not what you know, but what you teach."

Teaff, who in 2016 was given the prestigious Outstanding Contribution to Amateur Football Award by the National Football Foundation, looks to history to further make his point: "During World War II, General George Marshall once said, 'If I have a dangerous mission, give me an Army football player. Because those guys have already been in a different kind of trench.'"

CHAPTER 7

JACK LENGYEL—
WE WILL ALWAYS BE MARSHALL

"Football's a game that enhances so many of the characteristics you need to be successful in life," Jack Lengyel told *Arizona Images* for the magazine's May 2017 issue, in which he was featured.

He should know. Though he may not resemble Matthew McConaughey, the actor who played him in *We Are Marshall*, the themes that emerged from that film mirror his thoughts on what's best about the game of football. Lengyel wasn't Marshall Univrsity's first, second, or even third choice to rebuild a program that had nearly been ended by unspeakable tragedy and, in retrospect, he had no reason to leave the College of Wooster where he'd amassed a 23-13 record over his last four seasons. Well, maybe one.

"There's an old Chinese proverb," he's fond of saying. "If you're ever given something of value, you have a moral obligation to pass it on to others."

A head coach from the young age of 29, Jack passed his gift on to countless others. The players he coached for four years, the Marshall University community to whom he lent hope, the program that would go on to national prominence years later, and a nation shocked by the catastrophe that has earned him one of the most celebrated legacies in the history of college football.

"I was home watching television," he says. "It was the same day we'd lost to Wittenberg University for the conference title. Suddenly a crawl comes across the screen: MARSHALL UNIVERSITY FOOTBALL TEAM PLANE CRASHED. ALL 75 ABOARD PERISHED."

Here's how *ESPN Classic* recalls that fateful day in an article that ran on November 19, 2003:

> *When Marshall won its opening game of the 1970 season, the townsfolk of Huntington, West Virginia looked with anticipation at the possibility of the college's first winning season in five years, during which time it absorbed a winless streak of 27 games. Instead, a week before the final game of yet another losing year, the school and the residents of this quiet town on the Ohio River became bonded forever by the biggest tragedy in American sports.*
>
> *On November 14, 1970, a chartered Southern Airlines plane, transporting the players, coaches, wives, boosters, and officials from a Southern Conference game against East Carolina, crashed and burned into a wet, foggy hillside two miles from the runway of the Tri-State Airport. All 75 passengers aboard the DC-7 plane were killed instantly upon impact, five of whom were doctors, which was almost half of the town's registered physicians. The fiery furnace that once was a plane was so severe that the bodies of six players were never identified and were buried [at a memorial gravesite at Spring Hill Cemetery in Huntington that honors those that perished in the tragic plane crash].*
>
> *Amazingly, the exact cause of the crash was never determined.*

The entire state was shocked by the tragic event and suddenly the 3-6 record of another losing season didn't mean anything. A day after the crash, over 7,000 people, which was more than attended a football game, gathered with heads bowed in the Marshall Fieldhouse praying for the strength and courage to go on. The Today Show televised the memorial tribute that solemn day, a eulogy that has continued now for the last 30 years.

"Something like this had never happened before. Some of the faculty weren't all that supportive, and the administration came this close to just ending the football program," Jack relates today. "But the Marshall University's Big Green supporters and interim president, Dr. Don Dedmon, decided to honor the memory of all those 75 players and coaches by rebuilding the program instead of abandoning it. So, after allowing for the shock to wear off and the grieving to subside, they started the search for a coach to rebuild the program.

"A Penn State assistant turned the job down. Another coach took the position, then resigned after two days for personal reasons. That's when I decided to apply for the job and made the 230 mile drive south, had my interview, and was offered the position of head football coach at Marshall University on the spot. A week later, during my press conference I asked if there were any questions after I finished my remarks.

"'What's your goal for the team?' Ernie Salvatore asked me. Salvatore was a columnist for West Virginia's *Herald-Dispatch* who covered Marshall and the tragedy's aftermath in elegant detail.

"'To go undefeated,' I told him.

"'Isn't that a little unrealistic?'

"'Of course, it is. But we have to find the dedication, perseverance, and commitment needed to meet the unprecedented circumstances that are like nothing ever seen before in the history of college football. That's the kind of effort it's going to take and we're going to need if we're ever going to be successful.'"

And all Jack had to start with were the team's freshmen, along with three varsity players who were injured and hadn't made that fateful trip. So, too, he had three assistant coaches—Red Dawson, Mickey Jackson, and

Carl Kokor—who also hadn't been on the plane.

"Red Dawson had escaped from being on the doomed plane by driving to East Carolina, making some recruiting stops along the way," *ESPN Classic* has written of that night. "He heard news of the plane crash on his car radio during the drive home. Dawson arrived in Huntington in the middle of the night and found himself among the searchers gathering scattered bodies in the darkest night of his life. He saw the dead and later met with their families."

That number of remaining freshmen players quickly shrank when some were recruited by other schools and others opted to transfer on their own. Jack didn't fault or blame them, resigned to building upon whatever he had and grateful for the still shell-shocked players he had left who were as determined as he was to do right by the team's memory.

"We had a few receivers and a couple of quarterbacks with some experience," he recalls, "but most of the players had little college game experience. When I was the head coach at the College of Wooster, we ran a power offense, something we could not run with this team comprised of the current freshmen together with next year's incoming class that fall.

"Bobby Bowden was coaching at nearby West Virginia at the time and his offense had mastered the Houston veer, which was a system we thought we could install and teach before the coming season started. So our offensive coaching staff and I went to see Bobby to explain our dilemma. Let me tell you, that first season happened only because Bobby opened up his playbook and game films to us, along with all the secrets and tricks of the trade that made him an offensive master. He invited us to take it all, put no restrictions on us whatsoever. We spent three full days watching practice during the day. Then, during the evening, their quarterbacks coach Frank Cignetti taught us the offense and we'd watch film for hours into the night. While driving back to Marshall, I thought for the first time we had an offense that was going to score touchdowns and give us a chance."

* * *

"I was an assistant at West Virginia and actually interviewed for the head coaching job at Marshall that Rick Tolley got, after I turned it down," Bobby Bowden himself remembers. "If I hadn't, I would've been on that plane that night. The day of the plane crash, we'd played in the afternoon and won a big game, a big upset. So we were all at my house, the coaches and some of our boosters, when the story came over the television. They named everybody on the flight one by one, and I kept looking for Red Dawson's name because Red had played for me when I was an assistant coach and we'd stayed in contact after he took a job as an assistant at Marshall.

"So it turned out Red had stayed behind to do some recruiting and had never gotten on that flight. So once things got settled, it was Red who first came to me about getting a look at the offense we were playing so it could be incorporated by Marshall and they could put an offense on the field. And it all happened because I had this relationship with Red."

Bobby also recalls reaching out to Penn State coach Rip Engle himself years before.

"Joe Paterno was Penn State's offensive coordinator in those days and their offense was something special. I was coaching at Howard in Birmingham at the time, and I wrote Rip and asked if I could come up there and take a look. He said yes, and I rode the train up there, then thumbed a ride to College Station with this lady and her four sons. I stayed there for three days and watched them practice, then brought that offense back to Birmingham with me. They didn't have any problem doing that for me, so when the time came, I didn't have any trouble doing it for Jack Lengyel and Marshall."

* * *

Dear Coach Lengyel:

The 1970 varsity players could have little greater tribute paid to their memory than the determination to field a team this year. Friends across the land will be rooting for you, but whatever the season brings, you have already won your greatest victory by putting the 1971 varsity squad on the field.

That letter, from none other than President Richard Nixon, to the Marshall team arrived on September 7, 1971, just prior to the season opener.

Between then and that spring day when Lengyel first took the job, things hardly went smoothly, but all that work and preparation were about to pay dividends. Marshall, incredibly, managed to win an emotionally wrought season home opener, defeating Xavier of Ohio in a thriller 15–13 with no time left on the game clock, solidifying the school's, and Lengyel's, place in history. They won one other game in a season that, by all estimations, exceeded expectations in terms of the product the team was able to put on the field despite being severely overmatched.

"It wasn't about winning," Lengyel recounted in a 2006 article entitled "Former Coach Remembers His Own Marshall Plan" in *USA Today*. "It was about getting a team together to begin the process of rebuilding."

Lengyel expounds further on that "Marshall Plan" today.

"We realized we were going to have to change the way we coach. We had seven new coaches that had never worked together as a staff and a team that was comprised of mostly freshmen players the NCAA granted a waiver to so they could play. We took Bobby Bowden's Houston veer and simplified it, modified it, and taught it to the 'Young Thundering Herd,' at the same time the coaches were learning it ourselves. I told the whole team, 'You're all seniors. There are no freshmen here and think of yourselves all as first-team starters. Be ready to go into the game at any time.'

"We were going to be an unpredictable football team. That forced us to get at it every day, practice after practice, adjusting on the run. It was a true experience of all the best elements football embodies and exemplifies at its core. We were out there having fun and we gambled all the time. We gambled with our kicking game, our passing game, our blitzes. We were totally unpredictable, which worked to our advantage because there was no book on us, no tendencies—what we were likely to do in this situation or that. We tried to take advantage of field position in every way we could, including even punting on second or third down. It was tough and difficult, but we all came together like a fist. You could fault us for having less experience out there, but not for our tenacity, commitment, dedication, or conditioning."

But problems surfaced neither Jack nor anyone else could have anticipated, given the utterly unprecedented nature of Marshall's situation.

"In the fall, we had a squad of ninety players," Jack recalls, "almost all of them freshmen combined with the sophomores who had stuck with the program. So my first year as coach everybody on the team lettered. And everybody lettered again my second year. But then we started getting some freshmen with talent, so we would start working more new players we'd recruited into the mix. This new talent was getting the reps more than two-year lettermen. I had players come up to me and say, 'Coach, I'm not getting enough reps.' I'd talk to them and say, 'There's no "I" in team!' I said sometimes you're a small part of the puzzle and sometimes you're a big part of the puzzle, but we couldn't finish this puzzle called team without everyone doing their job. Some players bought into that concept and some didn't and left the team, and that broke my heart. We were rebuilding a program backwards, with freshmen who didn't have upperclassmen ahead of them. And that required players to play outside their normal positions and comfort zones. That wasn't easy for them, playing defensive end instead of tackle because that's where we needed them. And, in some cases, even switching to offense instead of defense where they'd played before."

Marshall never earned a winning record in Lengyel's four years at the helm. But the experience was a smashing success because he positioned the school for great things down the road.

"It was important that we played the game, not that we won. This team was going to lay the foundation for future generations of Marshall football teams, and my players would share in those victories as much as the players on the field at the time. At Marshall, we made a commitment to build a team, just like any other coaches would have done, no matter the circumstances. We were all dedicated players, coaches and staff, happy to have the opportunity to lay the groundwork for those who would follow in the future and be involved with successful football teams.

"But in the first game of the season, we still didn't have a kicker. So I put an ad in the Marshall student newspaper that read 'ROOM, BOARD, BOOKS AND FEES FOR ANYONE WHO CAN KICK AN EXTRA POINT OR FIELD GOAL.' A soccer player named Blake Smith showed up in a soccer uniform with long hair and a beard.

"'You ever kick a football?' I asked him.

"'Yeah.'

"'You ever kick a ball in a game?'

"'No.'

"So we placed the ball on the three-yard line and he made it," Jack continues. "We placed the ball on the right hash on the fifteen-yard line, and he made it. We put the ball on the left hash, and he made it. Then I told him to get a haircut and a shave, and you have a scholarship, room, board, books, and fees.

"In our first home game versus Xavier University, we were underdogs by several touchdowns but were leading at halftime three to nothing on a field goal by that former soccer player Blake Smith. In my halftime talk to the team I told them, 'Gentlemen, you have in the palm of your hands one of the greatest upsets in football history. All I want is for you to play the next half with the dedication, perseverance, and toughness that you played in the first half of the game and you will have a memory that will last a lifetime.' And, you know what? We won the game fifteen to thirteen on the last play of the game with no time left on the clock on another Blake Smith field goal."

Ultimately, thanks to Jack's efforts, a former Marshall player named Bobby Pruett would take the program to football heights never scaled before. He went 15-0 in 1996 and won a national title at the Division I-AA, while amassing a 94-23 record in the late 1990s and early 2000s. Pruett led Marshall to five straight bowl games and won six conference titles. And the team finished in the top 25 three times under him.

"We were always talking about Marshall rising from the ashes to become the Phoenix," Jack recalls with a smile. "And Bobby Pruett did just that."

As *ESPN Classic* has chronicled that storied history in its November 19, 2003 article, it was all made possible to a great degree by Lengyel along with his football teams, staff, and all the others involved in the program:

> *...Finally, in 1984, Marshall finished 6-5, its first winning season in 20 years. The Herd hasn't had a losing season since.*
>
> *George Chaump, who later coached at Navy [brought there by Jack Lengyel in his capacity as athletic director], brought Marshall its first national exposure on Division I-AA level with two playoff appearances as a member of the Southern Conference in 1987 and '88. Marshall emerged as a I-AA powerhouse under Jim Donnan, who coached for six years before leaving for Georgia. The Herd was 64-21 under Donnan, appearing in the*

Division I-AA championship game four times....

...In 1996, Bob Pruett gave an unwanted Randy Moss a chance to play after he had lost scholarships at Notre Dame and Florida State. Marshall went 15-0 and won the Division I-AA title for the second time.

That was only the beginning of Pruett's and Marshall's national prominence. In 1997, Marshall's first year in Division I-A, the Herd thundered to its first of three consecutive Mid-American Conference championships, led by Moss and 1999 Heisman Trophy finalist quarterback [as well as National Football Foundation high school national scholar athlete, one of only seventeen] Chad Pennington.

As a result, Marshall earned a spot in three straight Motor City Bowls. They lost to Mississippi, 34–31, in the 1997 Motor City Bowl, but went on to drub Louisville, 48–29, in 1998. In last year's appearance, Marshall dominated Brigham Young, 21–3. In the final college poll of the season, Marshall ranked 10th, the first time in school history that it ever cracked the Top 25.

For Jack Lengyel, though, the lessons that experience taught him would stay with him for the remainder of his coaching and athletics career, both on and off the field.

"I learned one thing especially. When you're interviewing players, I learned people don't care how much you know until they know how much you care. That has to be the philosophy of coaching. You learn from all of your experiences, positive and negative. You learn from winning and you learn from losing. The Marshall experience made me a better person, especially because I moved around a lot and did a lot of different things. But Marshall—that time was something special in my career."

Indeed. "For Huntington, a town of some 80,000 residents back then, Marshall football was what they lived for on Saturday nights in the fall," notes that same *ESPN Classic* 2003 article. "The Thundering Herd played in Fairfield Stadium, a rickety structure that could seat only 10,000 on a sellout, and was also the playing field of the city's two high school teams, Huntington Central and crosstown rival, Huntington East, on Friday nights. It was an antiquated stadium barely adequately illuminated, which housed a wooden press box that tightly accommodated 20 people."

More than anyone, and more than anything else, Jack Lengyel restored that experience and did so for the purest of reasons: his love of the game.

"Competitive football is a wonderful experience for young players and high school players," he reflects. "The lessons you learn on the field are so much different from the classroom. Competitiveness, perseverance, team-work, the importance of putting the team ahead of self. It takes partners all working together, and not just players and coaches either. It takes boosters, parents, and administrators. The game gives back a lot more than it takes, because of the experiences and friendships that last a lifetime."

He gets a kick out of the fact that he was played by Matthew McCo-naughey in the film, once voted the Sexiest Man Alive by *People* magazine. For the film, McConaughey was channeling his own father as much as Jack, and for good reason. His father, who coached high school football in Tex-as, died just before filming was set to begin on McConaughey's first film, *Dazed and Confused*. Director Richard Linklater recalls not being sure the actor was going to return in time to play Wooderson, the aging Lothario unabashedly clinging to his own high school glory days on the football field. But he did and, in many people's minds, stole the movie before years later going on to play a coach instead, in a testament to his own father.

"Football is different from other sports because of the nature of the game," Lengyel believes more than ever today. "It's the speed of the game, facets like blocking and tackling which are just as important as touch-downs. You've got eleven playing against eleven, always in search of the strategic advantage that can change the game. And that takes not only physical conditioning, but also mental, maybe even more so. As Napoleon once said, 'The mental is to the physical as two is to one.'

"I'm especially partial to high school football because they begin to understand teamwork, selflessness, physical conditioning, persistence, and dedication. Those that go on to play college football will continue to refine these core values and contribute to the opportunity to play on successful teams. Somewhere around 97 percent of players won't make it to the pros, but they'll all use the lessons they learned as a player to become a lawyer, a doctor, or, maybe, a coach. Whatever they end up doing, they're going to do it better because they played football. What we're doing as coaches is preparing kids for life, not just to play football. We are committed to creating student-athletes who can prosper on the field and off, become leaders.

"That's the way it was for me when I played for a pair of wonderful coaches, Babe Flossie and Tommy Evans, who changed my life. I loved those two people and they gave me an opportunity to succeed and I've never stopped emulating them, modeling myself after them. To this day, I still think if I could be half as good as those coaches, I'd consider myself a success.

"I played for Babe Flossie at Garfield High School in Akron, Ohio because he convinced me to play the game. 'Come over here, Lengyel,' he said to me one day. 'I want to make you a blocking back.' I just listened to him. I went out and did what he coached me to do. He made me a football player. Then, at the University of Akron, Tommy Evans took me and coached me and taught me how to play the game at the college level. He was one of the finest coaches and men anywhere anytime, one of the best I've ever been around. He taught me how to coach, so I was ready when the time came to go out on my own and cut my own spurs."

Interestingly enough, Jack's final game at Marshall was also the final game of his football coaching career. But he went on to leave his mark as athletic director at such schools as Louisville, Missouri, Fresno State, Temple, Eastern Kentucky, Colorado, and the United States Naval Academy. From that position, he was able to influence even more students and coaches, applying the lessons he'd learned in football across a much wider array of sports. Had the Marshall experience burned him out of coaching? Had he given up what he'd loved so much because he'd left so much on the field there?

"I don't think that was it," he says. "It just felt like something else I needed to do. I'd coached fifteen years at that point and could have done it forever. Then I was offered the associate athletic director position at Louisville University, and I saw the opportunity to get back to what I loved the most—football especially, sure, but athletics in general because people in sports, the players and coaches, are the finest people I've ever been around."

And then there's this: on January 12, 2008, seven members of a high school basketball team from Bathurst, New Brunswick up in Canada and their coach's wife were killed in a crash when the van in which they were traveling collided with a tractor-trailer while returning from a game in Moncton in snowy conditions. Drawing similarities between the two tragedies, on March 13, 2008, Jack Lengyel funded his own traveling expenses to New Brunswick to assist in counseling the grieving community. This man who'd achieved all of a 33-54 record in his head-coaching career nonetheless left an indelible mark on the game of football and beyond. Just like many who had come before, and more who would come after, Jack never considered himself bigger than the game.

That said, in 2018 he received the Tuss McLaughry Award, presented by the American Football Coaches Association to a distinguished American for highest distinction in service to others. The first recipient of the award was General Douglas MacArthur, and six of those who followed him, preceding Jack Lengyel, were past presidents of the United States.

And he will always be Marshall.

CHAPTER 8

FRANK CIGNETTI—
YOU CAN GO HOME AGAIN

College Football Hall of Fame member Frank Cignetti's coaching career has run the gamut of opportunities both big and small. And, quite amazingly, both his sons have followed him into the profession: Frank Jr. with various professional teams, most recently the New York Giants, and Curt with a series of successful college stops that included a stint at Indiana University of Pennsylvania, where Frank has twice led the Indians to the title game for the NCAA Division II championship.

"I didn't want them to do it," he reflects, "because I know the demands the lifestyle makes on you. You've got to be so committed to it with all the traveling and really no off-season anymore. I asked them, do you really want to do this? Do you love the game enough to give so much of yourself to it? When each of them said yes, I told them to learn both sides of the ball and start out as GAs [graduate assistants] to get their feet wet. And Curt was fortunate enough to be exposed to some great mentors like Nick Saban when he worked at Alabama. I interviewed Nick when he was a GA in 1976 and I was coaching West Virginia, but I didn't have a spot for him. As soon as one opened up, I hired him."

Frank had succeeded Bobby Bowden at West Virginia after Bowden left to take the Florida State job. He had previously coached with Bobby as an assistant for six years, from 1970 to 1975 after one stellar season at Princeton, working under that school's new head coach Jake McCandless after Dick Colman stepped down.

"I loved it up there," Frank says of his experience at Princeton, "and I might've stayed there forever if someone like Bobby Bowden hadn't called me. When Jake got the job, he knew he couldn't compete playing the old single wing, so he brought me in to install the split back veer."

The offense, run like an option as a forerunner of the now famous spread formation, relied far more on passing, and McCandless saw making the switch as an opportunity to reclaim Princeton's storied stature. But Frank faced a problem immediately. There was no spring practice in the Ivy League back then, so he gathered the offensive players together in *ad hoc* fashion on whatever field, parking lot, or gymnasium he could find and taught them the veer.

"One thing about Ivy League kids," he recalls of his experience at Princeton. "They play the game because they love it—they're not bound by the scholarship."

And teaching the veer to those Princeton kids allowed Frank to rediscover his roots coaching at Leechburg High School in western Pennsylvania, not far from where he was raised in Washington Township. It was there that he won a pair of state championships before moving on to take a job as an assistant at Pitt. In his first and only year at Princeton, the team went 6-3 and shared the Ivy League title in a season highlighted by a stunning victory against a much-vaunted Dartmouth squad considered by some to be the best team in the entire East.

Then Bobby Bowden called.

"Let me tell you, he was something special, truly special. Like I said, I thought I was going to be at Princeton forever. But the National Coaching Clinic was in Washington, DC that year and I ran into a friend, Jack Cloud, who'd just left Indiana University of Pennsylvania to go to West Virginia under Bobby and asked me if I'd be interested in coming along. Well, I went down to visit West Virginia with my wife, Marlene. First of all, it was freezing—everything was frozen, covered in ice and snow. And the facilities for a program of this level were in sad shape, including the 30,000-seat Mountaineer Stadium that looked like it needed someone to take a wrecking ball to it. Coming down there from Princeton, with all the great facilities that school had, I'll tell you, between that and the cold, it was all I could do not to just get back in the car and turn around."

But then Frank met Bowden.

"Bobby swayed me. That was number one. If he wasn't there, I never would've gone. I learned so much working for him. What a mentor, what a man! He was great with the players and the coaches. Bobby changed my whole concept about how to run a program. It was the first time I'd been around a head coach of that level, so detailed and so organized in everything, from how he prepared for practice to how he game-planned for Saturday. It was a tremendous learning experience for me from that standpoint. I don't know if the success I ended up having at IUP [Indiana University of Pennsylvania] would have happened if it wasn't for Bobby Bowden."

Bowden was already running an offense called the Houston veer that he'd learned from Bill Yeoman at Houston, so bringing Frank in as offensive coordinator made perfect sense for all concerned, in spite of that frigid first impression of West Virginia. Frank was such an expert on the famed scheme that when Jack Lengyel and his staff made the trip there, it was him they were sequestered with for three days to bring the offense back to Marshall to even make that season possible.

"But that was at Bobby's bequest," Frank notes, "because that's the kind of guy he is."

The feeling is mutual.

"Frank was a very good coach," Bobby Bowden recalls. "A good detail man and you couldn't beat him as a person. He studied the game and always tried to get better. But he was also a very good teacher because he could explain things to the players in language they could understand. He was a great communicator."

Frank went on to succeed Bobby Bowden at West Virginia when Bowden left for his legendary run at Florida State. Wrong place at the wrong time, as they say.

"We were coming off a bowl season, but had graduated 32 seniors, a whole bunch of them starters. There were highlights, like beating Pitt under Johnny Majors when Tony Dorsett was playing for them, but we finished at 5-6, nothing to brag about, except that it gave us plenty to build on. And the next year, we got off to a great start. Went over and beat Maryland and popped up to about eighteen in the polls. I really thought that team had a chance to be special, but we got hit by a rash of injuries that depleted our team and our talent. The problem was that we weren't that deep to begin with. Our recruiting efforts were limited mostly to West Virginia and, in my four years there, I'd say we had four really great players from the state. The rest were more developmental players we needed to coach up into their roles. And that might've worked just fine, if the injury bug hadn't bitten us so bad. What I learned in my time there wasn't really a surprise: you've gotta recruit good kids with good character, kids who love to play. But we didn't have the kind of facilities to make the school attractive enough to them."

Frank was relieved of his coaching duties at West Virginia after four seasons, right around the time he was diagnosed with a rare form of cancer. The school couldn't bear simply dismissing him, which would've left Frank without health care to cover the treatments he desperately needed to save his life. So they kept him on as a kind of special advisor in athletic administration. Not surprisingly, even while fighting cancer, Frank threw himself fully into his new role, dedicating all his efforts toward revamping and upgrading West Virginia's woefully lacking athletic facilities.

"How were we supposed to compete with the likes of Pitt, Ohio State, Penn State, Maryland, and Virginia Tech? We were surrounded by top-flight programs with top-notch weight rooms, stadiums, and practice fields. These were the teams we needed to recruit against. Finally, the state legislature in Charleston came up with the funding to upgrade our facilities and I oversaw the transition.

"But, once the doctors gave me a pretty good idea that things were under control with my cancer, I started to look at getting back into coaching. I thought about going back to Princeton, where the head coaching job had just opened up. I thought about rejoining Bobby Bowden at Florida State. But ultimately, I decided to come back to Pennsylvania for two reasons: first, the state had a retirement and health plan and, being a cancer survivor, I could be uninsurable in some places. Second, the state had great health care and hospitals. So going home turned out to be the best option."

"I also saw my alma mater Indiana University of Pennsylvania as a sleeping giant. IUP is a great school. I knew we could be very competitive from a recruiting standpoint, that the real potential was there for the school to take the next step. I came in as both athletic director and head football coach but decided to stick to being AD and hired my friend George Chaump, who'd just left Tampa Bay of the NFL, to coach football while I rebuilt the scholarship program. When George left after four seasons, I returned to the sidelines, and the program took off from there."

An understatement to say the least. Frank coached the Indians a stone's throw away from his native Washington Township for 20 seasons, amassing a 182-50-1 record from 1986 to 2005. Under Cignetti, the Indians made their first Division II postseason appearance in 1987. His 28 postseason games are a Division II coaching record, while his 15 playoff wins were second best when he retired in 2005. In 1991, he was named the Division II Coach of the Year. His teams won 10 Lambert Cups as the best Division II team in the eastern United States. And then there were those two national title games in 1990 and 1993. (Another IUP alum, Bernie Kish, served as executive director of the National Football Foundation's College Hall of Fame for 10 years in South Bend, Indiana until it moved to Atlanta in 2014.)

Frank coached Frank Jr. for three years, having little notion at that time of the career path his younger son was going to take. It was his oldest son Curt, though, who ultimately followed in his father's footsteps to the head coaching job at IUP. And, not long before Curt took over the IUP program, managing a stellar 19-5 record over two seasons, Frank was inducted into the College Football of Hall of Fame in 2013.

"It's great. It's humbling," he says. "When you think of all the coaches that coached football and the great coaches that are in the Hall of Fame, it's a great honor."

And much, much deserved.

"When I look back at my experience, I've had a great time every place I went. I've been truly blessed."

Included among the blessings he is most proud of is winning the Western Pennsylvania Division I championship at his beloved Leechburg High School. The size of the student body actually made them more fit for Division II, but Frank wanted them to play up against the best competition possible. So winning the title meant besting schools two, three, or even four times their size.

"They just wanted to win so bad," he recalls of his players from those years.

He also recalls his single Ivy League championship at Princeton, where he installed the veer and served as offensive coordinator. That huge win against Dartmouth stands out, sure. But there was another victory Frank credits even more with that team's success.

"We fell behind twenty-one to nothing against Cornell and had to throw the ball to come back and win the game. Jake McCandless came up to me after the game and said, 'You know, Frank, we never could've won this game in the past. We could never throw the ball like we did today.' That game gave us momentum, confidence, something to build on. If we hadn't have come back, I think the season might've turned out to be a struggle. That game changed everything."

And what does Frank Cignetti think of the state, or plight, of the game of football today?

"Obviously, you've got this concussion crisis making an impact. But I see other issues too. I see parental influence having a negative impact across all sports, soccer and football included. But what we're also dealing with is a decrease in the size of the student bodies at high schools that used to pride themselves on being football powerhouses. In western Pennsylvania, for example, all that has changed. A lot of the traditional steel town and coal town communities just don't have the great football players they used to. They don't have the populations they once had."

Frank is highlighting a societal trend exemplified by, but not limited to, the once thriving coal and steel towns of Pennsylvania. On June 26, 2017, the *New York Times* ran a front-page article entitled "Another Blow for a Battered Work Force" that covers the comparable loss of retail jobs in places like Johnstown, Pennsylvania.

"Small cities in the Midwest and Northeast are particularly vulnerable," the article notes of that growing reality. "When major industries left town, retail accounted for a growing share of the job market in places like Johnstown, Decatur, Illinois, and Saginaw, Michigan. Now the work force is getting hit a second time, and there is little to fall back on."

"'Every time you lose a corner store, every time you lose a restaurant, every time you lose a small clothing store, it detracts from the quality of life, as well as the job loss,'" John McGrath, professor of management at the University of Pittsburgh, Johnstown, told the *Times* for the same article.

"The demographics are changing and the sport has suffered as a result," Frank adds. "But the character aspect of the game hasn't changed. I believe that, number one, football still provides high school kids with an opportunity to get a great education they might not be able to get otherwise. And if they're good enough, they still have a chance to go Division I and maybe even play at the next level where they can make the kind of money that can really help their families. The whole thing about football is the mental and physical toughness you develop. You might be a part of a team that didn't win, but that doesn't mean you can't develop the same things, learn to be what a winner's all about. You just have to be there working hard every day, working to get better on every play you're on the field, in practice or in a game situation."

He stops briefly to reflect on his own upbringing, how unlikely it was to be where he is now compared to where he started. He speaks with pride over being a first generation Italian-American, how his father came to America at the age of twelve and worked in the coal mines, how his mother seldom spoke English. Then his father was seriously injured in a mining accident and could never work again. A pair of Frank's brothers and sisters (he was the youngest of six by thirteen years) basically took over the family.

That brother had won a football scholarship to Ohio State but had to stay home to work in the local mill to support the family "so the rest of us would have a chance," Frank says. "So my older brother and sister were instrumental in my life. Without their support, I don't know where I'd be today. Football teams are a family too, a brotherhood. People have been very fortunate in the game, and you want to be sure you can pass it on to the next guy coming along. You want every team to be better, just like my goal for my children was to make sure they had a better situation than I had, a better start in life.

"The beauty of the game, and the sport itself, is being part of a team, and football is the ultimate team sport since on any given day so many people play an important role. You start with eleven on offense, eleven on defense, and eleven on special teams—that's a lot of people, even before you get to the backups and subs. And football teaches you commitment, mental toughness, and giving great effort, starting with winter workouts in January. My philosophy has always been that when you come onto the football field, I want you to be ready to play. During the winter, I used to do mat training with my kids to teach them quickness and agility. Then you get to spring ball and really get into teaching the fundamentals of the game. That's what I love most, how football goes from one thing to another. No matter how the season went, it ends and you get excited about recruiting. Then you get excited about going indoors for the winter, then spring ball, then you're thinking about summer training camp leading up to the season. No matter how bad something may have gone, you've always got something ahead of you to look forward to."

CHAPTER 9

BOB HALL—
BROKEN BUT NOT BEATEN

On the occasion of the 125th anniversary of its storied football program in 2003, Brown University celebrated by compiling an assemblage of its greatest players of all time at every position. For a program that had played in the first ever Rose Bowl game in 1916 and compiled an undefeated season a decade later, led by the legendary "Ironmen," comprised of seven players who never came off the field for six consecutive games, making that list was no small feat.

The quarterback selected was Bob Hall, from the class of 1966, and rightfully so.

Hall was named an honorable mention All-American by the Associated Press and first-team All-Ivy in 1965. That year, he also won the George Bulger Lowe Award as the outstanding player in New England, only the second player from Brown to do so. Hall established fifteen school records and five Ivy League marks in just two seasons and part of a third. His records of 135 pass completions in one season and for career total offense stood, incredibly, for two decades, and he was drafted in the fifth round by the Minnesota Vikings of the NFL after his senior season in 1965. All that, in spite of the fact that Hall played only five games as a sophomore after suffering a devastating leg injury in a game at Princeton in 1963.

"We were 4-1 at the time," Bob recalls. "I was running an option play when three or four players tackled me. I heard a snap and knew it wasn't good. The ambulance came out onto the field because they were afraid to move me, and the team doctor, Eddie Crane, had tears in his eyes. One of my teammates who'd heard the snap, Kenny Neal, was holding my hand."

He had suffered a clean break between the tibia and fibula bones in his leg, not as serious as a compound fracture, but in those days often a career ender. He stayed in the Princeton infirmary for a week and was told by doctors, both there and later in Providence, that his athletic career was over and he'd likely be walking with a limp for the rest of his life.

"The whole Princeton team came to visit me, including Štas Maliszewski," he smiles. "There were so many flowers in the room, it looked like a wake. Princeton's president, Robert Goheen, came to see me. So did Princeton's great basketball player Bill Bradley. They couldn't have been nicer. I've still got a game ball, signed by the whole team."

Bob flew home to Providence first class because he needed to keep his leg, casted all the way up to the hip, elevated. His Delta Phi fraternity brothers met him at the airport and got him safely back to campus. He had an apartment off campus and couldn't attend class for the remainder of the semester, so a number of his Brown professors, including the legendary John Rowe Workman from the classics department, stopped by regularly to keep Bob up on his classwork. He couldn't wait to begin his rehab, which he did as soon as he could walk, without all the modern methods and technology used today.

"I might have been broken, but I wasn't beaten. I'd go to the old Marvel Gym across from Brown Stadium, where they had this elevated track that circled the basketball court. I started by walking as best I could, which wasn't much. I was still limping by the time I started jogging and the limp was gone by the time I started running."

Every day. No exceptions.

He defied the odds and was ready to play again, without a limp, by his junior season the following fall, alternating between quarterback and halfback before regaining his QB job after leading the Bears to a 36–0 win over the University of Rhode Island. But Bob saved the best for last, finishing eighth in the country in passing and ninth in total offense his senior season, despite a weaker Brown squad's record falling to 2-7. The season was highlighted when Bob, for the first time, returned to Princeton's Palmer Stadium, the figurative scene of the crime. That day, he broke the record for total offense in one game that had been held by Princeton great Dick Kazmaier, the only Ivy League player to ever win the Heisman Trophy. (Yale greats Larry Kelley and Clint Frank won back-to-back Heismans in 1936 and 1937, but that was almost twenty years before the Ivy League was formed.)

"There was one low light from that day," Bob recalls today, grinning. "Štas Maliszewski intercepted one of my passes from his linebacker position. But I got some satisfaction when I ran him down from behind and tackled him."

After one season on the Vikings' taxi squad, he was traded to the Vancouver franchise of the Canadian Football League for none other than Joe Kapp, who'd go on to lead Minnesota to its first ever Super Bowl appearance. Once his football career finished up, he rented an apartment with a former teammate outside of Boston where, one day, he found himself combing through a stack of letters he'd received while being laid up in the Princeton infirmary. One was from a Brown alum who'd been at Palmer Stadium to witness Bob's injury firsthand. The alum, who had a big position at the brokerage firm Paine Webber, went on to offer Bob his services in the financial sector, should he ever be interested. Bob was indeed interested and was hired the very same day he went in for an interview at the firm's office on Federal Street in Boston. It was also where he met his wife, Robin, who worked there.

All because of football.

* * *

"I wish I'd played with him," says Paul Choquette, another all-time great Brown football player. "Bob was such a threat, as great a runner as he was a passer. He was an old-fashioned triple threat who in the old days of the single wing offense would have been classified as a tailback. I can remember other players coming back from injuries, but never as devastating as the one Bob suffered and he returned to the field as skilled and fast as ever. He never lost his drive and spirit to put out for the team and leave it all on the field. And the teams around him weren't great teams, but he never let that affect his play or his attitude. So many times Bob walked off the field as the outstanding player even though he played for the losing side. That just doesn't happen all that often."

Choquette should know. A bruising fullback in the late 50s, he's one of three Brown players picked for the All-Ivy Team of the Decade. He long held the Brown career record for most rushing attempts and yards gained and led the team in rushing all three years. He was also among the top ten ball carriers in the nation in his junior and senior seasons, excelled at defensive back, as well as a steady punter. Choquette was a two-time All-Ivy selection, earned All-East honors, and was named Rhode Island Athlete of the Year by Words Unlimited. And, not surprisingly, he has strong feelings about the need to preserve the game of football, though not entirely in its current form.

"I don't think kids should play tackle football until high school. That said, I'm a strong believer in all the things the game stands for," says the current vice chair of the Gilbane Building Company, one of the largest construction firms in the country. "We're often asked in the early stages of a project how ready we are. Well, there's a moment before a football game when you're walking out through the tunnel to the sounds of the crowd, the clack of your cleats and patter of your heart beating, and you know you're ready to play. I tell clients when they ask about a project we're on, *that's* how ready we are. The emotion of football is incomparable; there's nothing else like it. You play once a week, ten games a year, after all that training, practice and preparation, and that experience sticks with you for the rest of your life. Those Saturdays aren't just games, they're events. It's good for kids to have that moment in their lives, and football asks more of our kids than other sports do."

Choquette speaks of how specialization in football has enhanced the game, not detracted from it.

"So many more kids are getting involved. And they're better prepared for what they're asked to do, because they're not being asked to do everything. It behooves coaches to get as many kids involved as they can and that leads to more kids staying with a program because they know they're going to get their chance."

Choquette came to Gilbane as General Counsel in 1969 after graduating Harvard Law School. He rose to become both the company's president and CEO and remains a key cog today at the age of 78. During his playing days, he was the recipient of the National Football Foundation Student-Athlete Award for New England and was inducted into the College Football Hall of Fame's first class ever in 1959. And he continues to apply the lessons he learned on the field to business and the boardroom.

"I've never lost the competitive fire, having transferred it from the field to the business environment. What you learn and nurture in football works as well off the field as on it. The ability to get along with different kinds of people; that camaraderie in the locker room is what you're looking for in the office. You learn not to let setbacks stop you from ultimately winning the day, learn to get along with people no matter where they came from or their backgrounds or the color of their skin. Football teaches you the ability to walk in somebody else's shoes, encourages you to have each other's back. Gilbane was just rated the best company to work for in the state of Rhode Island and I credit the lessons of football we employ every day for a great portion of that."

* * *

"It's the ultimate team sport," Bob Hall believes to this day. "It teaches you discipline and teamwork. You have a role and you adhere to that role, because you never want to let your teammates down. I was a victim of the so-called violence in the game, but I wouldn't change a thing. I would do the same thing all over."

Bob went on to serve as president of the Brown Football Association for fifteen years, during which time the Bears won three of their four Ivy League titles. He also spearheaded the group's first true fundraising efforts, beginning with a golf tournament he continued to chair through 2016 and of which he remains a primary organizer in his capacity as chairman of the association.

One of the most respected and beloved names ever in college sports, Donald "Dee" Rowe, has especially fond memories of Bob Hall.

"I don't think there could be a better competitor that I have coached," said the longtime basketball coach at the University of Connecticut and former athletic director at Worcester Academy, where his relationship with Hall was founded. "We had a very special bond. There was no better leader, and he was never captured by himself. His kindness and concern for all was a true inspiration. This 'old coach' could not have been more proud or grateful for the opportunity to get to know him. He has the desire, courage, attitude, pride, and character that simply would not let his team lose."

While at Worcester Academy, Bob captained the football and baseball teams and started in basketball. The overall record of those three sports during his two years at the school was 70-6, highlighted by a state championship in basketball. And the football squad lost only one game in those two years. He has remained close to the school ever since, serving as chairman of the board for twenty years.

"He was a treasure who has never stopped giving back," Rowe concludes. "No one is more admired or respected."

Bob never coached football, but his playing career actually extended into his late fifties and even early sixties thanks to a traditional fundraiser in his adopted hometown of Barrington, Rhode Island, in which the alumni would play the varsity team. Full pads before a packed house every year at Victory Field, where the team has long played its home games.

"It started out as two-hand touch, but it didn't stay that way for long, less and less as the years went on. They were surprised, because they didn't know I could still throw the ball."

The game ended maybe ten years back, and Bob recalls exactly why.

"We beat up on them too much," he laughs. "The coach didn't want to play us anymore."

CHAPTER 10

PAUL SAVIDGE—
"IT'S THE COLOR OF THE HEART"

There's a news clipping from January of 1966 that pictures Princeton University football players Bert Kerstetter and Kit Mill paying their daily respects to Paul Savidge in Princeton Hospital. We see the mustachioed Savidge wearing a high-tech (at the time) neck brace as he continued his recovery from the spinal injury suffered in the season finale against Dartmouth. At the point of that January visit, it was still unclear whether Savidge would ever regain complete mobility.

The injury occurred during the final minutes of defensive tackle Savidge's storied career. Few remember the actual collision or tackle. It seemed like nothing dramatic, even to Paul himself.

"I actually stayed in the game for another play," he recalls, "but something didn't feel right. There wasn't much pain in the area, just a real rigidity in the neck muscles. Nobody knew what was wrong, that I'd actually broken my neck, until the next day when the X-rays confirmed the initial diagnosis made at the Princeton infirmary. In retrospect, I clearly shouldn't have stayed in the game and should have gone to the hospital right away, but I sat on the bench until the end of the game that saw us lose the Ivy League championship to Dartmouth. It was the first game we'd lost in two seasons, and I was thinking more about that than how my neck felt."

In those days, Paul reflects, football training and medical staffs weren't nearly as skilled nor as educated on diagnosing and dealing with injuries as they are today.

"If an injury like that had happened today, you'd have medical assistants and team doctors on hand to immediately make a determination that something serious had happened. They'd take you for a more detailed evaluation right away. Back then, they were just not as organized and certain injuries were pretty much ignored. If you could walk, you were healthy enough to play. In high school, I was a day student at a boarding school. My coach, who doubled as the athletic director, was a big guy and tough as nails himself. If you got hurt, he'd say, 'Get back in there! It's a long way from your heart. It's not that serious.'"

As captain of the Hun School, Savidge learned that football is about respect, not intimidation. And that you earn respect not by winning so much as playing hard. Paul recalls a game where Hun was pitted against a local public high school with practically no budget for athletics, to the point where the players had to purchase much of their own equipment, including helmets.

"One of our assistant coaches warned us that they were going to come off the bus looking like a Polish Christmas tree and, sure enough, the players are wearing different colored helmets—red, yellow, blue, green, black—because they had to use what they had. You kind of feel bad and you wanna laugh at them. But they were well coached and played so hard. I left that game realizing it's not the color of your helmet that matters, it's the color of your heart."

Paul had heart and then some. His injury didn't reduce his love of the game one bit, but it did make him look at it differently.

"There's a famous story," Paul continues, "about Princeton playing a preseason scrimmage against Syracuse back in the days when Jim Brown was running for the Orangemen. The Princeton quarterback, in the old single wing, was more of a blocker and on this day he must've gotten his bell rung pretty good. He came back to the huddle a bit woozy but no one noticed, because no one noticed those kinds of things back then. He was so dazed, he forgot what play they were supposed to run and ended up calling the same exact play on second down. Then called it again on third down.

"It's hard to envision anything like that happening today. First off, you have much better medical game management from the sideline, medical and training staff erring on the side of caution. And teams have also started minimizing contact during practice to cut down especially on head injuries in high school and college. Add that to the fact there've been technical improvements to helmets and the game could really be considered safer today than back when I played."

Paired on defense with linebacker Štas Maliszewski, Princeton's coach Dick Colman called the two of them "the best defenders in the East," spearheading the team's incredible two-year run. That season was highlighted by Princeton's game against Rutgers in which Paul faced off against his twin brother, Peter (pictured together on the first page of this chapter; Paul is number 63). As *Sports Illustrated*'s vaunted "Football Week" review wrote on October 4, 1965:

> *...the referee last Saturday solemnly introduced George Peter Savidge, Rutgers' 205-pound center and captain, to George Paul Savidge, Princeton's 220-pound defensive right tackle and captain. Within minutes of the ceremony these fraternal twins were using their considerable talents to break each other in half. As usual, the brothers' battle ended in a rather bloody standoff, but Princeton's George Paul had the help of Charles Gogolak, a 155-pound place kicker who swipes at the ball sideways. The little monster kicked six field goals, including one that was recorded as 52 yards but carried nearly 70. George Peter had to swallow Rutgers' fourth straight loss, 32–6.*
>
> *Ask anyone on either campus, and he will tell you he would not trade his Savidge for the other, even if the other side threw in a*

platoon of 200-pound sprinters. Rutgers followers, for instance, are quick to point out that last year the fullback diving straight over center averaged more than five yards a crack, an amazing statistic when you consider it means running smack-bang into the most populated area on the field. Princeton people simply remind you that their Savidge led his team to an Ivy League title.

The fraternal twins, interestingly enough, were both christened with the first name "George," as were there two other brothers, after their father. George Sr. supervised operations on a 430-acre farm in Lambertville, New Jersey where Paul got his start building his future football prowess by piling sixty-pound bales of hay seven stacks deep atop a wagon. But his mother, as the same *Sports Illustrated* article notes, would often find him hiding in a tree when it was his turn to mow the lawn. Both Paul and Peter (their middle names) earned scholarships as day students at the Hun School and went on to become co-captains of the football team. But there was a problem: the farm chores had built them up to the point where no one else could match up against them in one-on-one drills, forcing the brothers to go up against each other much the same way they had when Princeton faced Rutgers.

"I never got out of it with less than a bloody nose," Pete recalled in 1965 to *Sports Illustrated.*

Paul's Princeton career was of such renown that he was named to the second team of the Ivy League Silver Anniversary Team in 1981. (Štas Maliszewski, his partner in crime on defense, was selected as a first-team linebacker.)

Their season-ending loss against Dartmouth notwithstanding, 1965 was otherwise a stellar year for Princeton, with the Tigers going 8-1. But the aftermath of the season was dominated by Savidge's prognosis and ultimate recovery. And on November 14, 2015, Savidge walked—yes, walked—onto the field along with teammates Ron Landeck and the aforementioned Štas Maliszewski to accept the John P. Poe–Richard W. Kazmaier, Jr. Football Trophy at the annual homecoming celebration. A fitting cap to a football career that had come to a premature finish.

"Playing football was and is a wonderful experience," Paul says today. "The values you can realize, the goals you can meet, the confidence you can build—it's hard to find another vehicle that can accomplish those kinds of things. But it has to be played, and practiced, sensibly and that's where the improved equipment and medical care come in. I can remember in high school sitting on the bench in the locker room unable to move—I mean I'd cramped up so bad, I couldn't move a muscle, because in those days we didn't know all we know now about fluid and salt intake, and I don't ever remember any talk about nutrition and the only sports drink we had was milk.

"Look, football is a very physical sport, and that's why it's so important to continue to address and mitigate injury issues, particularly when it comes to concussions. But the benefits you take from an experience in football can be applied to any endeavor you pursue afterwards. The lessons stay with you when you go into the world. In my case, I wasn't actually a pre-med major, but I decided to go to medical school anyway. It meant I had to do an extra year in college to accumulate the required course work before I applied. And it was football that gave me the strength to allow me to do that and know that my future was going to be a bright one."

Paul's life-changing decision to enter medicine was actually birthed during those long months he was hospitalized, in traction much of the time.

"I went from tackling ball carriers to tackling real-life challenges. I couldn't sleep, so I'd walk the halls in my underwear in the dead of night. Fortunately, there weren't many people about to see me. What such a long hospital stay did was force me to make a decision as to my career. My world had changed, and I needed to focus on my long-term goals. I'd always been enamored by medicine, the idea of working with and helping people. But I hadn't really considered medicine as a career until the way they took care of me in Princeton Hospital. They gave me my life back, and I realized that's what I wanted to do for others. And what I learned on the football field—about growth and courage and taking risks and pursuing your dream—allowed me to accomplish that."

He went into obstetrics and gynecology, instead of orthopedics or neurosurgery, and estimates he's probably delivered 2,500 babies in the course of a storied career that has also involved teaching and mentoring. Even now, needing some dental work performed, Paul opted to have it done at a school where future dentists are trained.

"Being a doctor," he says, "is all about the privilege of helping people."

And Dr. Savidge remains convinced that football can and will continue helping young people who have the privilege to play it.

"You learn to approach situations and challenges knowing the solution only comes through hard work and persistence, and you have a basic level of confidence that you can accomplish anything you set out to do. One success leads to another—that's what the game teaches you, but there are also these collateral benefits like building respect, helping others, making friendships.

"It's a wonderful game," he continues, "in large part because you're not going to be successful unless you have good team coordination. It's a game based on individual effort, but the individual has to do his job to achieve greatness. You have to perform like pistons firing in sequence inside an engine. I imagine myself as a coach sometimes after a difficult loss, maybe in a game we were supposed to win. I'd ask my players, 'Did you give a hundred percent? Because if you did, take those sad expressions off your faces, because you did what you were expected to do.'

"That doesn't always translate into success. The loss is only in the numbers, not in the person so much. You need to finish a game knowing that you gave your full effort and maybe you'll be more successful next time. You gain that foundation in football to allow you to travel through life successfully, like a road map. It's such a competitive game, and it doesn't just prepare you for life but also for all the challenges you face along the way."

CHAPTER 11

MURRY BOWDEN—
A REAL COWBOY

"The day of my acceptance to Dartmouth College in the spring of 1967, I spent the afternoon riding my horse gathering cattle on our ranch in West Texas," Murry Bowden said, opening his remarks upon being inducted into the College Football Hall of Fame in 2003. "My thoughts drifted that afternoon as I pondered whether I should leave Texas and head back east to college. I doubted there would be any real cowboys in my class. I tried to imagine what my classmates would be like and if I would actually fit into the Ivy League. I had no idea what to expect. I was very curious but slightly intimidated. I had to find out and decided to embark on what turned out to be the biggest adventure of my life."

At that point of his life, at eighteen, Murry had never been north of the Mason-Dixon Line. His interest in, and ultimate matriculation at, Dartmouth had started with one of the literally hundreds of letters famed coach Bob Blackman sent to high schools all over the country in search of recruits who otherwise might've never known the school existed.

"You learn leadership qualities in football," Bowden told *Football Matters* in October of 2015. "People are looking for somebody to say, 'Let's go take this mountain.' It is a little bit inspiration, a little bit intellectualism, and a lot of brute force. I just think it's a great sport. It's a very difficult sport, but it's played a big role in my development from growing up on a ranch in West Texas all the way to the Ivy League. It helped me get there."

And it was also instrumental in getting the glistening new Atlanta, Georgia headquarters of the College Football Hall of Fame built, since Bowden's business savvy and construction acumen were crucial to that process. But a long time passed from his initial visit to Dartmouth's campus in 1967 and the new hall's opening in 2015. Bowden actually visited Yale first with Coach Carmen Cozza hot after him too.

"My high school football coach had been in the army with a bunch of Dartmouth guys," he recalls today. "He said, 'You should consider Dartmouth College.' I was ranked number one in my class. Academics had always been as important to me as football, but my coach telling me that I could be All-Ivy by my sophomore year certainly stoked my interest."

He came to visit Yale on his recruiting trip north from West Texas, where his student host was none other than fellow West Texas native George W. Bush.

"You need to come to Yale," Murry recalls the future president telling him. "But Dartmouth has its redeeming qualities. For example, if you like reading poetry alone on Saturday nights, you'll love Dartmouth."

"Well," Murry picks up, "I grew up around cattle, riding in rodeos, so Yale was a bit different and intimidating for a kid from Snyder, Texas [the same hometown as Grant Teaff]. Dartmouth was too, but less so because it was located in the small town of Hanover."

Fortuitous indeed for Murry, but especially for Dartmouth. The year before Murry's arrival on the Dartmouth campus, the coaching staff had attended some spring practices of other teams, including Penn State that had just put in a new defense based on the eight-man front. Penn State was able to innovate because they had the personnel that allowed them to do so. For the eight-man front to work, for example, the Dartmouth staff identified the key position as the rover back who has to have the ability to play the pass and run equally well. The coaches brought that principle back to Hanover, just at the time the recruiting battle for Murry Bowden was heating up. And they saw in Bowden a rover back who fit the mold of that position to a T, enabling the school to play a defense it never had before, thanks to a bulk mail letter from Bob Blackman that ultimately brought a legitimate pro prospect into the Ivy League.

"I'd learned to play football early in life under a coach who'd played in the NFL," Murry says, of all those pieces falling into place. "He taught me how to tackle, pursue the football, and find the football. It sounds like a cliché because it is, but I just had a nose for the ball. Almost like a sixth sense. I knew where the ball carrier was going and I was going to beat him to the spot. And playing the rover back freed me up to pursue the football from the backside, and get the most from the quickness, speed, and agility with which I was blessed."

And playing at Dartmouth, in the Ivy League, exceeded his expectations.

"When I got there, there were a hundred kids on the team and two-thirds of them had been captains of their high school teams. We had one who'd turned down Notre Dame, another who chose Dartmouth over Arizona, and another who turned down Nebraska. In many ways it was culture shock, but it many ways it wasn't. There were a lot of teammates that looked like me. The football team was composed of the 'big fishes in little ponds' profile, a lot of guys from small-town public schools all across America who selected Dartmouth. It was truly a fantastic team. But we started slow. We had a losing season my sophomore year. That was devastating to me. Dartmouth did not have losing seasons. And I was on the first losing team Dartmouth had in long time. Ouch! An assistant coach tried to console me by saying, 'Don't worry, this will be the last game you lose in your career.' Small consolation, but you know what? It turned out he was almost right—we went on to lose only one more game through my junior and senior seasons."

Murry's senior season of 1970 the Dartmouth team went undefeated, won the Ivy League title, and finished ranked 13th in the country, just behind Nebraska.

"Only three teams that year even scored on us," he recalls proudly of the season that saw him selected as a First Team All-American. "That's how great our defense was."

But there was more to Murry's Dartmouth experience than just football.

"What's awesome about Ivy League football is there were all these great athletes, but they were committed to accomplish other things in life. They were smart and ambitious. They weren't about to let football be the end of their lives, just a part of their lives. I felt very fortunate to have made the choice to attend Dartmouth. It expanded my universe. The world was much bigger than I thought it was when I left Snyder, Texas."

And he loved playing for the great Bob Blackman.

"He was very, very focused," Murry told *Football Matters* a few years back. "He was a perfectionist. I learned a lot from him. He was a taskmaster in many ways who was very creative. All of those qualities helped make him successful. I felt very blessed to play for him."

At the same time, Murry correctly recognized that someday football was going to be over and he needed, wanted, to achieve other things in his life, as ambitious as he was competitive. Playing the rover back, roaming the field in search of the opening and angle to bring down the ball carrier, became a metaphor for his life. Bowden graduated with a degree in psychology, but opted to go to law school at the University of Texas rather than pursue a professional football career. After he finished law school in 1975, Bowden opened an Austin law firm with a group of guys he'd gone to school with at Texas. But that proved only to be a short chapter in his life.

It didn't take Murry long to learn practicing the law wasn't for him. He was somebody who'd grown up getting his hands dirty, taking great pride in having something tangible to show for all his efforts and hard work. The real estate development world beckoned and he plunged straight in, building his first apartments in 1976.

"I was twenty-five years old," Bowden told *Football Matters*, "and I took the full risk of building my first apartment complex. I had no partners. I did the legal work and the construction work. It was my first deal. And I've built over fifty thousand apartment units and counting since then. Eventually, I expanded my developments around the country. My company has developed projects in over thirty cities across the United States."

And the lessons learned from football have been key to that growth as well.

"I think the primary lesson I learned from football was that great accomplishment demands a maniacal focus. In the game, my focus was to get to the football. In business, same thing—I needed to focus on one thing, stay with it, improve every day. In football, tackling was my thing. In business, I decided it was apartments, and I have remained focused on that since inception. My company has developed over nine billion dollars-worth of apartment properties. I've had opportunities to expand my focus to other property types, but I decided to stay with one product. I realized that if you really want to be great, not good, you need focus. Live it, breathe it, perfect it."

This is the mantra Murry has lived by, both on and off the field. There is so much he loves about football and draws a clear connection between how running down ball carriers led him into another world he's tackled with comparable aplomb today.

"Being great at something is pretty darn important in life. Another way to insure success is to always be prepared. My senior year, before we played Harvard, Coach Blackman engaged a math professor who provided a statistical analysis on the Crimson's tendencies. For example, on third down and long, with five yards or more to go for a first down and the football situated on the hash mark, Harvard ran the fullback draw one hundred percent of the time! So, sure enough, I'm playing the backside linebacker position in the Harvard game, it's third and seven and the ball is on the hash mark. I start barking, 'Draw! Draw! Watch for the draw!' to all my teammates.

"Well, the quarterback, a fellow Texan, must've heard me because he stared at me with this mystified look on his face. Our eyes met and I yelled out, 'You're going to run the draw, aren't you?' And he yelled back, 'Yes!' And they did. Can you believe it? And we stuffed them."

Of course, Murry did deviate from apartment building for his Hanover Company (named for the town in which Dartmouth is located) when he chaired the Building Committee in the relocation of the College Football Hall of Fame from South Bend, Indiana to a gleaming new facility in Atlanta, Georgia in August of 2014. He was inducted into the College Football

Hall of Fame in 2003. He joined the board of the National Football Foundation in 2004 and began to serve the game of football in that capacity.

"I hadn't ever built anything quite like the College Football Hall of Fame," he told *Football Matters* at the time. "I had built a lot of apartments, but this was something different, terribly interesting and unique. It's a great building. The city of Atlanta really wanted to get this done, so we decided to build a new Hall of Fame there. Even though the National Football Foundation wants to be a representative of football border-to-border, coast-to-coast, you are limited to locating the actual Hall of Fame in one place. We chose Atlanta, because there are a lot of amusements, attractions, and sports venues in the downtown area. And the city is situated at the crossroads of the ACC (Atlantic Coast Conference) and SEC (Southeast Conference), so we thought this would be a really great location."

It has proven to be just that. Bowden serves as the Hall's chair, as well as vice-chairman of the entire National Football Foundation.

"The Hall's purpose is to preserve the history of this great game. We have different stakeholders in the game of football, including the players, coaches, media, colleges, fans, and all have different perspectives on the game. We need a single institution to serve as a representative of all with the intent of preserving the future of the game by continuing to look at its past; celebrate its great moments, players, heroes and traditions. Football is embedded in the fabric of our country. It is seared into the consciousness of our nation. Friday nights, Saturdays, Sundays. Tailgating. The whole experience, the whole spectacle creates community, excitement, and thrills. It is a positive distraction for people from their everyday lives. The Hall of Fame exists because we need to make sure all the great people in this sport are remembered, all the great games are remembered, and all the great teams are remembered. The tendency is to focus on what's going on today, but it's important that football's history is always available to its stakeholders to study, appreciate, remember, and celebrate."

It is indeed a different game today, more pass-oriented and less reliant on the big backs who dominated football for so many years, when the Single Wing, the T-formation, and Option were in favor.

"Defense today," Murry says, "is about containment. The game has changed."

Something doesn't necessarily bother him, so long as what he sees as the most important facet of the game is preserved above all else.

"If you don't have great people, great athletes coming into the game, it won't be the same and the sport will be minimized. Safety concerns will have a major impact on the future of football. We must objectively gather the facts surrounding player safety and respond appropriately to make the game safer. Our future rests on getting this right." He stops, then starts again. "At its heart, football is still this wonderful blend of brute strength and artistry. I don't know if there's another sport that so fully embraces these two diametrically opposed movements."

PART THREE:

SHINING STARS

"I've never been a fan of individual awards because football is such a team sport. There's so many things that goes into making plays. It's about teammates trusting one another and working together."

—Troy Polamalu

CHAPTER 12

STEVE JORDAN –
"I'VE BEEN SO FORTUNATE"

Between his 1979 freshman and 1980 sophomore seasons at Brown University, Steve Jordan bulked up and gained twenty pounds. That, though, didn't change the opinion of an assistant coach who famously said that the future NFL All-Pro "would never play a minute of varsity football."

He was right only in the sense that Jordan went on to play far more than a minute. By the time his Brown career had ended, the Phoenix, Arizona native had twice been named a first-team All-Ivy selection and honorable mention All-American his junior year. His 1,330 career receiving yards ranked third in the Brown record book upon graduation, while his eighteen yards per reception are still third in Brown football history. He also set single-season Brown records for receiving yards in one game (188 versus Penn in 1981) and the receiving record for yards in a season (693 in 1981). Finally, he was presented with the program's Tuss McLaughry Award, which was named after the school's legendary coach from 1926–1940 and was given to the player who contributes the most to the team through sportsmanship, performance, and influence.

"I was kind of a late bloomer in high school," Jordan said in a 2002 interview, quoted for the 2007 celebration of Black History Month. "I was about six foot three and about a hundred and ninety-five pounds. I honed the concepts of tenacity and made the best of every opportunity. I was mostly a JV as a sophomore, but I became a full-time starter on the varsity as a junior. The coaching there was great. When I earned All-Ivy as a junior it was the first time I got all anything."

And he wasn't done yet.

Jordan went on to enjoy a thirteen-year career with the Minnesota Vikings, during which he was picked for the Pro Bowl six times (1986–1991), was named All-Pro three times (1986, 1987, 1989), and was selected as one of the "50 Greatest Vikings" in 2010. He caught 498 passes for over 6,000 yards and 28 touchdowns, generally considered not just a great tight end but also one who helped both elevate and redefine the position forever.

We need to pause there. That an Ivy League player had such a lasting impact on the professional game is impressive in itself; the fact that he did it for one of the NFL's finest teams of the time, in often less than perfect Minnesota weather conditions under the legendary Vikings coach Bud Grant, makes that impact even more pronounced, spectacular even.

"I did an intense workout regimen before camp, and I was in the best shape of my life to that point," he said in the same interview noted above. "Then on one of my first days there we're doing a one-on-one blocking drill, and I'm up against Matt Blair. The whistle blows and Matt ran right through me. It was an eye-opening experience. Bud Grant didn't keep many rookies back then, but I'd made enough of an impression on offense and special teams that I made the team."

Jordan didn't play much his rookie year, but that changed the following year.

"We had some injuries that season and I luckily stayed healthy so they had to play me. By my third year, I became a starter. The Vikings' big acquisition that year was another tight end, Don Hasselbeck, and the word was that he was going to be the starter. I ended up having a great season and started every game for the next ten years."

In a June 2, 2015 article entitled "Minnesota Vikings: Best 5 Wide Receivers Ever," 247Sports named him number three on the storied franchise's all-time list, behind only Cris Carter and, of course, Randy Moss. Even though he played tight end.

"Steve Jordan was easily one of the best of all time and was, without a shadow of a doubt, the greatest to ever play the position for the Minnesota Vikings," the article's author, Shawn Muller, notes. "He is third all-time in franchise history with 6,307 yards and 498 receptions...both of which are tops for the tight end position. In today's NFL, you see the position serving as a focal point for a lot of offenses throughout the league. Jordan really was ahead of his time and will forever hold a place amongst the greatest pass catchers in franchise history."

And that distinguished, even exceptional career on the field has been equaled by what he's done off it since his retirement from the Vikings in 1994. But Jordan began building that road long before, first at Brown where he earned a degree in engineering and later with the Vikings as well. Even at the height of his career, he spent his summers working as an engineer for a construction firm in Minneapolis, building on his Brown degree and laying the foundation for the great things that were to come.

Such a path has taken him to director of development for Ryan Industries, US, based in his home state of Arizona. And Jordan draws a clear connection between his experience playing football and running a major department for one of the country's top construction firms.

"There were life lessons I learned playing the game I apply every day in business. Teamwork, discipline, being accountable to other people, developing a sense of responsibility—that's just part of what I learned in the game of football. Growing up as a kid, I wasn't an extrovert by any stretch. What football did for me was help me improve my social skills, particularly by playing the game with so many other kids and building a sense of self-esteem from interacting with them. Football gave me the opportunity to develop in that regard, and I continued to develop these skills when I was fortunate enough to play in the pros. I became a player rep and went on to serve on the executive council of the players' union. I not only refined my communication skills, I also learned the business side of the game, helping to resolve union and labor management disputes and strategizing on how best to get policies through the NFL Players Association. We set up a subsidiary to help us stabilize and strengthen the organization. I was still playing the game at the same time I was getting experience for the business career I'd end up pursuing after my football career ended."

He also sees clear similarities between being a football player and helping to run a major construction and real estate development company.

"I talk about this all the time. I try to dispel the myth of the dumb jock who lands a job just because he played the game. I look at sports in general, but especially football because it's the most team oriented of any of them and there are so many lessons you learn from the scope of that. It's a microcosm of society. How you deal and interact with diverse personalities to achieve what you want, always trying to bring people together to work toward a common goal. What I learned in football is that there are 'me' people and 'team' guys. The 'me' people tend to be the stars and you need to get them to perform to the level you want, but not to the detriment of the team, which is sometimes a fine line. You can't avoid being judged on the football field, because your performance is there for everyone to see. You set out a strategy for how we're going to win this week, and it's all about executing that strategy just like you practiced it. Same thing in business, when you take on long-term strategic planning. In football, sometimes you know a season is a growth season, so you can be better the next year. People have to believe in the plan and have the patience needed to achieve it. That, to a great extent, defines long-term success in the business world, just as it does on the football field. And you also learn to adjust on the fly, deal with disappointment, and move on."

Jordan attended the Pro Football Hall of Fame induction weekend in Canton, Ohio in August of 2005, there to represent Brown University and its long-overdue enshrinee, African-American football pioneer Fritz Pollard, who led Brown to an appearance in the first Rose Bowl game ever, versus Washington in 1916. But Steve never made the trip to Canton to celebrate his own induction, something many see as a gross oversight given how he stacks up against the competition.

Quoting from that same 2007 Black History Celebration memo, "Joe Horrigan, the Vice President for Communications & Exhibits at the Pro Football Hall of Fame in Canton, Ohio, cannot recall Jordan's name ever appearing on the Hall of Fame ballot. Yet, among the tight ends on the 2006 ballot, Jordan had more receiving yards and more Pro Bowl selections than all five (Mark Bavaro, Todd Christensen, Ben Coates, Russ Francis, and Brent Jones). In fact, Jordan went to more Pro Bowls than each of the six modern era tight ends who have been enshrined (Dave Casper, Mike Ditka, John Mackey, Ozzie Newsome, Jackie Smith, and Kellen Winslow)."

Does he feel slighted? No. Is he bitter? Also no.

"I give that one to God," Jordan says. "I've been so fortunate. At the end of the day, I may not get into the Hall of Fame. But I still had the benefit of playing a game that I love at a pretty high level for a significant amount of time, so I'm fortunate to have had all the experiences that I did. That can never be taken away from me. My contemporaries look back and say, 'That dude was a player.' If I get the recognition that comes with being inducted into the Hall of Flame, that's awesome. If not, that's fine too."

The year after representing Brown University in attending Fritz Pollard's Hall of Fame induction ceremony, Jordan won the NCAA's Silver Anniversary Award, and with good reason. The award recognizes former student-athletes 25 years after completing their successful collegiate careers, something that describes him to a T.

"It was really special because that award is not just about being a good college athlete, it also recognizes what they call 'useful purpose' at Brown, to achieve things off the field from a business and work standpoint, as well as on. It means so much because it's about being recognized for what you've contributed to the greater good, to society."

Jordan established the Steve R. Jordan Endowed Scholarship for Minority Athletes at Brown in 2000. Other professional and civic contributions have included being a member of the College Football Hall of Fame Advisory Board, Leukemia Golf Classic (as honorary chairman), Cystic Fibrosis Foundation (honorary board member), Special Olympics (volunteer), National Missing Children's Foundation, Multiple Sclerosis Society, Boys and Girls Clubs of America, Camp Confidence, and Minnesota Attorney General's Office Alliance for a Drug-Free Minnesota.

Of his many passions, Jordan ranks his contributions to his alma mater right near the top.

"I have a real passion for the school. I've served as a trustee, a fellow, and on the board of the Brown Sports Foundation. I want to make a positive impact, to give back."

Steve also speaks passionately about his association with the Phoenix Thunderbirds, a group of fellow local businessmen who've banded together, taking a true team approach to raise money for charitable causes primarily through their sponsorship of the Phoenix Open, regarded as one of the top golf tournaments on the pro tour.

"We've raised a boatload of money to support youth programs and social programs as well. When I got started, we were raising around three million dollars. Now, fifteen years later we're up to ten million, which allows us to do so many good things for the greater community. Like provide seed money for one Boys and Girls Club or computers for another. One of our local Little League baseball teams made it to the national playoffs and we were able to fund their travel. We developed a program that's now nationwide called First Tee, which provides golf instructions to disadvantaged kids for free. There's a program that goes along with it that serves a lot of need, stressing nine key character traits while exposing more kids to the game of golf. We've picked up the slack in a lot of local communities that have cut back on physical education classes. We have fifteen locations in the metro Phoenix area and have reached three hundred thousand kids. A couple years ago, a girl our program introduced to the game got a scholarship to play golf at Arizona State University."

Jordan enjoyed a long NFL career, but he knew when it was time to go.

"I could see the damage that artificial turf had done to me for thirteen years. Still, I was fortunate to have no major injuries. There was no way I was going to take drugs to play. I was in a cycle of whirlpools, massages, tape jobs like a mummy, playing with a neck brace, a knee brace."

Nonetheless, Jordan couldn't be more proud of the fact that his son Cam followed him into the NFL as a first-round draft pick of the New Orleans Saints in 2014 where he has become a star.

"I'm thrilled for him to play professionally. We all want our kids to be successful and achieve their dreams, and for Cam that was one of them. I'm doubly blessed because I have two sons; one followed me into football and the other into construction. I'm happy for Cam but I'm concerned as a parent, too, because there's an injury factor he has to get through. But the grace of God has given him the ability and capacity to play in the NFL, and I have faith that God will protect him, after giving him this chance."

He speaks of Cam's workout regimen that allows him to endure a twenty-game (including exhibition) season against players who are bigger and faster than the ones who Steve played against, proud of how his son manages and trains his body on a year-round basis to mitigate injury. And Jordan also speaks of how what he calls "high-performance training" has changed the game by allowing players to transform their bodies. How, at one point, players were either big or fast and now they're both, packing an incredible amount of muscle mass into every hit. But he is also proud of how steps are being taken to make the game safer.

"Inspired by the NFL, kids are being taught a safer way to hit and tackle. They're being taught and coached better on how to play the game."

And it's not just football either, Steve stresses, noting the example of some high school soccer programs that have outlawed heading the ball because of the same concussion issues that have plagued football. It's something else entirely, though, that he's taken from the game.

"It's realizing that a lot of people have invested in me so it's incumbent on me to invest in others the same way, to believe in them the way people believed in me. I look back at all the teachers and coaches who helped mentor me, who gave me so much. I need to pass that on. I want to help improve the lives of others."

CHAPTER 13

REGGIE WILLIAMS—
"I WOULD DO IT ALL OVER AGAIN"

"He was never meant to be ordinary," Paul Daugherty wrote of Reggie Williams for *USA Today* on August 25, 2013. "Not as a hearing-impaired youth growing up in Flint, Michigan, not as an African-American Ivy Leaguer at Dartmouth, not as arguably the most proficient linebacker in the 45-year history of the Cincinnati Bengals. Not as a vice president at Disney, who created the most extensive youth sports complex in the world."

Even all that, though, tells only a small part of Reggie's story, a very small part, starting with how he ended up at Dartmouth College.

"Dartmouth came to my rescue after one of the most embarrassing moments of my high school career," he recalls today. "I thought I had done everything right, in terms of academics, playing football, and staying away from trouble. I grew up in Flint, Michigan during the Vietnam War and the battle for civil rights. The next major riot after Watts was Detroit. During my childhood, civil rights marches were happening all the time, in response to all the turmoil the country was facing. I remember when four young girls died in a bombing in Birmingham, Alabama. I remember when Martin Luther King was assassinated. But I avoided the turmoil, with an eye toward going to Michigan. Until the school's coaching staff told me I wasn't good enough, even though I fit all the criteria.

"What I didn't know then was that my high school coach had given my name to Dartmouth's head coach, Bob Blackman, because he knew I qualified academically. I'd applied to Dartmouth as an afterthought, but the same day I got the bad news from Michigan, I got home to find a letter from Coach Blackman waiting saying they had a spot for me."

Quite a thing, Reggie Williams going to the Ivy League, given that neither of his parents had ever finished high school. He'd been born with a severe hearing impairment that had required several surgeries to give him the semblance of a normal life. Even then, he lagged behind his peers socially, focusing instead on reading and academics. He really didn't play football until high school, and not out of pure love for the game.

"I wanted to be more social. I wanted to be around kids outside of the classroom. I'd grown up going to both a regular public school and a school for the hearing impaired, so I'd never built a big circle of friends. Football gave me a chance to do that."

He speaks reverently of one of his idols, the Supreme Court justice Thurgood Marshall.

"The ability to pursue a quality education made a dramatic change in the chances an African-American kid had in life, and I was determined to take advantage of it."

So off Reggie went to Dartmouth, where Bob Blackman and his staff realized they had something special right from the start. So special that Lenny Nichols, an All-State linebacker out of New York State who'd received multiple scholarships offers but chose Dartmouth for academic reasons, was shifted to the offensive line to make room at linebacker for the budding star.

"He became my best friend and fraternity brother, in spite of that," Reggie says today. "We pledged Alpha Phi Alpha together. I wrestled one season because I promised one of our assistant coaches, who doubled as the wrestling coach, that I would. My first match I wrestled heavyweight against a kid from Harvard and he beat me badly, so badly I pretty much quit in the third period of the match. It was winter, freezing cold, and we headed back to Hanover from Cambridge. The bus's windows were frosted over and I wrote 'I quit' on the glass during the ride, and I was comfortable with that. But Lenny came into my room that night and wouldn't let me quit. He said it didn't matter if I lost every single match. I was the incoming captain of the football team, and he said he hadn't given up his position on the team to room with a quitter. So I stuck with it and never lost another match. Became the Ivy League champion and ended up going to the national championships in New Jersey."

Reggie speaks with reverence about Lenny Nichols, just as he speaks reverently about the idols in his life he's had the great fortune to actually meet, idols who became mentors. He remembers his senior year at Dartmouth, opting to forego his spot in the Senior Bowl to play in the Hula Bowl instead, because the organizer of the game was a Dartmouth alum.

"My team's defensive coordinator came from the Big Ten. As soon as we hit the practice field, he changed the defense and pretty much excluded my position. He treated me like an errand boy, even made me part of his pregame speech where he lambasted 'nerds' who had no place in the game. He basically made me a punch line. I only got in for one play where I ended up chasing Joe Washington all over the field. Got in on the tackle after missing him twice. I came off the field and the defensive coordinator just shook his head and said that's why I wasn't going to see the field again."

Maybe forever, Reggie figured, his dreams of playing pro football dashed. How could he play at the next level if he wasn't good enough to play in the Hula Bowl?

"I figured I should just get on the next plane and go home, after we landed. But as I was walking through a mostly empty terminal, who do I see but Muhammad Ali waiting for a flight too. Here it is 1976, Ali is still the Greatest, and I mustered up the courage to run up, not just to talk to him but to explain my situation. All he told me was to pursue my dream. I've been truly blessed by my heroes being there to give me direction."

And that wasn't the only time either. Reggie wore number 32 in high school because of the great Cleveland Browns running back Jim Brown. Having run ESPN's Wide World of Sports Academy for Youth after his playing career concluded, the league asked Reggie to put together an NFL Youth Education program in Compton, California in response to the Rodney King riots. But there was a problem, two in fact: the Bloods and the Crips.

"We needed their cooperation so everyone in the South Central Los Angeles area would be free to join the program. And to accomplish that, I needed to work side by side with Jim Brown, who'd gotten a big head start in trying to work with the gangs and show these disadvantaged kids there was hope for them, that they could get out of the ghetto."

Just like Ali and Brown, Reggie felt the need to give back.

"When I played football, I was playing for the community of people of color, both African-American and Puerto Rican, because that's where my mother came from. And I was also playing for those who were hearing impaired."

As a linebacker, he couldn't wear number 32 at Dartmouth, so he wore number 63 as a testament to another of his heroes, Willie Lanier, the All-Pro and Super Bowl–winning linebacker of the Kansas City Chiefs under Hank Stram.

"I believe strongly there is a God, that there's this thing called destiny. My father grew up in the heart of the Jim Crow South—Birmingham, Alabama to be specific. He had to hit the road with his brothers after getting into a fight with a white man. He ended up in Flint, where he met my mother. So, all these years later, I'm being inducted into the College Football Hall of Fame, and who comes down the stairs of this two-tier ballroom of the Waldorf Hotel but Willie Lanier, my hero. In that moment, I forgot about everything else and ran up to him. Began listing all his accomplishments and accolades, and I could see how much it meant to him. That in all those dark and lonely days that had followed the end of his career, somebody still knew who he was, somebody still remembered him. I always wanted someone to do that for me."

A perfunctory chore, given all he achieved with Dartmouth and especially during his 14-year career with the Cincinnati Bengals. He was a three-time All-Ivy League, All-New England selection from 1973–75, and was drafted by the Bengals in the third round. In addition to playing in the team's only two Super Bowls, 1981 and 1988, Reggie Williams recorded sixteen interceptions and 23 fumble recoveries (a franchise record). During his career Williams amassed 62.5 sacks, which is the second most in Bengals history. As further testament to his commitment to the community at large, in his final two seasons with the Bengals, Williams was appointed to an open seat on the Cincinnati City Council in 1988 and was elected for a second term in 1989 on the Charter Party ticket. He was selected to the NFL All-Rookie Team (1976), won the Byron "Whizzer" White Award for Humanitarian Service (1985), the NFL Walter Payton Man of the Year Award (1986), and was named *Sports Illustrated's* Co-Sportsman of the Year (1987).

"For the other opportunities in my life that football has brought, I would do it all over again," Williams said the night he was inducted into the College Football Hall of Fame and met Willie Lanier.

What followed in 2007 is not for the squeamish, perhaps the greatest testament to Reggie's character.

"He greets me at the elevator in the early afternoon," Paul Daugherty's 2013 article for *USA Today* opens. "He is on crutches, which he uses like dual canes. One in front of the other, step by step. He has spent the morning the way he spends every morning: perpetually stretching and gently twisting and patiently aligning his body, so his body will allow him to walk. He has eased the length of his six foot one frame across an adjustable bed, a sectional leather sofa, and a wooden chaise from Bali. With great effort, he has donned a pair of sneakers he designed for himself. The right sneaker's sole is bolstered with two and 5/8 inches of extra padding. That's because, after the 24 surgeries and multiple knee infections, and the osteomyelitis he says 'ate my femur like termites,' his right leg is precisely two and 5/8 inches shorter than his left."

What happened in the interim, even before 2007 and that day in 2013, can best be described as a hellish battle in which Reggie waged war with both his doctors and his own body to avoid amputation and save his ravaged leg.

"Now that he finds himself in acute pain and uncertain about the future," the *New York Daily News* pondered on July 26, 2008, "he is forced to confront a question that follows many athletes who played through injuries: was it worth it?"

Paul Daugherty's terrific article for *USA* Today from 2013 sees Reggie's physical plights a different way. "I asked Reggie how he did it. The pain, the surgeries, the delayed diagnosis. The wreckage of spirit, over and over. A loss of what seems an inalienable right to locomotion. 'I look at pain and pleasure as scales,' he says. 'The more pain you have, the more pleasure you need to balance it out.'"

All that pain he has endured now seems well worth it, much of the uncertainty removed from his future. He still has his right leg and, after another grueling series of procedures (including open heart surgery for a ruptured aorta), he feels better than he has in a decade.

"The music plays," Daugherty's *USA Today* article concludes. "It's the soundtrack of his life. Now, it's Billie Holiday. She knew some about pain. After three days, I make my way to the door. Reggie rises and stands. He waves goodbye: one crutch lifted to the sky."

He is still standing, albeit without crutches anymore. The many agonizing procedures he's endured have finally managed to straighten his legs, having to overcome being born severely bowlegged through all his playing days, which accounts in some portion for the physical trauma he faced. Football was indeed worth it for Reggie Williams, as he believes it continues to be for the youth of America today.

"Football's a game that's very instructive in team dynamics, the importance of working together toward a common goal, something that's otherwise very difficult to teach kids. How to interact in a manner that allows every individual to be better, and wouldn't that be a great thing as a mandate for society. I think there should be an appropriate discussion of when is the appropriate time to introduce the most physical aspects of the game versus when to learn the instructional aspects of football. You can learn a tremendous amount about the game, and experience much of the game, without the kind of hitting that has soured some parents and discouraged them from letting their kids play. But they can start learning before they start hitting. Part of our discussion on preserving and strengthening the game is that we can love the game of football, love the dynamics and education of the individual skill sets, without the hitting. So mark me down as an advocate of flag football until ninth grade."

No less a source than Warren Sapp, voted into the NFL Hall of Fame after a stellar 13-year career, agrees.

"The game is getting better; let's just make it all the way better for everybody involved, especially the youth," Sapp told *USA Today* in June of 2017. "I'm talking about seven, eight, nine, ten, eleven, thirteen. We eliminate the tackle football for all the kids, we put them on equal playing fields so all their brains develop and then, when they reach high school, now let's go. Now let's pick out a four-year plan for you to find the college you want to go to, play the game you know and love, and be good at it. That's the biggest thing. Make it safer for everybody that's involved. Let's get the research, let's apply the knowledge, and let's make it all better for everybody."

In the same article, Sapp reflects on his own career, seeing it now through the prism of experience with an eye on the bigger picture that was considerably smaller back then.

"It was just bad, it was Neanderthals, we were dinosaurs. We were doing Oklahoma drill, bull in the ring, all this crazy stuff that was just about being a tough guy. It wasn't about the skills you had. It was just the bare bones of bone-on-bone. That's not what this game should be. It's about skills."

Reggie Williams didn't play football his freshman year in high school, after suffering a severe concussion: not from football, but from falling out of a tree. Like Steve Jordan, he also mentions a local high school soccer league near his home that has outlawed heading due to the concussion issues that have sprung up in that sport as well. His status, the intelligence and experience he brings to a myriad of areas within football, led to Reggie being asked to interview for the job of commissioner of the NFL after Paul Tagliabue retired. And his vast experiences on so many sides of the game have given him a true worldview of football, including its future and how it can still be a positive force in the lives of young men.

"It's left for those of us who love the game to come out and defend the game. And I do love the game. I love the fact that there has yet to be a football season, whether it be college or the NFL, where you see something you've never seen before." He pauses. "I remember during the speech I gave when I went into the College Hall of Fame, I forgot a word. It felt forever before it came to me, and nobody knew how close I came to blowing it. Just like I came so close to winning two Super Bowls and so close to losing my leg. You see, at its most basic level football teaches you that no matter how many times you get knocked down, you've got to keep getting up. I take that lesson to heart every day of my life."

CHAPTER 14

MARK WHIPPLE—
WINNING AT EVERY LEVEL

"Mark has been successful in every phase of his career," Miami head coach Randy Shannon told *College Sports Live* on January 27, 2009, the day Mark Whipple was hired as offensive coordinator. "He developed a Super Bowl quarterback in Ben Roethlisberger, won a national championship as the head coach of UMass, and created an effective and potent offense most recently for the playoff-bound Philadelphia Eagles. Aside from being innovative at his craft, Mark is a tremendous individual who will positively impact our student-athletes on and off the field."

Press releases like that are nothing new for Mark Whipple, "Whip" to his friends, who has indeed won at every level. A high school championship, followed by an Ivy title at Brown University in 1976, and the afore-mentioned national championship as head coach at the University of Mas-sachusetts in 1998, all culminating in winning a Super Bowl ring as quar-terbacks coach of the Pittsburgh Steelers. So to say he has been successful at every stage of his career, as both player and coach, is an understatement; in fact, it's difficult to find other football lifers who can match that success across such a wide array of coaching levels.

What makes Whip special is he's such a bright guy, one of those rare Ivy League football alums who decided to dedicate his career to coaching. Good thing, because he's got all the qualities of a great coach, including a brilliant offensive mind. He parlayed his considerable strengths on the field to become a leader in the sport, building his success and reputation to the point where people at every level of the game wanted to work with him. They see him as a great teacher and leader, a man known for making a positive impact on kids, an exemplary individual the likes of which are just what football needs today.

"I agree the game is in trouble right now," he says. "I think that's accu-rate. Over time, football has always had its detractors. It's the greatest game of all and there's so much jealousy because of the power of the game, its vast reach and what it does for the human spirit. You play the game, you coach the game, and form lifelong bonds that are more like family.

"Let me give you an example. The great Chris Berman from ESPN cut his broadcasting teeth from the Brown University radio booth while I was playing. He became a virtual member of our team back when we won the '76 championship. And when Chris' wife died tragically, there were guys who flew across the country to be there for him. Look, I played base-ball and basketball in high school too, went on to play varsity baseball at Brown. And I can tell you, without any shred of doubt, that compared to any other sport there really is something special about football and the people who play the game.

"In football, you truly need a team to be successful. In baseball a pitch-er can dominate, and in basketball one superstar can take over a game. Not so in football. You can have the best quarterback on the planet. But he won't perform like that without solid receivers and an offensive line to keep him upright. By the same token, the great linebacker can thrive only if the defensive line does its job. You need everybody to be successful. And that includes the backups, the third string, the scout team guys. You need everybody on the same page. That's a huge challenge for coaches, and there's nothing else like it."

Whip gives great credit to his coaches at Brown for all the success he's had, reaching football career heights seldom achieved by players coming out of the Ivy League. His first year as the team's starting quarterback in 1977 as a junior, he led the Bears to a 7-2 record, coming literally one play away from winning the Ivy title. But the team didn't begin his senior season in the same fashion, and he recalls one especially pivotal moment that followed the disappointing start.

"I'd been picked as the preseason Ivy League Player of the Year," he recalls, "but I didn't play like that out of the gate. We got our butts kicked the first two games and started off 0-2. Well, Ray Tellier [who, ironically, was my starting quarterback for two years at the University of Connecticut and led us to a Yankee Conference title in 1971], Andy Talley, and my head coach John Anderson called me into the office and said they wanted me to start calling the plays myself. Talk about a vote of confidence! We went out the next week and beat Princeton something like 44–16. Ended up running the table until we lost to Dartmouth for the Ivy title on national television the second to last week of the season. And I never forgot what it felt like to have my coaches believe in me the way they did. That taught me more about how to coach than anything, the notion of how important it is to let your players know you believe in them."

John King, from King of Prussia, Pennsylvania, played fullback behind the Arizona born and raised Whipple. They both arrived at Brown when the school was generally regarded as the doormat of the Ivy League, a trend John Anderson was already beginning to turn around. Both had come from championship programs in high school and greeted the Brown mindset with obvious disdain.

"'This sucks,'" King recalls Whip saying when they were freshmen. "And it did. We were tired of being regarded as a bunch of losers, and we weren't going to be denied. We came close to winning the title our freshman year and were determined not to come up short again. We weren't used to losing and weren't about to take it."

In 1976, Brown went up to Harvard to play on national television before a sold-out stadium in the de facto Ivy League title game. From his fullback position, King barreled into the end zone from the three-yard line in the fourth quarter for the winning touchdown, what many call the most important score in Brown football history.

"We had beaten the big boys, the defending champs," he recalls. "It was the first time we'd ever beaten Harvard, Yale, Princeton, and Dartmouth en route to winning the title."

King also believes that "football helped create the kind of character on campus that complimented the course offerings."

He's not alone. In an article entitled "How a Successful College Football Season Will Affect Your Admissions Chances at Highly Selective Schools," the IvyWise Newsletter has reported that "widely known as the 'Flutie Effect' in college admissions, a winning football season usually results in a swell of applications. The increased attention given to these schools by sports media, coupled with increased campus morale among students, faculty, and alumni, affects prospective applicants positively. So, if such colleges continue winning on the football field this season, don't be surprised if their admissions offices reap the benefits. And if you're looking at one of these colleges, be advised: you may be facing an uphill battle to win admission."

Taking that concept even further, in a detailed study commissioned by the University of California at Berkley, Michael L. Anderson found "robust evidence that football success increases athletic donations, increases the number of applicants, lowers a school's acceptance rate, increases enrollment of in-state students, increases the average SAT score of incoming classes, and enhances a school's academic reputation."

John King also played varsity baseball at Brown alongside Whip—often literally, at third base while Whip played shortstop. They were playing a game in the spring of their junior season when Whip's knee twisted the wrong way as he went to field a ground ball.

"I heard it snap," King recalls. "He got up limping and I waited for him to wave to the trainer, but he just went back to his position. 'Don't you wanna get that checked out?' I asked him.

"'No,' Whip said. 'I'll just stretch it out.'

"'But I heard it snap,' I told him.

"'I'll be fine. I'll walk it off.'"

King shakes his head, grinning. "Turns out Whip had torn his ACL and he still finished the game. He had surgery later in, this would've been, April. Stayed in Providence over the summer to rehab and was ready for the start of his senior football season. Remember, this was 1978; no one had ever come back from reconstructive knee surgery that fast."

Maybe that's why Whip got off to a slow start his senior season but still came up just a few plays short of an Ivy title. Upon graduating, he went straight into coaching as an assistant at St. Lawrence, followed by stints at Union (offensive coordinator) and back for one season at Brown (working with the wide receivers) before becoming offensive coordinator at New Hampshire and then on to the head coaching job at the University of New Haven. It was there he won a title before heading back home again to Brown in 1994, where he took the reins of a moribund program that had won all of two games the previous two seasons.

That changed in a hurry, thanks in large part to the "Whiplash Offense" he installed that not only revived Brown's program and the school's football culture, but changed the Ivy League forever by injecting high-powered offense into the staid league, long based on a more conservative running attack. Whip didn't win a title in the four years he spent at his alma mater, but that all changed when he left Brown for UMass in 1998. That year he won a national title in what was then called Division I-AA, later renamed the FCS, the Football Championship Subdivision. Interestingly enough, that same year (1998) Brown won the Ivy League title under first-year coach Phil Estes, who had originally accompanied Whip to Brown and has gone on to win two more titles, in 2005 and 2008.

That 1998 UMass team broke school records in points scored (524), touchdowns (73), total yards (7,074), passing yards (4,050), completions (306), and first downs (354). An impressive offensive resume, to say the least, that put Whip on the NFL's radar. And among those paying the most attention was none other than Bill Cowher, head coach of the Pittsburgh Steelers, who personally recruited Whip to tutor his cherished number one draft pick in 2004, quarterback Ben Roethlisberger.

"Mark Whipple was without doubt instrumental in Ben's development," Cowher told *College Sports Live*. "He has a wealth of experience on the offensive side and is a great teacher and leader of young men."

Adds Roethlisberger himself, on the occasion of Mark being hired as the University of Miami's offensive coordinator following a stint with the Philadelphia Eagles, "Whip is a great coach and is the perfect fit for any coaching position at any school or team. I know he will do great things at Miami and help that program tremendously. He will help the players not just as a coach, but as a leader and a mentor to them. I have nothing but the utmost respect for Whip and what he stands for."

"Ben was the youngest quarterback to ever win a Super Bowl," Whip recalls. "And I was fortunate to have him when he was young enough to really listen. It means so much to me to see how he's grown his greatness and how far he's come. I tried to instill in him the same confidence that John Anderson, Ray Tellier, and Andy Talley instilled in me. And he's the only player I'll take time out of my preparation and film study to watch play on Sundays."

Whip followed up his stint as Miami's offensive coordinator with a return to UMass, where he'd won a national championship over a decade before. But the school had moved up to the Bowl Championship Series (BCS) and was still adjusting to the rigors of playing bowl-caliber, sometimes ranked teams. Newly invigorated by a few losing seasons out of the gate, Whip has redoubled his recruiting efforts toward lifting that program to the level of its competition.

In talking about his team, though, the first thing Whip raises is character. Like the award the UMass program recently created called the Michael Boland Inspirational Award to honor a player who tragically passed away while preparing for the NFL combine.

"He was so unselfish," Whip recalls. "A great teammate who never missed a play, a role model for our offensive linemen, and he was going to play in the NFL. He was that good, that talented. That's why you coach, because of kids like him. One of the best players and people I've ever been around. He exemplified everything you want in a college football player, which includes molding the next group of guys to carry the torch. That's part of building a program, being fortunate to have players who are great leaders and show up every day to work toward being successful. That was Michael."

Whip also enjoys telling the story of a highly recruited five-star player named Adam Breneman and the tight end's unlikely journey to UMass.

"He was my youngest son Austin's roommate at Penn State. They played football together and Adam had made All-American as a freshman, no small feat. Then he got hurt and wasn't sure if he was ever going to play again. So he focused on his studies and ended up graduating from Penn State in three years. Around this time, I signed his best friend, Andrew Ford, to play quarterback for us. So Andrew called Adam to see if he might be ready to play again. Adam enrolls in graduate school at UMass, resumes his football career, and, right out of the box, becomes the best tight end in the country, named as the New England Offensive Player of the Year. He could have entered the draft and gone to the NFL, but he decided to come back for one more year to be with his teammates and friends. He felt he owed it to both them and himself."

* * *

Whip's influence goes even further. One person not surprised by his success as a coach is Jerry Massa. Massa played with Whip briefly on that first Brown team ever to win an Ivy League title. Although a car accident in his junior year ended his career prematurely, he went on to organize a trio of successful reunions for that '76 championship team and served as president of the Brown Football Association from 2009 through his sudden and tragic death in the summer of 2017.

"He was a great leader," Massa recalled of Whip, "and coming back from that knee injury set an example for everyone. He never cared about individual records, the way so many players do. He cared about the team. He cared about winning and would do anything in his power to make that happen."

In 1996, Massa, whose relentless dedication to the Brown program exemplified the level of support alumni football boosters in general provide, nominated Whip for admission to Brown's Athletics Hall of Fame.

"No one was more vital to Brown's success under John Anderson in the '70s than Whip. He compiled a 13-5 record and was just a few plays, literally, from winning one Ivy League title and maybe two. You have to go a long way back in Brown football history to find a quarterback who achieved success comparable to that. And we were able to honor him in his third year as head coach of the program he had brought back to respectability and prominence. That made it truly special."

But Massa's efforts, as president of the BFA, toward enhancing Brown's football program didn't stop with the Hall of Fame. He was responsible for the school's first ever night game, the force behind renting portable light towers that spearheaded the Bears to a crushing victory over Harvard in 2010 before nearly 18,000 fans. More recently, he worked to build a new student section in one end zone to enhance the undergraduate game experience and boost attendance that was christened the "Bear Den."

Under Massa's leadership of the Brown Football Association, model programs in player mentoring and career counseling were expanded, and community-building events celebrating literacy for local Providence, Rhode Island schoolkids and recognizing Brown's veterans on Military Appreciation Day debuted and have continued to thrive. But perhaps his most vital contribution to Brown football, and football as a whole, was providing recognition for players from the past who'd gone on to parlay their success on the field to far greater things in life. Players like Tom Catena who used the game as a springboard to medical school and after medical school has spent the bulk of his life serving in overseas missions, most recently for the past decade as the only doctor for 400 square miles in war-torn Sudan. Thanks to Jerry, in 2014 "Dr. Tom," as he's known by his Sudanese patients, was given the National Football Foundation's highest honor, the Gold Medal Award, in recognition of his exceptional contribution to humanity, and he was the subject of a documentary by award-winning film director and fellow Brown University alum Ken Carlson entitled *The Heart of Nuba*.

So one person truly can make a real difference, on the field as well as off. Like Tom Catena. Or Jerry Massa.

"To me, all this is important because it makes football more than just a game. For our players, we strive to assist them in developing their career aspirations, providing leadership and guidance. We also provide them with a network after graduation as a medium to remain part of Brown's team off the field, just as they were on the field. Lessons to prepare them for the roles they're going to take on after graduation. Life, after all," Massa concluded, "is a team game."

* * *

And what does Mark Whipple think of that state of the game today?

"It's a work in progress," he says. "People who call football a profession, or an avocation, have to work together and stay together to keep growing the game. There are always detractors and, let's face it, there will always be people on the outside who really don't understand the game. Thanks to football, I was able get an Ivy League education. People who rail against the game have little or no idea how many people have parlayed their experience on the field with tremendous success off it.

"I could be wrong, I don't know. I think the NFL has a concussion problem; I don't think football has a concussion problem. I'm still in touch with maybe fifty of the guys I played with, won a title with at Brown, and I don't know of a single player who displays any of the issues with dementia, loss of memory, any of those things. When I'm around NFL people, that's different.

"Look, the league is chasing the money. But you can't play Sunday and Thursday, you just can't. Your body needs more time to recover, probably even more than the six days which is all that you get now. That to me is not a football issue, it's an NFL issue. Make the playoffs and you might find yourself playing 24 games. We played fifteen total the year UMass won the national championship. Consider that, when there were only thirty-six games scheduled my entire collegiate career at Brown."

Whip pauses.

"I just think of how much it means when you see your former players; it's how they look at you, how rewarding that is. You did something for them nobody else could do. You helped give them a chance to win a national championship, a Super Bowl, or go on to build a great life and family. It's not about teaching them how to throw a twelve-yard curl, it's about teaching them how to grow and deal with the problems life throws at them. I've had players tell me, 'Coach, I became a man under you.' That's incredibly rewarding, but even more rewarding is to watch them become great fathers."

CHAPTER 15

DON MCPHERSON—
COMPETING ON A DIFFERENT FIELD

The night Don McPherson was inducted into the College Football Hall of Fame in 2008, he found himself in a private reception at New York's Waldorf Astoria with the likes of Ronnie Lott and Lynn Swann. But it was two others there that night who really get him beaming.

"Here I am talking to John Glenn," he recalls. "John Glenn, a true American hero in every respect. That's the privilege and benefit that football has brought to my life. I was lucky enough to have been in the right place at the right time to maximize my talents."

But it was the presence of another man whom Don also considers a hero that really made the night.

"My father had just retired from the NYPD and here he was at the Waldorf to watch his son get inducted into the College Hall of Fame. That highlighted the fact that football also enabled me to transcend the racism that my father had experienced. Having the opportunity to meet John Glenn and Vice President Joe Biden, freed me from the bonds of being black in America."

McPherson applies a similar logic to the passion that has, to a large extent, replaced the passion he felt playing the game, specifically becoming an activist in the fight against violence toward women.

"Feminism freed me from the toxicity of masculinity. I was supposed to ignore my feelings and ignore my emotions. Everything was about being tough. My entire experience as an athlete was an exercise in learning to be a self-absorbed, egomaniacal person. Feminism freed me from the narrow definition of masculinity I saw affect so many of my friends. It opened up my perspective."

For Don, being a "feminist" is all about being a dedicated advocate on the subject of violence against women, something he and many others see as an anathema in society today. He titled a presentation he gives in speaking gigs all over the country "You Throw Like a Girl."

"First," he says today, "men must become part of the solution, with our voices. Most men are not violent, but our silence allows those who are to continue their abuse. We must recognize all forms of abuse [verbal, emotional, etc.] as precipitating and equally insidious as physical violence. In doing so, we can truly prevent violence from occurring. The underlying message in 'You Throw Like a Girl' is that girls and women are 'less than.' This attitude results in our silence as well as our overall devaluation of women.

"Second, the statement or challenge 'You Throw Like a Girl' is designed as a challenge to a boy's or man's understanding of masculinity. That perspective is typically quite narrow, especially in this context. We often hear men talk of having no choice [but to defend their manhood]. When that 'manhood' is narrowly defined, violence, excessive drinking, and risky behavior are more likely. My work is focused on giving boys and men more options based on a greater, broader understanding of what it really means to be a man. My quote, 'We don't raise boys to be men, we raise them not to be women,' came from hundreds of conversations with men as they expressed the limited understanding of how masculinity governed their lives."

What seems like a lifetime before he became a passionate advocate for a cause he truly believes in, Don played football and he played it very, very well. He was a unanimous All-American quarterback at Syracuse University and is a veteran of the NFL and Canadian Football League. As captain of the undefeated 1987 Syracuse football team, McPherson set 22 school records, led the nation in passing, and won more than 18 national "Player of the Year" awards, including the Maxwell Award as the nation's best player, the Davey O'Brien National Quarterback Award, and the inaugural Johnny Unitas Golden Arm Award. He was second in the Heisman Trophy voting, and in 2013 Syracuse University retired his number nine jersey, only the fourth number to be retired in the history of the school's storied football program. McPherson has worked as a college football analyst for ESPN, BET, and NBC and spent six seasons as the lead studio analyst for Sportsnet New York's coverage of Big East and American Athletic Conference football. In 2000, while a board member of the Nassau County (New York) Sports Commission, McPherson created the John Mackey Award, which recognizes college football's outstanding tight end.

Speaking of awards, Don has won as many of them off the field as on the field to recognize and commemorate his advocacy to fight violence against women, including the Frederick Douglas Men of Strength Award, Champions for Change (presented by Lifetime Television), the Creative Vision for Women's Justice, and a Leadership Award from the National Center for Victims of Crime. Most recently Don received the George Arents Award, Syracuse University's highest alumni honor, as well as being designated a Letter Winner of Distinction, the highest honor bestowed upon a former student-athlete.

"I don't really think I was a great player," Don says today. "I had a great senior season because I played on a great team. We were very good and, as a result, I got a lot of attention. We won all eleven of our games and we were as close to perfect as we could be on those eleven days. But we spent the other three hundred and fifty-four days that year preparing for those eleven. I once saw a statistical study of football that broke a game down into individual plays, each of which took an average of between four and six seconds. So when everything's said and done, when you're talking about being the better team on the football field, you're really talking about being better for those four minutes. And my senior season we were really, really good for those four minutes."

After graduating, Don was drafted by the Philadelphia Eagles and went on to play for the Houston Oilers as well. He later played with both the Hamilton Tiger-Cats and Ottawa Rough Riders of the Canadian Football League, after which the activist phase of his life beckoned.

"I happened to meet Richard Lapchick in 1994, who was the son of Joe Lapchick, considered to be one of the first great big men in the NBA playing for the New York Knicks, where he'd later become coach and general manager. The league was segregated back then, until Joe went out and signed a former Harlem Globetrotter named Nate 'Sweetwater' Clifton. So Richard grew up watching his father get death threats and bomb threats. He'd answer the phone and hear on the other end of the line, 'You're going to die tonight.' Richard experienced firsthand this incredible intersection of racism and sports and ended up dedicating himself to issues involving the two. This resonated with me from the first day I met Richard because I wasn't a quarterback, I was a *black* quarterback. He was running the Center for the Study of Sport in Society down at Northeastern University and offered me a position on the staff. I left Ottawa for Boston the next day and got there in time for the two o'clock staff meeting.

"Until that experience, I had never grasped the depths of the problem, how pervasive violence against women had become in our society. I'd seen evidence of sexual assault going through college but either ignored it or looked the other way. And now the issue of violence against women committed by men started resounding in me stronger than anything else, including racism. So I came to feminism in my work to end men's violence against women. As a society, we lay this burden on women; to fight all forms of oppression and violence waged against our mothers, daughters, grandmothers. While contemplating the work to which I had dedicated my life, I saw a bumper sticker that read, 'Feminism is the radical view that women are people too.' That day, I realized that I was a feminist. And I learned to respect a group of people for which I was raised not to respect. And those who took up the cause before me, regardless of what others said about them, were my comrades, my partners. We all fight for what we believe in and/or what we want the world to be like. We have environmentalists who work to save the earth and lobbyists to further their cause or product with the political elite. To me, a feminist is someone who cares about women and the issues that impact their lives."

Don pauses to catch his breath. He sounds like he might after chugging fifty yards for a touchdown, his words and this cause amounting to how he scores points today.

"When you think about violence today in general, in the workplace or in so many tragic school shootings, think about this: when was the last time one of them was committed by a woman? The two causes you always hear thrown around for such tragedies are accessibility to guns and mental health. Well, women have access to guns too and they are as riddled with mental health problems as men, but it's never women who are behind these shootings. It's men, because we live in a patriarchal society where men feel both a need and entitlement to be dominant.

"When I speak, the deeper I delve into the issue in a deliberate way I realize the men in the audience have never heard this before, because they have a narrow sense of what their own masculinity means. Before men can objectify women, we have to objectify ourselves. There's nothing more important in football than to understand what your role is in the larger scheme, and the same thing is true of life. One of the things I talk about with masculinity is that it's a performance, it's not real. The key is to be authentic. I tell players today that I want your life to be defined by things no one else told you to define them by. You can be a loving, caring man and also the toughest guy on the field. In football, the impossible can be made simple through preparation. The same thing can be true, for men, off the field."

He does not see football as necessarily a "violent" sport so much as a "collision" sport and stresses that what the game is really about is "executing your plan and imposing your will on another. When you're off the field, on the sidelines, I can see how someone watching thinks, 'God, this game is violent.' But when people are violent to each other, they don't hug each other when the game is over.

"And," Don adds, "I've taken a ton of lessons from the game. Maybe the greatest is learning how to recognize how to value the people who are in your orbit, in your world. Not just as teammates who help you get things accomplished, but people you listened to and learned from. You meet a lot of people from diverse backgrounds and different environments, and you have the opportunity to get to know them better. You've got kids who are from poverty-stricken areas and this is their only chance to get out. At the same time you've got rednecks. They care about each other and they love each other. They go into that locker room and they fight to get past that, a part of this game that often gets overlooked; how diverse it is and how many people of varied backgrounds and cultures football exposes you to."

For Don, it paid off and then some. Many will say he deserved the Heisman Trophy for his stellar senior season of 1987, when he went on to finish second in the balloting.

The only blemish on the Orangemen's undefeated season was a 16–16 tie against Auburn in the Sugar Bowl; remember, there was no overtime in 1988. But that does nothing to diminish the incredible run McPherson enjoyed to finish out his collegiate career, over not one but two seasons. As Syracuse.com notes, in compiling a 16-2 record over his final eighteen games, Don "completed 271 of his 498 passes for 4,168 yards, he ran 301 times for 722 more, and he accounted (by throwing, rushing, or catching) for 46 touchdowns during SU's twenty-two games. He was, simply, an offensive franchise."

But his size kept him from the bulk of NFL teams' draft boards and he never got the chance to play in the league on anything resembling a regular basis. Today he takes all that in stride, content to live his life much by a mantra taught to him by the late Dick MacPherson, his coach at Syracuse.

"Coach Mac always told me to play within myself. Recognize where your talents lie. Don't feel like you have to do everything. As much as I had the ability to take off and run, he convinced me I didn't need to do that. I needed to let someone else do that. My job wasn't to get first downs every play. My job as a QB was to put other players in a position where they could make the plays. Sure, I had the talent to play the game and do a lot of things others couldn't do. But Coach Mac showed me how my real strength was to let someone else go outside the tackle box, instead of me going outside the box. And I was able to better maximize my gifts by buying into that philosophy."

Almost immediately from the time his career ended, thanks to that fateful meeting with Richard Lapchick, Don began channeling those gifts in the direction that has become his life's passion: speaking out against, and fighting, violence against women.

"I was a unique guy at a unique time. I got a lot of media attention and became a well-known guy. And I took advantage of that by finding out during that time what I was passionate about. I benefitted so much from playing the game, and playing the game has enabled me to do what I'm doing today. When I think about the honor of getting into the College Hall of Fame, I don't picture the selection committee sitting around saying things like, 'He had a great career, consensus All-American.' I picture them saying, 'He's a good guy. We want him here, we want him in the Hall.' Being recognized for what I did on the field as well as off, in other words. I don't feel worthy as a football player to be in the Hall, so much as for what I've contributed afterward."

And those contributions run deep with a spate of speaking engagements across the country, addressing civic groups and football fans, sure, but also spending more than his share of time in college football locker rooms helping to educate players on the issue of violence against women—a scourge on many college campuses today, which Don is determined to do something about. The doubters, of course, remain; they're just not confined to NFL draft strategy rooms these days, and Don doesn't care much if they don't believe in the importance of the cause to which he's dedicated his life.

"The difference between a boss and leader is that a leader is behind making everyone else better. The leader, the guy who makes the biggest difference, is not necessarily the guy with C for 'captain' on his chest. When I received my first award for fighting violence against women, it was so much different from anything I'd ever won in football, because those awards are about numbers; games won, stats, how many passes I completed and how many yards I threw for. It's quantifiable. When you get an award for your contribution to an issue, though, you take stock in why you're doing it, what you've accomplished, and what you'd like to continue accomplishing.

"I've been blessed beyond my own comprehension. I'm a guy who grew up on Long Island. My father, who died four years ago, was a cop his whole adult life. My mother was a school nurse at the middle school I went to. I grew up in a loving household and got a chance to play a great game that has its own night named after it—Monday Night Football. I know I've been blessed because playing football has allowed me to exponentially exceed what people normally get out of life, so I can make an impact far away from the fields I used to play on. When people ask me, 'What do you think your legacy is?' I tell them I don't think I've come close to it, I don't think I've started it. I just want to be worthy of the blessings I've received."

CHAPTER 16

BOB EHRLICH—FROM THE GRIDIRON TO THE GOVERNOR'S MANSION

"Many of you know I was fortunate enough to play high school football at the Gilman School and college football at Princeton," Bob Ehrlich, former governor of Maryland, wrote for the *Baltimore Sun* on May 6, 2012, in a column that was later included in his book *Turning Point*. "What most of you do not know is that I worked as a graduate assistant on the Wake Forest football staff to pay for my room and board during law school. These experiences instilled in me a strong sense of the appropriate role of academics and athletics in our secondary schools and colleges."

It comes as no surprise, then, that football played an important, if not vital, part of Bob's life. He played for me when I assumed the head coaching duties at Princeton. A tough, hard-nosed kid who captained our 1978 squad, Bob was a working-class success story, having earned a scholarship to the prestigious Gilman School not far from his hometown. His father sold cars and his mother was a legal secretary. So in looking at the state of the game today, particularly youth football, the governor offers an interesting perspective.

"I have a minimum of two or three conversations a month about the state of the game," he says. "So many conversations that it scares me in large part because this has become a class issue. Working-class kids like I was are still playing the game, because they still see football as a means to escape their environment. But we're losing the upper and upper-middle-class, mostly white kids, from both the cities and the suburbs. The sport at the youth level has too often become defined by a class divide, and that threatens the future of the game. And I take it personally, because I owe so much to the game. Without football, I don't become a politician, don't become part of a big-time law firm, don't become an author."

But the governor clearly recognizes the problems confronting the game.

"We are typically attracted to aggressive sports," Ehrlich writes in another column on September 29, 2013, also for the *Baltimore Sun* and also included in *Turning Point*. "In fact, it was not so long ago that the NFL spent part of its advertising budget marketing 'best hits' videos to its fans. And the toughest, hardest hitting players (Dick Butkus, Ronnie Lott, Jack Tatum) were used to market the league's tough guy image. Alas, such promotion will go the way of the dinosaur in light of the new litigious era of player protection and large fines for helmet-to-helmet hits."

We can hope so, and the trend lines are indeed already moving in that direction.

"I wouldn't say the bad guys are winning," the governor continues, "because they're not, except for that upper-middle-class fear that has spawned the haters. Hey, football's not alone—there are plenty of places where that same mentality applies and has led to the elimination of dodgeball in some school districts. What I don't get is how these same football haters can let their kids play soccer, lacrosse, or hockey instead. It seems like those sports carry a similar risk of injury as football."

* * *

The governor raises an excellent point. Take, for example, Brant Wilkerson-New's article that ran in the June 1, 2015 edition of the *Winston-Salem Journal* entitled "Concussions More Prevalent in Girls' Soccer Than Football."

> *Football has been at the forefront of the national discussion regarding head injuries in recent years, but it's actually the other football that is just as dangerous to high school athletes.*
>
> *In particular, girls' soccer players suffer concussions at a higher rate than football players, according to statistics from the National Federation of State High School Associations from the 2013–14 season.*
>
> *In a population of 374,565 players across the nation, there were an estimated 55,598 concussions—a rate of 14.8 percent. Football players suffered concussions at a rate of 13.5 percent in 1,094,949 players....*
>
> *Asked whether concussions have reached the point where the issue needs to be seriously addressed, Coach Scott Bilton of both the boys' and girls' soccer teams at West Forsyth didn't hesitate.*
>
> *"Yes. I do think so, and I think it's becoming more and more common," he said.*

Add to that an even more persuasive argument that the risks of playing football are actually no greater statistically than a number of other sports, as compiled in a study undertaken by Property Casualty 360. In their most recent listing of the "10 Most Dangerous Youth Sports in America," the insurance-oriented study notes that in 2012, there were 394,500 injuries logged in football. Right below it was basketball at 389,610. Given the fact that there are so many more players on a football team than a basketball team, basketball would be the more dangerous sport by a mile, according to that metric alone.

The Livestrong.com report, "Do You Get Hurt More in Soccer or Football?" concluded that concussion injuries, sometimes referred to as "preconcussive impacts," are equally likely in soccer and football players.

Also detailed on Livestrong.com is a recent study by neurologists at the Albert Einstein College of Medicine that determined, "Repetitive heading could set a cascade of response that can lead to degeneration of brain cells over time." The study was conducted on both men and women who had spent more than two decades playing soccer. As the *Huffington Post* explains in the same Livestrong.com post, "Frequent headers were found to have low fractional anisotropy (FA), which measures how water moves along the brain's nerve fibers. When white matter in the brain is healthy, FA measures are high, indicating that water is flowing in a uniform way. But when FA levels are low, it's indicative that the water is moving in a more random pattern. Abnormally low FA levels have been linked in the past with thinking troubles in people who have experienced brain injury."

Okay, we're getting a bit technical here, wading into the weeds as they say, but the point is clear: while the risks of playing football are most certainly present, there are risks of comparable or even equal levels to playing other sports. And don't forget that article in a previous chapter that noted how a girls' cheerleading team cheering for a Pop Warner football team suffered more injuries than the football players themselves.

* * *

Dan Fournier, who captained the Princeton Tigers his senior season of 1976 when the governor was a sophomore, remembers Bob Ehrlich as "tough as nails and a bit of a grinder who never had a clean uniform in his life." Though never making a career out of it as the governor did, Dan enjoyed a flirtation with politics north of the border back home in Montreal. But he has since moved on to a fabulously successful career in finance, specifically running a 65-billion-dollar company, Ivanhoe Cambridge, whose clients include the pension funds that support all of Canada's public employees and is generally considered to be one of the top ten real estate investors in the world according to the *Globe and Mail* newspaper. And he's quick to say that the roots of his success go all the way back to his experience on the football field.

"Playing football affected the way I think, what I've chosen to do, and how I've chosen to do it. I always liken the game to the brilliant book by Doris Kearns Goodwin called *Team of Rivals* about Abraham Lincoln. How someone who was never supposed to be president became a great one by assembling a team who were far better at what they did than he was. Similarly, football teaches us about the importance of having the capacity to work as a group, to put the group's results ahead of individuals. In the business world, I'm dealing with people's lives every day, their futures. When we don't succeed, we have to correct ourselves quickly. Same thing is true on the football field: you'd better be working as a group, and how you work as a group determines the success of your team. You can't win as a team of individuals in football any more than you can in business. It comes down to getting the best talent you can and building the system around that talent. That helps define success in business and life in general, but the game embodies it better than anything I've ever experienced. It's mind-boggling that playing it gave me all these opportunities."

This former Rhodes Scholar parlayed his stellar career at Princeton into a stint playing in the Canadian Football League and has since helped the rector of the Université de Montréal to establish a collegiate program from scratch—no easy task.

"I take pride in giving back to my community," he says today, "because people gave so much to me. I believe in paying it forward. Remembering what the people ahead of us did for us and now doing it for the people who are coming behind us. I got the chances I had at Exeter, Princeton, and then Oxford because of the people who'd set up endowments from which I received scholarships. It's nice to be on the other end of that, to help open the same doors for others that people opened for me."

Dan was raised by a single mother and considers himself blessed for all the doors that football opened for him. At Exeter, one of his mentors was Roger Staubach's center at the Naval Academy, Walter Pierce. Another Exeter alum introduced him to Princeton and the rest, as they say, is history.

But not all of that history from a football standpoint is rosy. Dan's own son had his career ended before his senior year in high school by recurring concussions.

"It broke his heart, but it was the right thing to do. He just couldn't play the game anymore without risking further damage. I apologized to him at the time because I knew the risks and still let him play. He'd say to me, 'Don't go there, Dad. This has been the best experience of my life.'"

Indeed, after his son was ruled out for his senior season, the boy's coaches suggested he coach the defensive line for the school's freshman team.

"So you had a kid who couldn't play any longer still contributing, still a part of the team, by coaching, instead of playing, that final season. I don't think I've ever been prouder of him."

* * *

That said, plenty of football coaches are being proactive to reduce injuries, CTE and beyond. In 2016, for example, the Ivy League banned tackling entirely in all practices.

"We're not trying to change the nature of the game," Robin Harris, the league's executive director, told the *New York Times* at the time. "We're just trying to make it safer."

The eight Ivy League coaches were unanimously in favor of the measure. But one, Brown University's three-time title winning head coach Phil Estes, didn't wait for such an edict to make Brown's one of the first programs in the country to incorporate the new policy without being told to.

"We're not doing anything that we haven't been doing already," Estes notes in an interview with *Brown Alumni Magazine*. "The only thing that's changed is this will make our game safer and the Ivy League is leading the nation in how to do it."

To that point, in July of 2011, five years prior to the Ivy League's formal adoption of that rule change, Estes advocated for the elimination of tackling in Pop Warner football.

"The coach's feeling," reported Ask Coach Wolff, a website dedicated to dealing with athletic issues of prime concern to parents, "is that kids can still learn the basics of fundamental football while playing flag football and then can learn to tackle opponents when they get to be in the eighth or ninth grade. Coach Estes says he didn't start to learn how to tackle until he was that old himself, and he played four years of high school ball and then played at the University of New Hampshire."

The *New York Times* takes that one step further in a September 2017 article entitled "Playing Tackle Football Before 12 Is Tied to Brain Problems Later."

"Athletes who began playing tackle football before the age of 12," the article begins, "had more behavioral and cognitive problems later in life than those who started playing after they turned 12, a new study released on Tuesday showed. The findings, from a long-term study conducted by researchers at Boston University, are likely to add to the debate over when, or even if, children should be allowed to begin playing tackle football. The study, published in the journal *Nature's Translational Psychiatry*, was based on a sample of 214 former players, with an average age of 51. Of those, 43 played through high school, 103 played through college, and the remaining 68 played in the NFL. In phone interviews and online surveys, the researchers found that players in all three groups who participated in youth football before the age of 12 had a twofold 'risk of problems with behavioral regulation, apathy, and executive function' and a threefold risk of 'clinically elevated depression scores.'

"'The brain is going through this incredible time of growth between the years of 10 and 12, and if you subject that developing brain to repetitive head impacts, it may cause problems later in life,' Robert Stern, one of the authors of the study, said of the findings."

Phil Estes, though, enjoys a personal stake in the issue because his own son Brett saw his high school football career nearly ended by concussions. I say "nearly" because Brett opted to fight his way back onto the field by remaking himself as a kicker. This after his father advised him to give up the game he so dearly loved. And then two years later he found himself on the Brown football team, playing for that father, as a punter and placekicker.

"I love the game," Brett told the *Providence Journal* in October of 2014. "And I was born into the Brown football tradition. It's amazing," he adds of playing for his dad at Brown. "It's a dream come true."

The elder Estes' counterpart at Dartmouth, Buddy Teevens, finds himself similarly ahead of the curve. Teevens has become a regular participant on panels for the advocacy group Practice Like Pros "to extol the virtues of cutting down on full-contact practices by focusing on technique, which in turn limits injuries suffered in practice and in games." Teevens said that his team hasn't tackled in practice in five years, and the results have been statistically better when it comes to tackling. Alternatively, Teevens explained that they use robots to practice tackling. And he said that his practices closely resemble what they do in the NFL.

"A Dartmouth football player," he says, "will never tackle or be tackled by a teammate during his four-year career. But we average five hundred to eight hundred tackles per year per defensive player. We do it in tackle circuits, on bags, and a mobile tackling device that allows us to hit a moving target. We're doing more tacking than most people in the country; we just don't hit each other."

Toward that end, Teevens has taken the traditional football tackling "donut" to the next level by mechanizing it into that "mobile tackling device" to enable rubber to stand in for flesh, bone, muscle, and pads.

"I tell coaches," Teevens continues, "either we change the way we coach the game or we won't have a game to coach. If everyone stepped away from the paranoia and said do we really need this much contact? Tackling is like riding a bike; you don't forget how to do it."

"It's not just about the wins and losses," Brown's Phil Estes adds. "It's about trying to keep the players healthy. It's about their quality of life. It's the only way we're going to save the game."

While acknowledging Estes' points about CTE, Bob Surace, head coach of Princeton University, offers a slightly different perspective.

"I keep a Google Drive with every living Princeton football alum. I use it to help our players make career connections in their chosen fields, for recruiting purposes and other things. A couple of thousand names now and it seems every one of them is a president, a vice president, a head coach, a headmaster, a CEO. I believe there is no better study group for success than Ivy League football players. Many of these Princeton alums played in the fifties, sixties, and seventies before attention was paid to player safety, the way it is now. We monitor the way we practice, the health of our players, the amount of hitting we do, the conditioning, the amount of time we're on the field. So today's players are getting the best of both worlds, taking out of the game everything past generations have been able to in a far safer environment."

Prior to his days playing for the Tigers in Palmer Stadium, Bob played for his father, a high school football coach in working class, hardscrabble Millville, New Jersey, so you can justifiably say that football is in his blood.

"I grew up going from water boy, to team manager, to putting the playbooks together, to being a statistician, to actually playing for my dad. And I saw the impact first-hand he and his staff had on twenty-five seniors every year. How you make a difference in the lives of these players by instilling in them the values I watched my dad instill in so many others."

Upon leaving Western Connecticut State University, where he'd won a title and advanced to the second round of the Division III playoffs, Bob became an assistant with the Cincinnati Bengals to better position himself to be considered for a Division I coaching job.

"We had just lost to the Raiders," he recalls, during his eighth and final season with the Bengals, "and my phone was blowing up with the news that the Princeton job had opened up. I sent a text to my wife at the very same time she was sending me one. Dozens of my old teammates, the best friends I'd ever made, were already asking, 'Are you going to do this?' And I really wasn't sure, given the great field of candidates who applied for the job. But when I was named head coach, getting that opportunity, coaching at the great school where I'd played, was a dream come true."

As a center during his playing days for Princeton, Bob snapped the ball to none other than Jason Garrett, current head coach of the Dallas Cowboys. Garrett continues to maintain close ties with the Princeton community, hosting an annual Play It Smart Camp and Leadership Forum. Houston Texans head coach Bill O'Brien has built an equally strong relationship with his alma mater Brown University. The man responsible for rebuilding Penn State's storied football program also coordinated the Texans' relief efforts after Hurricane Harvey devastated Houston in 2017. Both coaches will be their respective schools' honorees at the 2019 Ivy Football Dinner.

* * *

None of this is lost on Governor Ehrlich either, who credits football with much of the great success he has achieved in life.

"Playing the game was the foundation of my personality," he explains. "It defines my character, it defines my worldview. Playing the game is all about a willingness to prepare, to compete, to be disciplined. In this case, all the clichés you hear are true. I'm a creature of how I was brought up and the people who influenced me: my coaches and teachers, the Gilman School, where I met a host of strong male role models who were jocks but also smart. They preached ethics above everything, turning boys into men in the classroom and on the athletic fields."

The governor speaks with great fondness and affinity for the school's legendary headmaster Reddy Finney, a three-sport varsity athlete at Princeton who made All-American in both football and lacrosse (something done only by one other athlete, the great Jim Brown). The year he graduated in 1951, Finney received the prestigious William Winston Roper Trophy, which is awarded to a Princeton man of high scholastic rank, outstanding qualities of sportsmanship, and general proficiency in athletics.

"He had a profound, truly profound, effect on my life. After serving in the U.S. Navy in Korea, he came home to become Mr. Chips, teaching and coaching at Gilman before becoming its headmaster. He used to stop by the field at practice and participate in drills with us, wearing a suit and tie. In college I wore his number, 51. His style was leadership by example. When you screwed up, when you made a mistake either on the field or off it, you were upset because you knew you had let Mr. Finney down. He ran Gilman for almost thirty years and made a huge difference in the lives of everyone he touched.

"Reddy Finney's ideas were radical because he decided he wanted this elite prep school in Baltimore to look more like Baltimore. So he recruited kids of different races and socioeconomic levels, including the first black athlete to really star at Gilman, quarterback Stuart Simms, who'd later become captain of the football team and went on to Dartmouth [recruited by me when I was an assistant coach in 1968], where he also captained their football team. These ideas were radical at the time, and I was actually part of the second generation of diverse kids Mr. Finney brought to the school. A lot of kids had their tuitions paid by Reddy through an entity called 'Desire Foundation.' What I didn't know then, and wouldn't learn until many years later, was that I was one of them."

So for Governor Bob Ehrlich, without football there is no Reddy Finney, no Gilman, no Princeton, and no political career. The future governor's coach had summoned me to Gilman with the admonition that "you have to see this kid." What I saw was a very aggressive linebacker with good movement. Not a big guy, but full of heart and very tough, a good, solid football player who'd been named captain his senior year. An emotional kid who impressed me as a natural leader.

"I like analogizing football to politics," Ehrlich says today. "When I see politicians who are self-absorbed and comfortable acting as free agents, it's pretty clear they never played a team sport, never mind football. Playing football, the ultimate team sport, instills a selflessness, makes you more appreciative of the people working together with you toward the same goal: to win. And I was so fortunate that football opened the door for someone like me to attend Gilman first, and then on to Princeton. As I said before, none of who I am happens if not for that, which means if not for football."

And, like politics, Ehrlich stresses that the state of football today (particularly regarding CTE) remains somewhat open to interpretation. As he wrote on July 31, 2017, in his column for the *Washington Examiner*:

> *Two major football-related studies have been published in recent weeks, but you likely have not heard about one of them. The highly-publicized one is an updated study by the Journal of the American Medical Association that found 88 percent of 202 brains taken from deceased former football players (at all levels) revealed some degree of Chronic Traumatic Encephalopathy. The other was an analysis of multi-decade survey data of men who played Wisconsin high school football in 1957, published in the estimable JAMA Neurology.*
>
> *The reason you have not heard of this second study has more to do with its counterintuitive conclusions than anything else: Researchers found that former football players did not have higher incidences of cognitive impairment at age 65 as opposed to non-football players; former players were in fact slightly less likely to suffer from depression.*
>
> *Both studies are newsworthy given the tenor of our nascent national conversation about football's future, an issue that has resonated with some (especially on the Left) who want to outlaw what in their eyes is a game grown too violent.*

The governor does not at all mean to suggest that concussions are not a problem in football, even a major one; only that alone, the undeniable scourge they represent, among especially NFL players, should be kept in perspective and within the bigger picture that includes all the good football can do for those who partake in the sport.

I convey these thoughts with appropriate reference to the realities of a violent game. All involved must recognize that a collision sport can be dangerous and accordingly is not for every boy, and made more so by the "bigger, stronger, faster" nature of today's training regimes. The bottom line: Kids susceptible to concussions or those who have suffered numerous concussions should not play.

Further, we should all support additional research into the science of brain trauma and further safety measures. (In this respect, I for one would be happy to revisit the issue of artificial turf, an invention borne of convenience, but that has made a fast game faster and more dangerous. Note the Baltimore Ravens made the switch back to grass last year after its players had had enough of the fake stuff.)

Another move in the right direction is an increased focus on player safety in youth leagues, especially a new emphasis on experienced coaching. This is not a game where well-intentioned dads should simply show up to lend a hand. The teaching of proper technique has never been more important given what we now know about injury prevention and treatment.

Those who profess to love football should not be threatened, but rather welcome further study into how to make our game safer.

Indeed, the governor is a prime advocate for all that's good in the game he's most comfortable making a case for.

"I'll never forget when standout wide receiver Pat McInally of Harvard, who'd go on to play in the NFL for the Cincinnati Bengals [and was inducted into the College Football Hall of Fame in 2016] was asked what the Crimson's offensive line averaged. 'Oh,' he said, referring instead to the line's Grade Point Average 'about 3.85.'"

To that point, that same July 2017 column the governor penned for the *Washington Examiner* concludes, "Those who are engaged in a campaign of cultural assassination directed at America's favorite sport should remember that millions of young men have played the game at all levels over the past 150 years. The vast majority are far better off for the experience."

CHAPTER 17

CHAD HENNINGS—
MISSION ACCOMPLISHED

Chad Hennings won three Super Bowls over his nine years with the Dallas Cowboys. This after he was a U.S. Air Force fighter pilot during the Gulf War, Operation Desert Storm.

"For me," he says, "football was the greatest leadership lab there was. I learned so many lessons about teamwork, about commitment, about overcoming obstacles. How you prepare and how you succeed as an individual in the context of a team. That carried over for me when I was flying jets. And it's also translated into business. We need football, the opportunity it provides for young men and boys to learn what it's like to be a man."

What it means to be a man has actually become a mantra in Chad's life. In addition to running a successful commercial real estate company, he's a minister and boasts two books to his credit. The first, *Rules of Engagement: Finding Faith and Purpose in a Disconnected World*, deals heavily with what it means to be a man. And, coming from a fighter pilot who played defensive lineman in the NFL, Chad's thoughts may surprise you.

"I want this book to make a difference," he writes in the introduction, "to tear down the walls that separate men from each other and from our true selves. I want to offer a plan for men that gives them an alternative to suffering in silence, feeling disconnected from their spouses and families, seeking to numb themselves through unhealthy coping mechanisms, whether it's alcohol, drugs, extramarital affairs, workaholism, addiction to pornography, prescription painkillers, or a combination thereof. A man's legacy must be more than killing time through work and killing pain through distraction. Men may be able to point with pride to their work, but what else in their lives do they have? If work is the only measure of a man's success, then the result is depression, disconnection, and at the extreme, even suicide."

The roots of the book's message, and Chad's mission, date back not only to his military and football experience, but also to his son Chase being diagnosed with an autoimmune disease that attacked his joints as a toddler.

"That experience helped me formulate an identity," he recalls today. "Focus my priorities. Put life in perspective. It helped me get over myself. My whole existence, both personal and professional, up to that point had been based on performance: achieving goals and overcoming obstacles. I was dominated by what I did. Suddenly, I realized that what you do does not define who you are. There's gotta be more to life than playing football or flying jets. When you can't overcome something, when you realize you have no power at all, you get over yourself pretty quick."

Chad talks about finding Christ, about seeing life in the world through a whole different lens and filter. And that new mindset, that new sensibility, remained after Chase recovered. Twenty years later, he still has some mobility issues, challenges in getting around, but not enough to stop him from working with his father in that commercial real estate firm that Chad founded.

"I want men to find the joy and excitement in life that I have been privileged to experience in so many ways, public and private," he continues in the introduction to *Rules of Engagement*. "This book is that plan. I have known the kind of friendships, mentoring relationships, and accountability rarely found in our society outside the arenas of war and sport. Again, it was never just about flying jets in combat or being a Super Bowl champion. As I said, I've always seen these experiences as preparation for something greater down the road. For me, that something is the ability to speak to men and inspire them to greatness, not just in their outer lives but in their hearts. Not just in their business dealings but in their marriages and in their relationships with their children. Not just in their workplaces but in their communities and in their countries."

Chad speaks as a father, as well as a football player and fighter pilot, about what stands out the most from his exceptionally rare combination of experiences.

"Relationships—teammates—would be the number one thing, and that started with football. The guys I played the game with are still my best friends and closest contacts. Developing a work ethic to achieve victory translates onto a whole other level. It's the ultimate team sport, both during the season as well as the off season. When you work out with guys, when you've sweated together, gotten dirty and bloody together, you know you're not going to give up on one another. You know the character of your teammates, know what makes them tick, and you know you can trust them. For me, that carried over into the military and into business."

Chad starred at the Air Force Academy, an almost certain number one draft pick in 1988 if it hadn't been for the eight-year commitment he'd made once he chose to become a pilot. The Cowboys president and general manager at the time, Tex Schramm, rolled the dice in the eleventh round and signed Chad to a multiyear contract, knowing his potential star would be thirty years old as a rookie.

The Gulf War's wake, though, led to a series of military cutbacks that allowed him to leave active duty after only four years and begin his football career in 1992 at the age of 2. Interestingly enough, he remained in the Air Force Reserve as a liaison officer for the nine years he spent in the NFL. The Cowboys were in the process of building one of the league's best defensive lines that included the likes of Leon Lett and Russell Maryland. Chad became a key reserve on that team early on and became a starter while Lett served a four-game suspension in 1995. The following year, he became a full-time starter when Maryland opted to join the Oakland Raiders as a free agent. Nine years later he'd registered 27.5 sacks and boasted those three Super Bowl rings.

His senior season at Air Force, Chad won the Outland Trophy that recognizes the nation's best interior lineman. He'd recorded twenty-four sacks that season and is generally regarded as one of the best players in the academy's storied history. He was inducted into the College Football Hall of Fame in 2005, and in 2013, he was awarded the NCAA Silver Anniversary Award, presented each year to six outstanding college student-athletes on the twenty-fifth anniversary of their graduation. He was inducted into the Air Force Academy Athletics Hall of Fame as a member of its inaugural class in 2007 and, in 2014, received the Walter Camp Football Foundation's alumni award, "bestowed on a worthy individual who has distinguished himself in the pursuit of excellence as an athlete, in his personal career, and in doing good works for others."

As for his experience flying A-10 Thunderbolts, affectionately known as the "Warthog," in Operation Desert Storm, he tempted Iraqi ground fire by flying 45 combat sorties over two deployments. He was twice awarded the Air Force Achievement Medal, a humanitarian award, and an Outstanding Unit Award for his actions in the service.

Chad enjoys talking about the indelible link, the commonality, between football and the military. And, having experienced them both at the highest of levels, he should know.

"The two go hand-in-hand. It's one thing to sit in a classroom and have someone tell you what it means to be a leader from a cerebral standpoint. But actually employing those traits on the field, or in combat, is something entirely different. It's about mentoring a younger player or officer. It's about overcoming odds, demonstrating a work ethic, showing grit and determination. Being under stress and duress while playing football helped me so much in the air force with training and combat missions. Football and combat are all about preparation. Evaluating film to be a better pilot and a better defensive lineman. Dropping opponents or dropping bombs. That's how I got better at both. In the air force, learning what the enemy had from a standpoint of ground assets. In football, learning offensive back sets, different formations, an opponent's tendencies to run or pass in certain situations. But you can't succeed alone. You need wingmen, in the cockpit and on the field."

To that point, Chad established Wingmen Ministries to mesh the lessons gleaned from his dual experiences, in large part to dispel the "go it alone" macho creed too many men, in his mind, live by. He seeks to redefine what it means to be a man by defining masculinity on an emotional level based on the nurturing of relationships, while learning to rely upon and accept others into your life. Lessons culled from his own experiences as a football player, a fighter pilot, and a man.

"People ask me what I want to be remembered as. That would never be one single play or a game or a Super Bowl victory. It's always about the relationships. The greatest compliment I could ever receive was that I was a good teammate. That would mean mission accomplished for me. People forget how much money you have, your stats, how many sacks you recorded and fumbles you recovered. Instead, what they remember most is the product of those relationships. When I get together with the teammates I played with, we never talk about individual games or plays. We talk about the fun we had that we shared."

Which is why the man behind Wingmen Ministries preaches the value of the game.

"I think football has become a victim of its own success," Chad reflects. "There's a lot of misinformation out there, when the reality is the game is safer today than it's ever been, thanks to the implementation of safety protocols, restrictions on contact drills, and more protective equipment. The game is taking care of guys who've been injured at a whole new level, giving them time to heal. And that's true even of concussions, because the brain's ability to heal post-concussion is a proven fact so long as the player receives the kind of treatment dominating football today.

"I love watching kids play the game at the high school or even junior high level. They play it for the love of the game. And that grounds me, reminds me why I love the game. The problem we face is that the influence of football has skewed its true value. You turn on the television or open the newspaper and there's always a story about some college team did this or some NFL player did that. You know what they say about the squeaky wheel. And that means we need to be better guardians of the game, to spread the lessons of all the good that is football."

Chad followed up *Rules of Engagement* with *Forces of Character: Conversations about Building a Life of Impact,* a Studs Terkel–like oral history assemblage celebrating the wisdom and advice of those who've made the biggest impact upon him.

"Chad has brought together a truly astonishing collection of individuals to share their personal stories about a critical topic for our times: character," Kurt Warner, a Super Bowl and NFL MVP winning quarterback himself, notes. "This book is just as important to society as it is to sports."

The book includes chapters on very well-known names like Roger Staubach, Troy Aikman, and San Antonio Spurs head coach Gregg Popovich, as well a number of others you've probably never heard of like Tom Henricks and Virginia Prodan. It doesn't matter that we may not know them, because Chad does and wants us to learn from them just as he did.

"My mission in life is about spreading the word that you are more than what you do; you are what you believe. Determining your identity determines your mission, your avocation, wherever you want to take it. I want to encourage individuals to define who they are, to discover their identity and not be afraid to accept it. Character is about choice. You decide who you are and who you want to be."

Like him, Staubach and Aikman have won Super Bowls, something Chad does not take lightly.

"As a kid growing up, all your heroes, the role models that you looked up to on the gridiron—you know those guys—they were able to hold that trophy up," Chad told the publication *U.S. Air Force* in February of 2016. "I was a Minnesota Vikings fan, and they went there four years and they never won one. That's where I realized how difficult it is, not only to just get to the Super Bowl, but also to win."

Chad sums up his thoughts on preserving the game largely responsible for making him who he is in the simplest of terms.

"We need football more than ever."

PART FOUR:

GIVING BACK

"I have loved football as an almost mythic game since I was in the fourth grade. To me, the game wasn't even grounded in reality. The uniform turned you into a warrior. Being on a team, the mythology of physical combat, the struggle against the elements, the narrative of the game."

—Steve Sabol

CHAPTER 18

TOM CATENA—
"GIVING UP IS NOT AN OPTION"

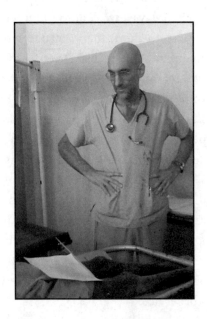

"Dr. Catena embodies the spirit of the Aurora Prize, and we extend our deepest gratitude to him and the people and organizations around the world that support and inspire him to continue his noble work despite immensely challenging conditions," said Ruben Vardanyan, co-founder of the Aurora Humanitarian Initiative and United World College at Dilijan. "We are honored to share his story with the world to shed light on the

goodwill that exists in the world so that helping others becomes part of our global culture."

—Citation for the 2017 Aurora Prize, presented annually to an individual "whose actions have had an exceptional impact on preserving human life and advancing humanitarian causes."

For nearly a decade now, the man known as "Dr. Tom" to the thousands of Sudanese natives for whom he is the only physician, has been on call 24 hours a day, seven days a week at the Mother of Mercy Catholic Hospital in Nuba, home to more than 750,000 citizens mired in the ongoing civil war in Sudan. Patients have been known to walk for up to seven days to receive treatment for injuries from bombing attacks and ailments varying from bone fractures to malnourishment and malaria. It's estimated that Dr. Tom treats 500 patients per day and performs more than 1,000 operations each year—always at the risk of his life and never giving consideration to abandoning his post as the only physician within roughly 400 square miles.

And what does he think about the lofty praise above and being named the Aurora Prize Lauriat in 2017 "for rekindling faith in humanity"?

"Like many people, I'm a bit shy when praise is directed my way—sure it feels good but never fully comfortable. I hope that these kind words can be turned into tangible results and that others can perhaps follow our example and lead lives of service."

Catena, who enjoyed a stellar career playing nose guard for Brown University, was one of 550 nominations for the Aurora Prize submitted from 66 countries. The prize brings with it a grant of one million dollars that Dr. Tom has already apportioned equally among three different charities that support bringing modern-day medicine to the Third World.

"His service to others is an inspiration, and it is our hope that the individuals he has saved will continue the cycle of gratitude by becoming saviors themselves," said Vartan Gregorian, president of the Carnegie Corporation of New York, cofounder of the Aurora Humanitarian Initiative, and Aurora Prize Selection Committee member.

Coincidentally, Gregorian once served as president of Brown University where, years before, Dr. Tom had provided a different kind of inspiration for his fellow Bear football players.

"I loved everything about Ivy League football—the history, traditions, focus on academics. We normally played in quaint old stadiums, but we did have one game in the 'big time' when we played Penn State at State College during my sophomore year. I only got in for three plays but even being on the sidelines in such an arena was an experience not to be forgotten. Road trips, staying at the hotel, ice cream sundaes the night before the game, laughing at the antics of teammates are all cherished memories."

"We all have an obligation to look after our brothers and sisters," Dr. Tom says of his experiences today. "It is possible that every single person can make a contribution, and to recognize that shared humanity can lead to a brighter future. With my faith as my guide, I am honored to continue to serve the world and make it a better place."

Of his work in the Sudan, no less a source than Nicholas Kristof wrote for the *New York Times* on June 13, 2015, that "he does all this off the electrical grid, without running water, a telephone, or so much as an X-ray machine—while under constant threat of bombing.... The first time, Dr. Tom sheltered, terrified, in a newly dug pit for an outhouse, but the hospital is now surrounded by foxholes in which patients and the staff crouch when military aircraft approach."

"We're in a place where the government is not trying to help us," Catena told Kristof, when the reporter visited a region the rest of the world has forgotten. "It's trying to kill us."

Before he became "Dr. Tom," Catena made All-Ivy and was an honorable mention All-American his senior season in 1985, while being named a Rhodes Scholar candidate.

"We had a very strong defensive line in those days," recalls Walt Cataldo, a two-time All-Ivy, All-ECAC at safety who played with Catena for two years. "But Tom was a key cog and, as nose guard, everything revolved around him. He wasn't a big rah-rah guy, but he showed up for every practice and every game, and never took a play off. He was very humble, very focused, and came ready to play all the time. He was never after the limelight, content to handle all the ugly assignments so us linebackers and safeties could make the tackles. I remember him in the trenches, covered in mud, somebody comfortable with doing the dirty work, getting down and dirty. And he was also a great human being. He treated us very well as underclassmen. Took us under his wing and embraced us, made us feel part of the team. Tommy never had one ounce of 'what's in it for me?' in him. That's what I remember most about Catman."

Not surprisingly, "Catman" wholeheartedly agrees with Jack Lengyel's previously noted quote that "if you're ever given something of value, you have a moral obligation to pass it on to others."

"What I have to offer," he says, "is my medical knowledge and skills which have been honed over the past twenty-five years. I do believe that I have an obligation to pass on this knowledge to our Nuba staff. We are sponsoring two local Nuba men for medical school and several others in medical-related fields. I plan to continue training them when they return to Nuba Mountains until they are prepared to take over the reins of the hospital."

After graduating Brown, Catena decided to pursue a career in medicine and enrolled at the Duke University School of Medicine on a U.S. Navy scholarship. He entered the United States Navy in 1992, becoming a naval flight surgeon. After fulfilling his navy obligation, he completed a residency in family medicine and during his residency, he began his medical foray into the developing world with mission trips to Guyana and Honduras before spending six years in Nairobi and then moving on to the Sudan.

But the game of football remains close to his heart.

"Playing college football was the experience of a lifetime and I wouldn't exchange it for anything," he reflects. "There is a special camaraderie among football players that transcends age, race, and degree of ability. The friendships made on the football field are there for life as they are among people with shared goals and interests."

More pointedly, Dr. Tom draws a clear connection between the lessons he learned on the football field and the selfless work he's performing today for the people of the Sudan.

"The lessons learned on the football field have a direct correlation with my work as a physician and surgeon in a war zone. Teamwork is an important lesson learned in a team sport such as football. Working as a surgeon in a war zone, coordinated teamwork saves lives. I was a nose guard and a big part of my job was to take on double teams so that the linebackers could roam free. Not very exciting, but it was what had to be done for the defense to work. This idea of sacrificing for the good of the team is essential in my line of work. We often have to do unpleasant jobs and give up most of the finer things in life to work in our impoverished environment. Playing hurt, giving your all in the fourth quarter despite being exhausted, are part of football that players at all levels are well acquainted. There have been innumerable occasions when fifty to eighty wounded would come to our hospital after a battle. Being the sole surgeon at the hospital, I am responsible for each one of these casualties. Sometimes we're up all night operating on the wounded, and we know there is no other option. We keep working until all of the wounded are treated. Giving up is not an option."

Dr. Tom is succinct regarding his thoughts on the game today, as both a former player and physician.

"As a physician I must admit that I am concerned about the reports of former players suffering from chronic traumatic encephalopathy [CTE], although I think it would be a shame to prohibit young people from playing the game. Football is much more than a game, as the values of teamwork, sacrifice, camaraderie, and pushing oneself beyond one's limits will stay with the athlete for life."

The Aurora Prize is only the most recent accolade acknowledging Tom Catena's incredible contribution to humanity. In 2013, Brown University awarded him the William Rogers Award, given to a Brown graduate who exemplifies the university's mission to prepare alumni for lives of "usefulness and reputation." He was also named one of twelve Catholic Heroes for America and the World by *Catholic Digest* in 2010. And the National Football Foundation gave Dr. Tom its highest honor, the Gold Medal Award, in 2014 in recognition of building on his stellar performance on the football field with an extraordinary contribution to humanity.

"Tom Catena symbolizes everything that our organization represents," NFF president and CEO Steve Hatchell said at the time. "He was a powerhouse as a football player who distinguished himself as an exceptional leader at Brown. He took those same skills and turned himself into a doctor, helping the less fortunate in the war-torn region of the Sudan. Many of us dream of making the world a better place. Tom Catena has given up all his earthly possessions to do that every day of his life. He is off the charts in making the world a better place."

"A truly remarkable individual, Tom Catena stands as an inspiration to us all," adds NFF chairman Archie Manning, who would be given the foundation's Gold Medal Award himself two years later, "having created a powerful path for making a difference in one of the bleakest places on earth. His role in the Sudan in providing medical care has become so critical that it has taken us more than a year to arrange to bring him back for the event, and this December marks the first Christmas in thirteen years that he will be able to spend with his family in America."

Dr. Gus White, a fellow Brown alumnus who also appears in this section of the book, sums up Dr. Tom's life and career by saying, "Tom is a modern-day Albert Schweitzer."

Corry Chapman witnessed the work of this modern-day Schweitzer up close and personal when he worked by Dr. Tom's side for a time in the Sudan, an experience he brilliantly recounted in an award-winning 2008 article entitled "Always on Call" for *The Lancet*, England's premier medical journal.

"Those first months took a toll on Catena," he writes. "He got malaria twice. He dropped 50 pounds. He never left the compound. Surgical emergencies arrived daily, often nightly. Catena worked in an isolated region with no cities or government and no other doctors nearby. He managed a hospital that relied on solar power, pumped water, and pit latrines, its small storehouse of supplies replenished only twice a year by cargo plane from Nairobi. Everything was limited, nothing could be wasted. Catena stretched his drugs, suture, and physical energy as far as they could go to treat overwhelming need. It nearly broke him, but the effort paid off."

Just as it had on the football field a generation before.

"I've been living in Africa for the past seventeen-plus years so I have not been able to follow the game as much as I'd like," Tom says today, aptly encapsulating the experiences that earned him inclusion as one of *Time* magazine's "100 Most Influential People of 2015" and he is rumored to be under active consideration for a Nobel Prize. "However, from my far vantage point, it seems football has maintained its essence as a rough-and-tumble team sport played by energetic young men. My father keeps me updated on my high school team [Amsterdam High School in Amsterdam, New York] and I can keep up with Brown football through the internet. Certainly, as I get older, my appreciation for the game has increased immensely as I see how the lessons learned on the gridiron have been so invaluable to my career."

"People in the Nuba Mountains will never forget his name," Lt. Col. Aburass Albino Kuku of a Sudanese rebel military force told Nicholas Kristof for that June 13, 2015 *New York Times* article. "People are praying that he never dies."

A Muslim paramount chief named Hussein Nalukuri Cuppi was even more lavish with his praise of Dr. Tom to Kristof.

"He's Jesus Christ," he said.

The chief elaborated to Kristof that "Jesus healed the sick, made the blind see, and helped the lame walk."

Just another day at the office for Dr. Tom Catena.

CHAPTER 19

GUS WHITE—
"YOU STAND UP AND FIGHT"

"Football," says Doctor Augustus White, "gives you the opportunities to stand up before others and put yourself on the line, to meet a challenge. You stand up and fight. Sometimes you win and sometimes you lose, but you know what it's all about. Football is one of many wonderful ways to prepare oneself for those day-to-day, moment-to-moment, year-to-year life challenges."

He should know, although the life challenges Gus has faced have been considerably more than what can be remotely described as "day to day."

"When Augustus A. White III arrived at Brown in 1953," the *Brown Alumni Magazine* wrote in a fall 2011 issue, "he joined a student body as whitewashed and WASPy as a beach house in Kennebunkport, Maine. The Hillel House wouldn't open for another decade. The first woman, the first African-American, and the first Jew on the Corporation's Board of Fellows would have to wait until 1969. White was one of only five African-Americans in his class."

"We, Brown's African-American students, didn't feel affronted by this plain discrimination," he told the magazine for that same article. "Quite the opposite. We felt happy to be at a place so liberal that it accepted Negroes at all."

"The influence White has had on Brown's racial and ethnic diversity reflects the steady, deliberate effort of an unlikely pioneer," the article continues. "A groundbreaking orthopedic surgeon, he was the first African-American medical student at Stanford, the first black surgical resident at Yale, the first black professor of medicine at Yale, and the first black department chief at a Harvard teaching hospital. One of the nation's preeminent experts on the biomechanics of the spine, White has coauthored textbooks that remain seminal references for surgeons and clinicians. When his book for a popular audience, *Your Aching Back: A Doctor's Guide to Relief*, appeared in 1990, the *New England Journal of Medicine* decreed that it 'should be read by every person afflicted with low back pain, and perhaps everybody.'"

Little did Gus know when his stellar defensive play against the Crimson his senior year earned him a game ball in a 26–18 win that he'd eventually be returning to Harvard to climb another rung in his storied, if not legendary, career that began with a childhood spent in Memphis, Tennessee.

"In the black south, when I was a child," Gus writes in *Seeing Patients*, his superb professional biography published in 2011, "the first thing an adult person would ask you was: 'Well, boy, what are you going to be when you grow up?' Or in my case, since my father had been a physician, 'Your father was a fine man, a great doctor. You going to be a doctor like him?' My physician father died when I was eight, but some of his influence must have rubbed off, because in our playground games of Cowboys and Indians I seemed to naturally want to take care of those who might have been hurt or wounded in the action."

That inclination gave way to a journey north, to the Mount Hermon School for Boys, a prestigious boarding school which accepted blacks and set Gus White on the road to breaking down numerous color barriers deemed unthinkable at the time. After his father's death, he and his mother were forced to move from their two-bedroom house into the home of Aunt Addie and her husband, Uncle Doc, a pharmacist. The family doubled up on couches and cots, and White's college-educated mother got a job as a secretary at a high school, where she eventually became a teacher.

At the Mount Hermon School for Boys (now Northfield Mount Hermon), Gus earned tuition money by waiting tables and sweeping floors. He sang in the choir, excelled academically, and was the only member of his class to earn letters in three different sports: wrestling and lacrosse, in addition to football.

Once at Brown, Gus worked grueling hours in order to play football—defensive end and wide receiver—in a career highlighted by a game against Dartmouth his senior season that found the Big Green driving for a winning touchdown in the game's waning minutes.

"They had gotten down to our six or seven-yard line and seemed certain to be going in," Gus recalls. "I'd been badly beaten on an earlier running play and they came out in the same formation. As the ball was snapped, the offensive lineman tried to hook me to get me out of the way again. But this time I was ready. I threw him aside, made the tackle, and the clock ran out."

Also during his senior year, Gus caught a twice-deflected pass and ran it in for a touchdown in a crucial victory against Cornell. Quite an accomplishment for a player who hadn't even made the travel squad as a sophomore. And yet the 1954 season held one of his most indelible highlights: the day when Brown's, and the country's, first great African-American player, Fritz Pollard, was inducted into the College Football Hall of Fame at Brown Stadium. Gus and teammate Archie Williams '56 were standing on the sidelines when the man who'd led Brown to an appearance in the first-ever Rose Bowl game in 1916 came strolling past them.

"The excitement of Fritz Pollard coming back and walking the sidelines and talking to Archie and to me—that was invigorating.

"I don't know what life would've been like if I hadn't played football, if I'd focused on another sport instead," Gus reflects. "A lot of that has to do with the culture in which I grew up, how important football was to the culture of the South in a middle-class black community. Football was lauded. People respected and looked up to people who played the game. And that was so important to my identity as a young boy playing pick-up games with my friends. I thought I was tough, even though I was a pip-squeak at the time. When I think of all the things I took from football, the first one that comes to mind is resilience."

Gus showers praise on many of those who helped him along the way, particularly a stepfather who came into his life after the death of his own father.

"All the schools in the South were segregated back then," the man long known as "the Jackie Robinson of orthopedics" recalls. "And the high school I attended was considered the best in terms of sports. My stepfather coached boxing and also served as an assistant coach on the football team. He was very generous with his time to me. He taught me how to box and how to catch a football. I learned so much from him, including how important it is when an adult takes an interest in you. He taught me to love the game."

And yet as a renowned orthopedist specializing in the spine and biomechanics, Gus has serious concerns about the state of football today.

"I see CTE, chronic traumatic encephalopathy, as a real calamity, a real issue. I agree with Dr. Robert Cantu of the Concussion Legacy Foundation and co-director of the Neurological Sports Injury Center at Brigham and Women's Hospital in Boston that there should be no contact prior to high school. That alone would greatly diminish the risk of injury for players. The major thing that Dr. Cantu's work has concluded is that if you avoid contact before your teenage years, you're much less likely to have a problem down the road. But the problem isn't limited to football. Heading a soccer ball repeatedly can be traumatic to the brain too, and there are issues with lacrosse and hockey as well. It's now somewhat a matter of medical management."

Somewhat, Gus stresses, adding, "No doubt, playing the game of football historically for many athletes has accrued tremendous benefits for them. Nevertheless, all potential participants should be warned and advised to make a thorough, thoughtful, well-informed, and well-assisted analysis of the risk benefits of playing the game."

According to the Black History Timeline for Brown University, compiled by the Ivy League website, "Augustus A. White III, in playing for the Bruins' football team, discovered his career path, orthopedics over psychiatry. Seeing many an injury that was not prevented by the inferior equipment of the day, White became a world-renowned expert on spinal cord injuries."

Gus mostly agrees with that assessment. Mostly.

"Yes and no. My mentor at Brown was a wonderful man named Tony Davis, who was in the psychology department. He noticed me because I was a football player and wrestler and took an interest in me. Walking out of class one day he said, 'Mr. White, may I speak with you? You're a good student and you might want to consider writing a thesis. Please make an appointment to come see me.' Well, I did and down the road we ended up publishing a paper together. That was so important to me, because no one besides my family had ever told me I was a good student before. Life has that way of bringing people to you who have a huge impact sometimes. Years later, he became my patient. He died recently and I read in his obituary that he was a fighter pilot in the Korean War. I wish I'd known that when he was alive."

Gus also fondly recalls the relationship he built with Joe Restic, then an assistant coach for Brown under Alva Kelley prior to going on to a remarkable career as head coach of the Harvard Crimson. Gus calls him a "friend and mentor."

This after Restic referred to Gus as a "real team guy" in a November 1956 article that appeared in the *Providence Journal*. Gus earned an 80 percent defensive rating that season, highest on the team.

"A significant portion of the great defensive job by the Bruins last Saturday [against Cornell]," the same article went on to say, "can be traced to a rangy senior end who was starting his first game. He was no slouch on offense either. In fact, he was the hero who grabbed a twice-deflected forward pass and turned tail for the tying touchdown."

The article concluded by noting that, as a pre-medical student, "Gus probably is the busiest man on the Brown campus."

And that hasn't changed in all the years since.

"As we grew up in college, particularly as seniors, in our early twenties," Gus said upon being Brown's honoree at the Ivy League Football Dinner in January of 2011, "we sometimes questioned the extent to which coaches are just doing their job; when they give us a lot of emotional stuff we wondered sometimes if they sincerely believed it. So I couldn't wait to meet my friend and coach, Joe Restic, again when I was in my early forties, after some years of experience, including Vietnam. I thought now that I've got a little maturity and a war on my belly, let's see how he sounds. Joe was then Harvard's head coach, and I had come to the medical school to start an orthopedic department at the Beth Israel Hospital. We had lunch at the Faculty Club. Well, Coach 'rang true'—he sounded powerfully sincere.

"One of the things he said in that conversation was, 'Gus, you know it's really good for you to have played football; for example, as you're out there defending the line and there are a whole bunch of people coming at you, you have to 'stand up and be counted.' You have to work through it and find the ball carrier and take him down. It's good for you to have to stand up and be counted, to get out there and put yourself on the line and test your mettle. That is very transferable to a lot of situations, far beyond the football field."

Including Vietnam. In August 1966, Gus arrived there as a combat surgeon. Subject to a special doctors' draft, he could have found alternative service but opted not to. He wanted to "jump over there and do what I could," he writes in *Seeing Patients*. But Gus' Vietnam experience didn't stop in the operating room. He also volunteered at a nearby leprosarium, doing the best he could to help the unfortunate lot confined there.

"What was going on at the St. Francis Leprosarium made for quite a contrast with the Eighty-Fifth EVAC Hospital," he recalls today. "We'd operate at times for forty to fifty straight hours, awash in blood and gore in the center of the worst of that war. Then I'd volunteer at the leper colony two half days a week, where I saw a different kind of tragedy. I saw victims who had a hole in their face where their mouth and nose had once been. And here are these Franciscan nuns running the colony, preserving human dignity at all costs. What I experienced firsthand as a result was the amazing contrast between what nature can do to man, and what man can do to man."

"In many cultures," Gus writes in *Seeing Patients*, "leprosy is regarded with such horror that if anybody just makes eye contact and looks at lepers and acknowledges them as human beings, they are profoundly grateful. And if you help them? You fix them up? The feedback is incomparable.... I didn't know who was helped most at that leper colony, the helpers or the helpees."

Given all that, but for chance Gus would likely have followed the path laid out by his Brown mentor, Tony Davis.

"I went to med school with an eye on practicing psychiatry. But I was able to get a residency with the chief of orthopedics at Yale University, one of the leading spinal orthopedists at the time. A wonderful opportunity I couldn't turn down and I ended up finding my calling. The rest is history."

And throughout that history, Gus White has shown himself time and time again to be a man of unparalleled principles, the many examples of which would fill an entire book. So let's look at just one, specifically when he applied for the presidency of the University of Maryland, a campus consisting of seven top-notch graduate schools, in 1989. The search committee supported his nomination and he got the job as an African-American university president. Quite an accomplishment, right?

Except Gus never filled the position he had applied for, been offered, and accepted.

"Two months later," he writes in *Seeing Patients*, "before I had even taken office, I handed the chancellor my resignation. It was a particularly hard decision, but unavoidable, I thought. What had happened was that a few days earlier the chairman of the board of regents had abruptly informed me that the law school and school of social work would be removed administratively from the university at Baltimore and relocated outside of the city. I had been talking and negotiating about the presidency of seven schools; now the seven were suddenly reduced to five. Just as significantly, the two that were to be removed—law and social work—provided extensive services and programs for the city's minority community. It was, I thought, a truly awful decision."

Awful enough for Gus to turn away from a life-capping opportunity because the writing on the wall was too clear to ignore, although that wouldn't have stopped many from looking in the other direction. Gus always has put character first, and his character would never have allowed him to compromise his principles.

In his commencement address before the Stanford School of Medicine in June of 2017, he finished with the following axioms:

- Make it a goal to have some fun every day.

- Seize upon and celebrate the privilege, joy, and satisfaction of earning your livelihood by helping your fellow humans!

- The book on resilience by Southwick and Charney emphasizes the importance of helping others as an enhancement of one's own resilience. This brings to mind another quote from Dr. Martin Luther King, Jr.: "An individual has not started living until he can rise above the narrow confines of his individualistic concerns to the broader concerns of all."

- I will leave you now as I offer my very best wishes for your happiness and success! I share with you a poem that was frequently recited by Dr. Benjamin Mays, one of the distinguished presidents of Morehouse College and a mentor for Dr. King.

> *I have just one minute,*
> *Only sixty seconds in it.*
> *Forced upon me—Can't refuse it,*
> *Didn't seek it, didn't choose it,*
> *But it's up to me to use it.*
> *I must suffer if I lose it,*
> *Give an account if I abuse it.*
> *Just a tiny little minute,*
> *But all eternity is in it.*

"This may sound corny," he reflects, on the sum total of his multitude of experiences, of which football remains a prime component, "but what I'm most proud of is how close I've come to fulfilling my mother's teaching and the admonition to treat all people with respect. As I look back, what football does is provide an enhanced environment for people to gain mutual respect across racial lines. It nurtures cross-cultural relationships and friendships like nothing else I've ever experienced."

The teachings of his mother gained special meaning for Gus when she was there to watch him play at Brown Stadium as a senior.

"She had not seen any games because she still lived in Memphis," he said in that same January 2011 address at the Ivy League Football Dinner. "And my hometown was too far from Massachusetts and Rhode Island, where I played prep school and college football respectively. We simply did not have the travel money. But we were playing Colgate Thanksgiving Day that year at Brown Stadium, and she made the trip. It was the first and final game she ever saw me play, and Brown won. I wrote her this prayer before the game."

Oh God,
When the final gun is shot and my final football game is over.
May I please know that on every play I had done my very best.
This way may I leave football and life.

Amen.

CHAPTER 20

DANNY WUERFFEL— TWO STEPS AT A TIME

When Danny Wuerffel led the University of Florida onto the field against the Seminoles of Florida State, coached by the great Bobby Bowden, late in the 1996 college football season, the Gators were 10-0 and looking at a cherished undefeated season, along with an undisputed national championship. Sixty minutes later, the quarterback who a few weeks later would go on to win the Heisman Trophy would find himself knocked to the turf a staggering 32 times, some of the hits truly jaw rattling. The Gators went on to lose the game 24–21 to the Seminoles, who remained undefeated and on the fast track to the title.

"Life is tough," Danny says today in recalling that game, "but when you get knocked down, you just have to get back up."

The following week Florida hammered Alabama 45–30 for the Southeast Conference (SEC) title, earning them a rematch against FSU in the Sugar Bowl in a de facto national championship game that saw the Gators crush the Seminoles 52–20 in the Superdome.

"I don't know how many times I got knocked down that day," Danny recalls, "but it certainly wasn't thirty-two. Now I'm forty-three and looking at my life in all sorts of ways. I still get knocked down, but it's football that taught me getting back up to try again is the greatest thing in the world."

And Danny Wuerffel lives his life off the field the very same way he lived his life on it.

"He's had a wonderful career here, leading us to three conference championships," Danny's coach at Florida, Steve Spurrier, said to WUFT radio station in December of 1996, the week before the Gators won their fourth in a row against the Crimson Tide. "But he's probably an even better person than he is a football player. He's been a wonderful student-athlete and a great role model for the younger guys."

The pairing became fortuitous for both Danny and his coach, who'd won his own Heisman while quarterbacking the Gators way back in 1966. When Danny was named winner for the 1996 season, it marked the first time ever one Heisman Trophy winner had ever coached another. Even before he was named winner of the most cherished trophy in all of college sports, Danny had been awarded the Draddy Trophy, presented by the National Football Foundation and generally considered to be the academic Heisman, in recognition of his 3.7 grade point average. The Draddy would later be renamed the William V. Campbell Trophy and stands out to this day for honoring "the American college football [at the BCS level] player with the best combination of academics, community service, and on-field performance." Danny had also already been awarded the Walter Camp Award as the Collegiate Player of the Year, along with the comparably defined Johnny Unitas Golden Arm and Maxwell Awards.

No shortage of platitudes, in other words, for which Danny was the recipient.

Today, in the wake of Danny being one of the most decorated players in the history of college football, he finds himself on the other side of the awards, specifically the Wuerffel Trophy, described as "college football's premier award for community service. The All Sports Association presents the Wuerffel Trophy to the Football Bowl Subdivision player who best exhibits exemplary community service, along with qualifying academic and athletic achievement."

Since its inception in 2005, thirteen college players have received the award for representing the best the sport has to offer. And for Tom Brassell, executive director of the Wuerffel Trophy, the person for whom the award is named still exemplifies those qualities better than anyone.

"It was all about establishing a national football award that was more than just about football," Brassell recalls. "It was about recognizing the kind of qualities that Danny exemplifies in other football players, as much for what they do on the field as off it. So we said, 'Let's talk to Danny and see what he thinks.' He was living in New Orleans at the time and said the award sounded great, but he wasn't interested in having it named after him. There were already so many awards named after so many people, Danny said, and he just didn't feel worthy of joining that roster. We convinced him that the award was bigger than football, capable of recognizing people who've done great things and inspiring others to do great things. I think it was the latter that got him on board more than anything—not recognizing players for what they'd done, so much as encouraging others to follow in that path by drawing attention to the importance of giving back. To inspire young people to do great things while they're playing sports. So it's not just about the collegiate player who wins the Wuerffel Trophy, it's about all the nominees and the dozens of others who didn't quite make the short list; all the good each and every one of them is doing. That's what the award represents and what it recognizes."

Brassell talks about Paul Smith as a typical recipient of the Wuerffel and shining example for all football players, relating how Paul's coach at Tulsa, Todd Graham, often mentioned how Paul would go straight to the local children's hospital after practice instead of eating. In addition to Smith's considerable achievements on the playing field and in the classroom, he remains actively involved in the Fellowship of Christian Athletes, having served as the Tulsa University FCA president the last three years. He was a popular speaker and singer throughout the Tulsa area and participated in inner city ministry and in programs that educate young people so they can make positive choices about drugs and alcohol. He's a truly model citizen, on top of being a quarterback who set a Conference USA record with 4,327 yards and 39 touchdowns while passing for more than 300 yards in each of Tulsa's regular season games his senior season in 2006. Smith was named the Conference USA Co-Offensive Player of the Year and garnered first-team All-Conference honors at quarterback. And all this while being named a first-team Academic All-American and boasting a 3.84 GPA.

"The character of the modern-day football player is more exceptional than it's ever been," Brassell says. "The challenge is getting that out there. In general, networks don't cover that. They're more interested in covering the train wrecks. That's what sizzles, not football players going to visit kids in a cancer hospital or building wells in Haiti."

What's getting lost here, in the minds of those like Tom Brassell and Danny Wuerffel, is how many football players at the collegiate level are accomplishing even more off the field than on it.

"The Wuerffel Trophy is meant to highlight the quality individuals playing the game today," Danny adds. "And that's so important in an era where negative behavior and the negative aspects of the game garner the bulk of the attention. Beyond football, my hope is that the award represents what all of us would aspire to, how all of us would go out of our way to help a fellow human in need."

Take a look at just some of the accomplishments of the thirteen recipients of the Wuerffel Trophy. Emphasis on "some" since there are simply too many to list for each of the individual award winners.

- 2017—Courtney Love, University of Kentucky: Love, a native of Youngstown, Ohio, has a passion for mentoring children especially those living in a one-parent household or children who have parents who are incarcerated. Because of his passion, he currently volunteers at Amachi Central Kentucky, a mentoring program that seeks to pair caring, positive adults with children and youth in the Bluegrass state who have one or both parents in state or federal prison or are affected by incarceration in some way. He also has served in a Skype mentoring program with area high school students, and has taken part in many events with the UK Children's Hospital, Read Across America, and Special Olympics, along with many other service activities. In May of 2016, Love was chosen to participate in a service/educational trip to Ethiopia where he helped build houses as well as shoe-shining boxes for men to be able to work and provide for their families.

- 2016—Trevor Knight, Texas A&M: Currently playing in the NFL for the Arizona Cardinals, Trevor was part of a contingent that worked with orphanages and other charitable organizations in Haiti. He was a frequent visitor to area children's hospitals as well as an active speaker on the Fellowship of Christian Athletes circuit. He also helped his father battle throat cancer in 2012 after graduating early from high school, giving his dad a pair of boxing gloves before treatments began to inspire him to have a "fighter's mentality."

- 2015—Ty Darlington, Oklahoma: Ty received the 2015 University of Oklahoma Letzeiser Award, one of the highest student awards at OU based on leadership, scholarship, and service. He served as president of the Big 12 Student-Athlete Advisory Committee and led Oklahoma's Fellowship of Christian Athletes chapter as its president his junior and senior years. Darlington twice visited Haiti as part of the Mission of Hope program, repairing damage caused by a massive earthquake.

- 2014—Deterrian Shackelford, Ole Miss: A rare sixth-year senior, Deterrian boasts two degrees, a bachelor's degree in history and a master's degree in higher education. The Decatur, Alabama native helped lead two mission trips to Haiti and Panama while also mentoring local Oxford, Mississippi youth. He was actively involved in the Oxford community, helping lead efforts to fight hunger and raise funds for cancer research.

- 2013—Gabe Ikard, Oklahoma: "Coach (Bob) Stoops consistently preaches to us about being active in the community and being dedicated in the classroom," Gabe said upon receiving the award. "And to receive this honor is unbelievable. I've been fortunate to have been given an amazing platform as a student-athlete, and I'm proud to be standing here today." A 2013 Big Man on Campus at Oklahoma, Ikard serves on the OU leadership team for the Fellowship of Christian Athletes and was lauded by the school for his leadership in responding to the tragic Oklahoma City tornado disaster in 2012.

- 2012—Matt Barkley, USC: A fixture in Los Angeles, Barkley worked with children from seventeen local elementary schools around USC in a variety of ways, and he has volunteered with S.C.O.R.E. (Service, Community, Outreach, Responsibility, and Education, based out of USC), helping to encourage inner city kids to pursue their education. Barkley has also made an impact abroad. In May of 2012, Matt helped spearhead a trip with his family and fifteen teammates for a week working in Sous Savanne, Haiti, building houses for underprivileged families.

- 2011—Barrett Jones, Alabama: This All-SEC lineman was extremely active in the community as well. Jones made two mission trips to Haiti to help people struggling with daily life and helped build a school and orphanage. He also actively participated in tornado cleanup in Tuscaloosa and worked with countless other community organizations in his time at Alabama. "I think being a student-athlete is a lot about time management," Jones said. "You really have to learn how to balance your time and prioritize the things you think are important."

- 2010—Sam Acho, Texas: Currently playing in the NFL for the Chicago Bears, Sam went to Nigeria during his college years to participate in Living Hope Christian Ministries' medical mission Operation Hope, something he continues doing today. "I travel with over thirty medical professionals overseas and we spend two weeks in remote villages in Nigeria to serve people."

- 2009—Tim Hiller, Western Michigan: Along with a slew of other community-service activities, he joined 23 other college students on a faith-based mission to Trinidad where, among other things, he visited youth prisons and drug clinics, witnessing firsthand the devastating impact of poverty on a nation. Hiller's Western Michigan coach Bill Cubit said of him, "This kid is really something special."

- 2008—Tim Tebow, Florida: His celebrity status makes it easy to forget that he spent almost every summer of his life, through college, preaching and providing support, not only in the Philippines where he was born, but across the world as well. He understood that football provided him the opportunity to make positive changes in peoples' lives, and he still takes advantage of that platform every chance he gets, to the point where Danny himself says, "Maybe one day my son will win the Tebow Trophy."

- 2007—Paul Smith, Tulsa: In addition to serving as the president of the Fellowship of Christian Athletes for three years, he made himself available for dozens of speaking engagements at area churches. Chris Kaiser, the Northeast Oklahoma FCA Area Director, calls Paul among the top three volunteers he'd ever worked with and possibly the very best because of the lives he touched.

- 2006—Joel Penton, Ohio State: Joel managed to work more than a hundred local speaking engagements into his jam-packed collegiate career. He also planned and launched an outreach called the "Main Event." And he gained commitments from 300 students to volunteer for the event along with members of the OSU Marching Band and Cheerleading Squad. The event drew over 13,000 people.

- 2005—Rudy Niswanger, LSU: The award's first ever recipient distinguished himself for, among other things, volunteering his time at area shelters following Hurricane Katrina to provide emotional support for survivors. He also organized a clothing and bedding drive to support evacuees and was known for both visiting local children's hospitals and spending time with underprivileged children.

The Wuerffel Trophy, in other words, is about the spirit of using football as a platform to do greater things, and nobody encompasses that spirit more than Danny himself. Take his association with the New Orleans–based Desire Street Ministries, for example, a nonprofit organization that seeks to help impoverished neighborhoods through spiritual and community development. Danny first became involved with the organization while playing for the Saints in the late 1990s. After his NFL career ended, he returned to New Orleans to become the organization's executive director as it struggled to recover from the devastation of Hurricane Katrina. Under Wuerffel, Desire Street Ministries not only recovered, it moved its headquarters to Atlanta and expanded its programs to other inner cities in the South.

"Being in New Orleans and having been exposed to the challenges facing the city's under-resourced neighborhoods, it wasn't hard to get motivated to do something about it," he recalls today. "Desire Street is all about the passionate pursuit of positively impacting lives in those kinds of impoverished neighborhoods. This is the platform I've chosen to use as best I can to impact those who live in places that don't offer the kinds of opportunities available to me or my kids.

"Hardwired into each of our hearts is to be thankful for what we have and to want to help others who don't have as much. It comes down to living for a cause bigger than yourself, getting the opportunity to experience something bigger than yourself while helping others to have a shot at their slice of the American Dream instead of just pursuing your own. Part of the beauty of playing football is that you realize you're all in it together. But life is the same way. It's not something you have to do, or feel compelled to do, it's just something you do. I was able to discover Desire Street through football and leverage those platforms on behalf of others."

Also, as in football, Danny knows he can't do it alone.

"Our model at its base is to find leaders in the neighborhood from nonprofits or churches and help them lead their own transformations of where they live. I was so blessed in my football career by having coaches who helped me develop my potential, and in a sense we use a little bit of the coaching models to work with urban ministries to effect change. We help them develop their neighborhoods' full potential."

Given all that he's accomplished off the field, it's easy to overlook Danny's achievements on it. He led the nation in touchdown passes in 1995 and 1996 and set numerous school and conference records. Besides his many awards, Danny was a two-time SEC Player of the Year and first-team All-American in 1995 and 1996, as well as a first-team Academic All-American. He is one of only two Heisman Trophy winners to also win the Draddy. He finished his Gator career by completing 708 of 1,170 passes for 10,875 yards and 114 touchdowns, the best in SEC history and second most in major college history. His career pass efficiency rating of 163.56 was the best in major college history, and his percentage of passes that went for a touchdown (9.74) ranked first in collegiate history. In 1995, his efficiency rating of 178.4 set a single-season collegiate record. During his Heisman-winning season of 1996, he completed 207 of 360 passes for 3,625 yards (an SEC record at the time) for 39 touchdowns (leading the nation), and his efficiency rating of 170.6 made him the first quarterback to ever post a rating of 170 or better in back-to-back years.

About which Danny says simply, "I've been really blessed."

He says the same thing about his recovery from Guillain-Barré syndrome, an autoimmune disorder that left him bedridden and nearly paralyzed for a prolonged period that began in 2011.

"I went from being active and busy to not being able to move and just sitting, or lying, still. One conscious decision I made was not to watch movies or gorge myself with TV, but to reflect, to write, and read. It was incredibly difficult, emotionally and spiritually. If I could sum it up, six years later I feel like I've changed a ton. I'm probably just starting to become the person I always thought I was."

He talks about mining his own motives and attitudes from that stillness, talks about how much the experience allowed him to grow in what Danny calls "emotional intelligence."

This coming from a man who got knocked down 32 times in that 1996 loss to Florida State. But he got up from each and every one of them, just as he did from Guillain-Barré, a metaphor he believes extends deeper so far as the game of football is concerned.

"The uniqueness of football often lies in the ability to work with an incredibly diverse group toward a common goal. Sure, America has made many strides over the years in terms of race relations, but unfortunately it's still all too rare to see the kind of diversity I experienced that helps define football. It very much helped shape who I am today and to inspire what I do. Yes, life is tough, and, as I always say, when you get knocked down, you just have to get back up. At the age of forty-three, I still get knocked down, but the biggest thing I learned from football is that getting back up to try again is the greatest of all accomplishments."

* * *

Among those on the selection committee for the Wuerffel Trophy is none other than legendary two-time national title winning coach Bobby Bowden.

"In my opinion," he says, "college football's the best it's ever been on the field. It's in great shape; I don't think it's ever been better as far as popularity goes with defenses having so much trouble stopping the wide-open, fast-paced offenses of today. I don't see a decline at all. As far as player behavior goes, well, I can remember a time that when one of my players got in trouble or had some issue, I'd get a call from the police or some such asking, 'Coach, what do you wanna do with this guy?' Later on, I'd find out a kid had got himself into trouble when I read about it in the paper.

"As far as concussions go, I've got a theory on that. Back when I played in high school and college, I wore a leather helmet without a face mask. So back in those days we couldn't stick our heads in there on first contact. Never hit with the head; we hit with the shoulders. I remember a coach saying something like you paid two hundred bucks for those shoulder pads, so you better darn well use them. And I think if we went back to tackling with the shoulders, we'd solve a great many of the problems relating to concussions. Eliminate leading with the head and you eliminate a whole host of problems.

"Back when I was an assistant at Dartmouth in the mid-1960s and there was no spring practice in the Ivy League, we'd use that time to visit other campuses to watch them prepare for the upcoming season. Some of our coaches spent a week down in the south. They came back north with several ideas they'd glimpsed, most notably a tackling technique many schools were using in which the emphasis was placed on leading with the head. The idea stressed balance by putting the head to the chest of the ball carrier, a technique that would soon be copied throughout the South and the nation, setting the stage for many of the issues the game is encountering today."

Rocky Seto, a former assistant coach at USC and for the Seattle Seahawks, who's studied how helmetless rugby players tackle, concurs.

"As soon as the face masks improved, coaching techniques and principles changed," he told *Sports Illustrated* in August of 2017. "Get your head across. See what you hit. Eyes to the ball. In essence, putting your head in the line of fire. That messed up the fundamentals of the game. The game was meant to be played with our shoulders and having good leverage. We got away from that for about thirty years. The game is correcting itself."

Bobby Bowden, meanwhile, speaks with passion about the game he loves now as much as ever, about how the veer offense he became famous for using over decades became the forerunner of the spread, the widely popular offense of today. How the spread's very origins may well go back to Florida State when Bobby had a running quarterback named Charlie Ward behind center.

"We started Charlie under center running the option. But we put him in the shotgun for the two-minute offense. Well, it turned out he threw the ball a heck of a lot better from the shotgun because he could see the field better. So we started putting him in the shotgun the whole game, running our whole offense from there, so he could beat the coverages he couldn't beat from under the center. And that's a big part of the reason why we won a national championship with Charlie in 1993 and why Charlie ended up winning the Heisman Trophy."

Bobby left coaching after the Seminoles compiled a 7-6 record during a 2009 season highlighted by a come-from-behind Gator Bowl win against Miami. He was eighty at the time and believes he could have continued coaching then and maybe even now.

"I could still do it mentally," he reflects, "but not physically, I think. See, the head coach doesn't just coach, he organizes. The thing I'm most proud of when I look back is that I coached fifty-seven years in college football. And I had thirty-three straight winning seasons, including those two titles at Florida State. I might not have been ready to go after 2009, but I couldn't argue with the decision. 7-6 isn't terrible, but something I learned was that once you win a national championship, people expect you to do it every year. And I hadn't won a title since 1999.

"I never planned on going into coaching," he continues after a pause. "I wasn't sure what I was going to do after graduation. But I'd majored in physical education and once the season ended, the athletic director came to me and said, 'Bobby, if you get your master's degree, we'll hire you as an assistant coach here at Howard College.' I took him up on his offer and coached for fifty-seven straight years."

* * *

"There are some challenges to the game," Danny Wuerffel concedes, "both in the negative behavior of some of the players as well as growing awareness of risks involved in a collision sport. Those are risks to the game we need to counter by highlighting the positive things so many of the players are doing, which is far more reflective of the character of the game today. I think everyone, including the most ardent football supporters out there, are open to pursuing ways to make the game safer, including continued research on how best to reduce the risks. Like a lot of things in life, I don't think this is an either/or situation. I think we can have it both ways."

Danny's attitude is relentlessly positive, as he's parlayed all the success he achieved on the field to all he has subsequently achieved off it, especially in coming up with the "Two Steps at a Time" approach to community service at Desire Street.

"Two Steps," he explains, "just emphasizes the fact that you're not walking alone. If someone's walking with you, you're taking a step and they're taking a step. Most of the people who've impacted your life have been through the good and also through the bad. And the Two Steps approach highlights the significance of authentic relationships in the journey of life."

In that respect, what Danny's coach Steve Spurrier said about him in 1996 rings equally true today:

"He's really what football stands for."

CHAPTER 21

BUFF DONELLI– "A PLAYER'S COACH"

Aldo "Buff" Donelli was the only man ever to coach a college (Duquesne) and professional team (the Pittsburgh Steelers) at the same time. It happened during the 1941 season, and although the results on both fronts weren't necessarily stellar, they were certainly historic.

"It was exhausting, but when you're young [34], you can do a lot of things," Donelli told the *Pittsburgh Press* in 1989. "I'd coach the Steelers in the morning at St. Vincent. I would finish with them about twelve or twelve-thirty, jump in the car, have a bite to eat and drive to Duquesne. I would get my athletic duties out of the way from one to three and then go to football practice until around six. Before I signed to coach them, I had an agreement with the Steelers that if there was a great improvement I would go with them. But if Duquesne was in a position to do something, I would go with them instead. Art Rooney, the Steelers' owner, understood the whole thing."

Well, on the college side of things Buff guided the Dukes to undefeated seasons in 1939 (8-0-1) and 1941 (8-0-0), the latter in which they surrendered only 21 points, a mark matched only once in college ball since then. The Dukes finished in the Associated Press top ten both years. Buff's professional experience was considerably different, his tenure abbreviated when the Steelers lost their first five games of 1941 and the so-called "experiment" was deemed a failure, freeing him to dedicate himself to his collegiate duties right up until a stint overseas in World War II. Upon getting home, he returned to the NFL to coach the Cleveland Rams, but he built his name and reputation back in the college ranks at Boston University beginning in 1947 and then, later, at Columbia University.

At BU, the majority of the players he inherited or recruited came with a military service background. They were veterans like himself, and his own experiences provided a keen understanding of the young men who assembled for that first practice on Braves Field in the fall of 1947, where Babe Ruth had played his last game as a baseball player with the Boston Braves. The group included the great Harry Agganis ("the Golden Greek") out of Lynn Classical High School, a left-handed quarterback who was one of the most sought-after high school prospects in the country and went on to become an All-American before transferring his skills to the Boston Red Sox, where he played alongside Ted Williams. They were older and well disciplined, used to following orders and giving no quarter. Young men already battle-tested in a literal sense who found opportunity in the GI Bill and considerable solace on the gridiron. They had already fought to preserve the very nature of the American Dream and were now prepared to chase their own version of it in unbridled fashion. That reflects not only on Buff Donelli personally, but also the indelible mark these returning veterans had on the game of football. The impact they left on the character of the game remains to this day. And Buff, and other coaches like him, was the right man for the job at the right time.

None other than former Secretary of State Condoleezza Rice beautifully summed up the impact of football on American culture in remarks on December 8, 2015 upon receiving the National Football Foundation highest and most prestigious award, the Gold Medal:

My father was a football coach, and I was actually supposed to be his All-American linebacker. And he was a little disappointed when he learned he was going to indeed have a girl, but decided he would teach this little girl everything about this sport instead. And so, football matters to me because it is first and foremost the greatest set of memories with my dad. My dad went to the Lord in 2001, but in those years, we loved football. It was about going down to the drugstore the minute that Street & Smith Pro Football Report and College Football Report appeared on the newsstand. It was my father, an offensive lineman, who said,

"Always watch the offensive line, Condoleezza. That is really where it happens. What kind of block was that, Condoleezza?"

"That was a trap block, Daddy."

"What are they getting set up now?"

"That's a screen, Daddy."

That's how we spent our Saturdays and our Sundays. It was recognizing that this was a very special bond between a very special man and his little girl and for that I will be always grateful to this game.

Football also matters to me because it is a reflection of how far our country has come. As a little girl growing up in segregated Birmingham, Alabama, where black players did not and could not play at the University of Alabama or at Auburn. Where they went far afield to play because our country was not yet ready to accept that "We the People" had to be an inclusive concept, and look at how far we have come.

As I watched those teams and others, as I watch young men of all backgrounds and all religions of all races and all ethnicities pulling together, working together as teammates, loving each

other, respecting each other, it is a reflection of America's jour-
ney. And it is a wonderful story of the incredible ability of the
human spirit to overcome. And for people to overcome their
prejudices and their history in favor of a common good. We are
a better country for the role that football has played in bringing
us together....

That football is played on the field, but it is also preparation for
life, for meeting that aspiration, for attaining that goal that is
so uniquely America.

It was legendary writer Studs Terkel, though, who perhaps best explained the reason so many returning veterans of World War II were drawn to the gridiron upon their return from the war.

"For the typical American soldier, despite the perverted film sermons, it wasn't 'getting another Jap' or 'getting another Nazi' that impelled him up front," he wrote in 2007's *The Great War: An Oral History of World War II*, before relating the words of one of that book's subjects. "'The reason you storm the beaches is not patriotism or bravery,' reflects the tall rifleman. 'It's that sense of not wanting to fail your buddies. There's sort of a special sense of a kinship.'"

Football provided a comparable sense of kinship, filling an inevitable void and at least partially explaining the character of the players who ushered in the modern era of the game. Playing became the best therapy, the best treatment imaginable, to help those veterans turned Boston University Terriers deal with the unthinkable that they had experienced. Men like Doctor Titus Plomaritis, Frank Guiliano, and Billy Tighe who himself would go on to coach high school football for 36 years, before retiring in 1986.

"We never had a discipline problem," Tighe noted of his experience playing for Donelli to Boston.com. "We all wanted to get an education and catch up with our lives. Buff was a player's coach. He gave us the opportunity to develop and be ourselves. The program was successful, and many of us, remarkably, decided to go on into education as teachers and coaches."

Donelli's influence is unmatched when you consider that nearly thirty of his players over the course of his storied career took on coaching positions throughout New England, forming "a union" that prided itself on being BU graduates and "Buff's Boys." Some worked in high school programs and others in college, but all brought to the sideline the same values that Buff had instilled in them. Here are some examples of those inspired enough by Donelli to follow him to the sidelines, all in Massachusetts unless otherwise noted:

- Billy Tighe—Wakefield, Malden, and Lexington High Schools

- Silvio Cella—Revere High School

- Bob Whelan—Lynn English High School

- John Toner—New Britain (Connecticut) High School, Columbia University, University of Connecticut,

- Wally Anderson—Hingham High School

- Al Stewart—Foxboro High School

- "Evie" Doerr—Cohasset High School

- Arthur Boyle—Malden High School

- Bill Pavkowski—Thornton Academy (Maine)

- Jim Maloney—Needham High School

- George Winkler—Newton South High School

- Chris Crasafi—St. Mary's Lynn and Revere High Schools

- Jim Wheeler—Weymouth High School

- John Simpson—Holy Cross College, Colby College

- Bob Hatch—Bates College

- George Ramacorto—Braintree High School

- Pete Sarno—Revere and Christopher Columbus High Schools

- Dick Fecteau—Boston University Football Hall of Fame

Buff's boys, indeed. Imagine for a moment how many lives these and other coaches touched and affected, because Buff had affected them. Would any of them not have gone into coaching otherwise? We'll never know for sure. What we do know for sure is that their version of the American Dream, in the wake of their service in World War II, allowed countless other young men and boys to chase theirs.

"Buff was a straight shooter," recalls Emo DiNitto, who's spent a lifetime in the game, most recently as head of the Rhode Island chapter of the National Football Foundation. "He told you how he felt. He was a personable guy who came from a tough background growing up in western Pennsylvania to immigrant parents. Growing up in a hard-nosed, working-class area meant he had to be tough, and the kind of personalities he coached at Boston University, these young veterans coming back from Europe, could appreciate that. These were tough guys.

"But, like Vince Lombardi, family was everything to Buff. It constituted and defined his very heritage, and he was able to translate that family concept to football, that sense of camaraderie the cast of players he coached knew from the war. I think that's why so many of his players went on to become coaches. Buff had made the kind of impression on them they wanted to make on others."

Emo, who'd played quarterback in high school, came to BU as a walk-on because there was no money left for scholarships.

"So I had some extra incentive. I was a little more hungry than the scholarship players at the time, and needing to prove myself enough to get that scholarship was a great motivation for me."

When the freshman quarterback ahead of him went down with an ankle injury, Emo stepped in, earned his scholarship, and didn't step out for the next three years, starting at quarterback for the Terriers the whole time after Buff had left to take over the Columbia program.

"Everything I have is possible because of football," DiNitto, recipient of the National Football Foundation's Chapter Leadership Award, says of his lifetime association with the game. "Getting involved with the NFF is a way to give back to the kids for a lot of the stuff that I got as a player."

And what does he think of today's high school football player?

"So much about the game has changed, like the way kids train, but not the character of the kids playing it. Football still teaches the same lessons it always has and is still the same microcosm for life it's always been. It still encompasses everything, every aspect of life."

A fact encapsulated in brilliant fashion by none other than Don DeLillo, arguably America's greatest living novelist, in his 1972 novel *End Zone*. "Football players are simple folk," wrote the two-time finalist for the Pulitzer Prize for Fiction and winner of both the National Book Award and PEN/Faulkner Award. "Whatever complexities, whatever dark politics of the human mind, the heart—these are noted only within the chalked borders of the playing field. At times strange visions ripple across that turf; madness leaks out. But wherever else he goes, the football player travels the straightest of lines. His thoughts are wholesomely commonplace, his actions uncomplicated by history, enigma, holocaust or dream. A passion for simplicity, for the true old things, as of boys on bicycles delivering newspapers, filled our days and nights that fierce summer. We practiced in the undulating heat with nothing to sustain us but the conviction that things here were simple. Hit and get hit; key the pulling guard, run over people; suck some ice and re-assume the three-point stance. We were a lean and dedicated squad run by a hungry coach and his seven oppressive assistants. Some of us were more simple than others; a few might be called outcasts or exiles; three or four, as on every football team, were crazy. But we were all—even myself—we were all dedicated."

And Buff Donelli's contribution to the game personified that kind of dedication, a fact that he made his first athletic bones not on the football field, but the soccer pitch.

"Born on July 22, 1907," the *Guardian* reported in April of 2015, "Donelli started playing soccer in the western Pennsylvania coal-mining area when he was fifteen and forged a reputation as a lethal goal-scorer. As a nineteen-year-old he tallied four times in Cuddy's 10–3 triumph over Westinghouse in the second round of the West Penn Cup on October 31, 1926. Playing for Morgan Strasser, Donelli led the Pittsburgh area in scoring from 1922 through 1928. While wearing the colors of the Heidelberg Soccer Club in 1929, he struck five times in a 9–0 win over the First Germans of Newark in the National Amateur Cup final in Irvington, New Jersey. Some reports had Donelli scoring his goals within an eight-minute span, though that could not be confirmed. Regardless, news of Donelli's exploits reached Preston North End of the English Football League, which reportedly had promised him a contract."

Buff, incredibly, also starred for Duquesne in football, as that same article in the *Guardian* notes.

"Donelli had a full plate with another brand of football, turning heads as captain and as a five foot, seven inches tall, 170 pound halfback and ambidextrous kicker for Duquesne University. His duties included punting—his kicking played a vital role in a 12–6 upset of Washington & Jefferson College in 1928. He also was known to drop-kick a field goal (while adding a point-after touchdown as well) in a 10–0 victory over St. Thomas College on Oct. 6, 1928."

After leading the Dukes to 8-1 and 9-0-1 records in his junior and senior years respectively, Donelli became an assistant coach, beginning the part of his life for which he is best remembered. He remained involved with soccer as well, never losing his love for either sport, although it was through football he touched thousands of lives via both his own efforts and those who played for him at BU.

Buff finished his coaching career at Columbia University, where the highlight was winning what is still the school's only Ivy League title in 1961.

"Pennsylvania born and tough as nails," Al Butts, a sophomore on that team, says of Donelli. "Kind of from the Vince Lombardi school."

Also part of that championship team was a young man Buff recruited out of Homestead, Pennsylvania named Bill Campbell, who went on to captain the '61 team and was called by Donelli "the best captain I ever had."

Campbell found Buff to be just what Columbia needed to build a new mindset, a winning mindset. Buff knew "to break the [losing] mold you were going to have to allow yourself not to go over to the whiny side of making excuses of why we can't win. He wouldn't listen to them."

To that point, the Lions' Ivy championship team was comprised entirely of players Buff himself had recruited, a squad that, indeed, fit his mold.

"One of our problems the last couple of years was that the seniors wouldn't set a good example," Bill Campbell told *Sports Illustrated* in November of 1961. "Seniors must lead a team or else there's no discipline."

The same article continues, "Last June, Campbell and the other seniors held a meeting of the team at which the law was laid down. Players were told to get into top condition during the summer. When practice began in the fall, training habits were strictly enforced. 'We didn't even permit pastries or soft bread. Just melba toast,' said Campbell."

After graduation, Bill Campbell became one of Buff's assistants, then moved on to a successful stint as an assistant with Boston College before taking over Columbia's head coaching job in 1974.

"I felt that we had won when I was there and there was no reason we couldn't win again," Bill told *Columbia College Today* in May of 2005.

"When he came back, we were all so happy," says John Cirigliano '64 and a close friend of Campbell's. "He was going to take the program beyond where it had been."

Bill threw all his efforts into building a program just as Buff Donelli had: from the ground up, recruiting from the same kind of haunts Donelli once did.

"There was a high degree of intensity and enthusiasm and energy. He got everyone focused," says Marty Cicco from the class of 1978, who was one of Bill's first recruits. "He worked harder than anybody. He was always motivating."

Bill was one of Buff's boys and then some, because today the National Football Foundation awards the William V. Campbell Trophy to college football's premier scholar-athlete. After leaving Columbia, and coaching, following the 1979 season, Campbell went on to enjoy a spectacular career in business, where he earned the nickname the "Coach of Silicon Valley."

Both fitting, and ironic, given the credit he gives his own coach.

"I came to Columbia to play for Buff Donelli," Bill said upon receiving the Gold Medal Award from the National Football Foundation in 2004. "And so much of what I am today, I owe to him."

CHAPTER 22

BILL CAMPBELL—
THE COACH OF SILICON VALLEY

Bill Campbell may have encountered far more success as the coach of Silicon Valley than coach of the Columbia Lions. But that hardly defines the contribution he made to football before his death in 2016 at the age of 75. Seven years before his passing, the National Football Foundation recognized that contribution by renaming the Draddy Trophy the William V. Campbell Trophy, now widely considered to be the academic Heisman.

"Rather than gazing into a mirror, one must look instead at what's beyond the window," Campbell said in the ceremony announcing the award's debut. "When an athlete unleashes the academic within, lives are affected, communities impacted, worlds forever changed. The William V. Campbell

Trophy honors scholar athletes who excel at athletics, academics, and community leadership."

An especially fitting testament to the man for whom it was named. The Lions struggled on the field in the six years their former captain coached them. But as far as Campbell's association with the school, the best was yet to come.

"He was a member of the University's Board of Trustees from 2003 until 2014 and chair from 2005 until 2014," *Columbia College Today* wrote in his obituary in their Summer 2016 issue. "In 2013, the Campbell Sports Center, a state-of-the-art 50,000 square foot facility at the Baker Athletics Complex, made possible by a 10 million dollar donation from Campbell, was dedicated. In fall 2014, Athletics retired Campbell's number, 67, and at the 2015 Varsity C Celebration introduced a new award, the William V. Campbell Performer of the Year, to be presented annually to the top male and female student-athletes of the academic year.

"Campbell also endowed the Roberta and William Campbell Professorship in Contemporary Civilization and the Campbell Family Professorship in Anthropology. He gave one million dollars to The Austin E. Quigley Endowment for Student Success and he recently had committed $10 million dollars to the Core to Commencement campaign. Campbell was presented the Varsity C Alumni Athletics Award in 1988, a John Jay Award for distinguished professional achievement in 1991, and the 2000 Alexander Hamilton Medal. In 2011 he received the Community Impact Award and in 2015 was awarded an Alumni Medal as well as an honorary doctor of laws degree at Commencement."

Contrast that with this recollection from Bill's Columbia classmate John Cirigliano as told to Columbia College Today in 2005, when John realized the school's new football coach had bald tires on his car.

"He was making 35,000 dollars a year. I went to the athletics department and said, 'You need to get him a set of new tires. He's going to drive off the road.'"

"Both of us come from backgrounds without any money," his first wife Roberta recalled in that same *Columbia College Today* article. "Bill comes from a Western Pennsylvania steel town, and I come from Irvington, NJ. Although his father was educated, neither of my parents went to college. So to go to a school like Columbia, well, we didn't even know people like that existed—the diversity, from all over the world, and certainly from all over the United States. The whole experience was profound for us. The associations we made at Columbia changed our lives and gave us the opportunities that we've enjoyed. All of the big opportunities in Bill's life were the result of knowing someone at Columbia or the education that he received there."

A school he decided to attend, and an education he received, thanks to football. Bill never did drive off the road; in point of fact, his life's work, metaphorically, was to keep so many of those with whom he came into contact on it.

"We are devastated by the loss of Bill Campbell," said Columbia dean James J. Valentini in the wake of Campbell's death in 2016. "Bill was a remarkable entrepreneur, a dedicated and generous Columbia College alumnus, and a committed friend, adviser, and mentor to me. He enriched the lives of many at Columbia and throughout the world, and he will be missed by all who knew him."

And that long list is hardly limited to Columbia. Being an early pioneer at Apple, and then serving as advisor for the likes of Amazon, Google, Facebook, and Twitter, led to him being proclaimed "the coach of Silicon Valley," in a clear allusion to Campbell's past life roaming the football sidelines. A man, in short, as generous with his time as he was with his money.

"Whenever you watch a world-class athlete perform, you can be sure that there is a great coach behind his or her success," Eric Schmidt and Jonathan Rosenberg wrote in *How Google Works*. "It's not that the coach is better at playing the sport than the player, in fact that is almost never the case. But the coaches have a different skill: they can observe players in action and tell them how to be better. So why is it that in the business world coaches are so unusual? As a business leader, you need a coach. The first ingredient of a successful coaching relationship is a student who is willing to listen and learn. Just like there are hard-to-coach athletes, there are hard-to-coach executives. But once they get past that initial reticence, they find there are always things to learn. Business coaches, like all coaches, are at heart teachers, and Bill Campbell, the best coach around, tells us he believes that management is a skill that is completely learnable."

Simply stated, no one ever has better applied the principles he learned playing and coaching football to everyday life. Though Bill himself never directly intoned that equivalency, the effusiveness with which he expresses his feelings for his coaches and reverence for the game itself certainly implies that very thing. And more than anything, that suggests an indelible link between the philosophy of football in particular, athletics in general, and life as a whole.

"Today, in sports, what you are is what you make yourself into," James Surowiecki wrote in an article entitled "Better All the Time" for the *New Yorker* in November of 2014. "Innate athletic ability matters, but it's taken to be the base from which you have to ascend. Training efforts that forty years ago would have seemed unimaginably sophisticated and obsessive are now what it takes to stay in the game. Athletes don't merely work harder than they once did. As Mark McClusky documents in his fascinating new book, *Faster, Higher, Stronger* (Hudson Street), they also work smarter, using science and technology to enhance the way they train and perform."

Surowiecki's superb article goes on to draw the link between the importance of enhancing performance on the playing field and within the ivory towers of business. Not only did Bill Campbell's ethos help define this movement, he pretty much became the spokesman for it.

"Bill Campbell became one of our country's most influential business leaders, playing critical roles in the success of Apple, Google, Intuit, and countless other high-tech companies," the National Football Foundation notes on its Website. "The captain of the 1961 Columbia Ivy League championship team, he found his true calling after an unlikely career change at age thirty-nine from football coach to advertising executive. His ability to recruit, develop, and manage talented executives—all lessons learned on the gridiron—proved to be a critical component of his ability to inspire his business teams to the highest levels of success. Later in life, Campbell was driven by a heartfelt desire to give back, and he quietly gave away tens of millions of dollars to multiple charities while also finding an hour and half each autumn weekday to coach an eighth-grade boys and girls flag-football team near his home in Palo Alto, California."

Pat Gallagher, executive vice president of the Super Bowl 50 Host Committee and former president of the San Francisco Giants, puts it another way. "You talk about the perfect guy and the perfect intersection when Silicon Valley needed someone like that. He was an instinctive sales and marketing guy, but he was also instinctive about what made people tick and what would motivate them."

Adds John Hennessy, director of Knight-Hennessy Scholars and former president of Stanford University, "How do you take somebody who's really exceptional and help them be better? That was a skill I think Bill had probably better than anyone I've ever seen."

Then there's this from John Doerr, chair of Kleiner Perkins Caulfield & Byers: "He envisioned success. He had a very clear picture of what it meant to win. And then he had an unusual ability to translate that into a personal development plan. So he didn't just run the same play over and over and over again. He assessed the individual, he assessed the business situation, and very importantly he assessed the team. Not only did he coach the CEO, he coached the whole team around the CEO. That was part of his magic."

Eric Schmidt, former executive chairman of Google, reflects that "somehow, [Bill] managed to make everyone his best friend. Somehow he managed to inspire each and every one of us by making us exceed everything we possibly could have thought."

"Together as a group, you will enjoy life more and you will accomplish far more," Lee Bollinger, president of Columbia University, says in summing up William Campbell's philosophy of life. "That was Bill's essential quality. The group for good purposes rather than the individual."

"This is a wonderful award for me," Campbell said of the trophy that bears his name, "because it recognizes college football. More importantly, it recognizes that there should be academic stature as a crucial component of college football's success. We at the National Football Foundation really believe in that linkage. And the purpose, the goal, the mission of that organization is to try to blend academic excellence with on-the-field achievement. This award serves to drive the recognition of this obligation we all have."

For Bill Campbell, the indelible link between life and football, matching talent on the field with talent off the field, came to define his philosophy of life.

"I can't even imagine a better experience playing at Columbia under coaches like Buff Donelli and John Toner, winning Columbia's only Ivy League title in football in 1961," Bill said upon receiving the NFF's highest award, the Gold Medal, on December 7, 2004. "We played together and we learned together. We learned the selflessness of our game allows for our young men to understand that the team approach applies to everything we do in our lives. But my wife reminds me frequently that it's more than that. The selflessness is even harder when giving your body is part of it. I am ultimately a businessman, and my sense of accomplishment rests on being a good teammate. I believe in selflessness and ensuring that the group, the unit, the business, the team succeeds. I have learned that from this team, and I so desperately want others to have the opportunity to learn that as well."

Everything you need to know about Bill Campbell is summed up by the seminal article on him by Charles Butler in that May 2005 *Columbia College Today* article:

> *Chiodo's Tavern is in gritty Homestead, Pa., a nine-mile drive from downtown Pittsburgh and a zillion miles from snooty. It's on West 8th Street, not far from where U.S. Steel used to employ a lot of folks when the town had 20,000 or so people. After work, guys from the mill would come to Chiodo's for a beer and rage on about the Steelers or the Pirates or their crummy bosses at the mill—and laugh a lot. Even after U.S. Steel shut down in 1987, accelerating an exodus that now leaves the town with about 4,000 residents, the regulars still come into Chiodo's.*
>
> *"It's a working man's bar," says owner Joe Chiodo. "I have a lot of things hanging from the walls. Footballs, baseballs, trophies, and apparel that young ladies wear." Chiodo has been collecting this stuff since he opened the place in 1947. He tells a visitor about a picture on a wall, a picture of the guy this story is about. The guy grew up in Homestead, son of a mill worker, watched the Homestead Grays go up against other Negro League teams with his dad, played guard and linebacker at Homestead High, then went off to college in New York City. He played football there with some success and coached football there with less success, then scrapped the coaching and went into business—and made a big deal of himself.*
>
> *But even though he never moved back to Homestead, the guy in the photo didn't forget Homestead, either. "My place has been here 58 years, and I'm always proud to say, 'This is Billy Camp-*

bell,'" Chiodo says as a way of introducing the photo and the guy in it, "the young man from our hometown who gave so much to our hometown."

"Each of us who has played this game carries the responsibility to give something back," Bill Campbell continued in his December 2004 speech. "This is the simplest thing—to give back. Yes, we are here tonight to honor our stars, but we are also here to honor the game and, ultimately, the unsung. Each of us has labored in the sweaty weight rooms, hot practice fields as teammates, to make our teams better. The unsung heroes are those teammates, those people that play on our teams who make us all better, who took our team's teaching and are now applying it in their daily lives. It should be what we all do."

Think of a world full of people like Bill Campbell, who toiled on playing fields that left them crusted with dirt, mud, and chalk, before leaving the gridiron to make the world a better place too.

CHAPTER 23

STEVE HATCHELL AND THE NATIONAL FOOTBALL FOUNDATION—CARRYING THE TORCH

"Look at the National Football Foundation," says the organization's president, Steve Hatchell, "and you'll see people who love the game and are devoted to pouring in the concrete to shore up the basic foundation as it's constructed. We're here to highlight the past, promote the present, and prepare for the future. That's what we're about, advocating for the creation of the right environment in which the game can thrive."

No easy task given the pressures the game is under today, especially, Hatchell notes, with mothers faced with the ultimate decision of whether or not to let their sons embrace football.

"The good stuff about the game doesn't get a lot of traction," he laments. "But the bad stuff has a megaphone, like the naysayers who came up with the catchphrase, 'Friends don't let friends play football.' The forces lined up against football are strategic and committed, and we have to be very two-fisted, very aggressive, in countering their arguments. What we are about is promoting the lifelong experience football offers, along with the value of a college education many players get as a result of playing the game."

Founded in 1947 with early leadership from General Douglas MacArthur, legendary Army coach Earl "Red" Blaik, and immortal journalist Grantland Rice, the National Football Foundation remains a nonprofit educational organization that runs programs designed to use the power of amateur football in developing scholarship, citizenship, and athletic achievement in young people. With 121 chapters and 12,000 members nationwide, NFF programs include the College Football Hall of Fame in Atlanta, the NFF Scholar-Athlete Awards presented by Fidelity Investments, the NFF Hampshire Honor Society (endowed by former NFF chairman Jon Hanson to honor players from all divisions who distinguish themselves academically), and the NFF National Scholar-Athlete Alumni Association which provides more than 1.3 million dollars in scholarships for college and high school scholar-athletes. The NFF presents the MacArthur Bowl (awarded to the national champion in the college ranks) and the William V. Campbell Trophy (awarded to the top college scholar-athlete), endowed by HealthSouth. The NFF also releases the Bowl Championship Series (BCS) Standings leading up to the semifinal and final game of the college football season.

Steve came to the National Football Foundation as my successor in 2014, after serving six years as the commissioner of the Professional Rodeo Cowboys Association. Prior to that, he served as the first commissioner of the Big 12 Conference, which he actually helped to establish in 1995. He also headed the Orange Bowl for six years. So he's hardly a stranger to running complex athletic organizations and is well suited for piloting the NFF through today's increasingly challenging waters.

Hatchell's and the NFF's strategy for changing the narrative on football today centers to a great extent on showcasing examples of what's best about the character of the game through many of those who've played it. Further, the foundation coordinates nationwide programs designed to use the power of amateur football in developing scholarship, citizenship, and athletic achievement in young people.

"Our goal," Steve says, "our mission, is to provide a counterargument to all the negative that's out there regarding injuries. We concede that football is a tough sport. Playing the game on the field teaches you about adversity, learning to pick yourself up after you've been knocked down. We stress that especially with the moms. We sit down with them and address their concerns. We stress the medical procedures and precautions undertaken at practices and during games. We review the increasing safety of helmets, heat protocol, concussion protocol."

Hatchell stresses that the foundation has undertaken a multifaceted approach to promoting the good in the game and its future with a major yearly outreach to coaches to provide guidance aimed at focusing on the positive and countering the negative. Among other strategies under his tenure, that outreach takes the form of a document circulated to thousands of coaches nationwide:

SUGGESTED GUIDELINES FOR HIGH SCHOOL FOOTBALL COACHES FOR PRESEASON PARENTS' MEETING

PROMOTE YOUR FOOTBALL PROGRAM WITH SAFETY AS THE PRIORITY

- Emphasize that safety is first and foremost in your program. Their son's health is a top priority.

- Discuss the training your coaches receive (ASEP, head coaches certification, Keep the Head Out of Football, etc.).

- Review your preseason and in-season practice policy (amount of contact, full pads, etc.).

- Discuss your heat policy relative to all activities.

- Thoroughly review your Concussion Management Policy and protocols, e.g., removed from practice or game, no participation until cleared by Concussion Oversight Team, etc.

- If applicable, discuss your baseline concussion testing program.

- Discuss your helmet and equipment safety standards and procedures (i.e., quality helmets that are certified every year and fitted by a trained professional).

- Discuss the critical importance of a quality mouthpiece (invest in a mouthpiece for better protection).

- Inform them of the safety personnel available at practices and games (physicians, trainers, ambulances, etc.).

- Discuss and review your emergency management plans and protocol concerning major injuries, lightning, etc.

- Emphasize the benefits of playing football (discipline, teamwork, increased focus on academics, etc.).

"You need to be able to get a group of guys to play together," Stanford head coach David Shaw told the AFCA Weekly in July of 2017. "The only way that any of those things happen is if those players trust you, trust what you're saying, and believe what you are trying to relate to them. That's why it's so important to be yourself as a coach, instead of trying to emulate someone else. If, as a coach, you are a yeller and a screamer, then that is who you are and that is how you should coach. If you speak softly, then you must coach that way. This is a violent, fast-moving sport that entails so much and is so demanding of players. They need a coach that is on their side and giving them the information to be successful. I am going to communicate to a guy and tell him what he needs to do and how he needs to do it for his benefit. And when you can be honest and earnest with that, and your players feel that this guy is trying to help me be a better player, that's when you get the best results."

* * *

Frank Vuono offers a different perspective, one born of being one of the foremost sports marketing experts in the country. Having consulted for more than half of the teams in the NFL, Vuono has negotiated record-breaking partnerships in naming rights, sponsorship, licensing, merchandising, and ticket and suite sales. Intimately acquainted with the game from a business standpoint, he wonders if the NFL has followed the right path in addressing the CTE crisis.

"I wish they'd spend more money, and put more emphasis, on player safety by researching better equipment," says the 1978 graduate of Princeton, where he played for me during my time there as head coach. "They've done great outreach to youth programs to emphasize player safety but haven't taken the more important step of putting more resources into R & D. Look, concussions aren't new; we just had other terms to describe them. You got 'dinged,' got 'your bell rung,' and we've come a long way from those days at all levels, including the NFL. You look at how the game has evolved over the years, and yet there haven't been a lot of advances at all, nothing dramatically different, when it comes to equipment. And I have to figure that there must be a way to design equipment, especially, that's just as light but more protective."

Frank also stresses the all-encompassing desire on the part of the NFL to protect its brand, an effort that seldom extends down to the level where the initial decision by a boy and his family to start playing the game is made.

"If I'm a single mom, and I've got a boy entering his teens and looking at football, where do I go to get information that's both accurate and a counter to the narrative that's dominant out there? Where do I go to learn where my son should play and for whom? What kind of shoes should he wear, what kind of helmet? Hey, I've got three daughters who've played soccer, basketball, and field hockey. And I've seen more injuries in any of those sports than I see with boys the same age playing football. But there aren't a lot of people talking about that. There's no narrative to that effect."

Tom Olivadotti, who's spent a career in football coaching at every level, including a stint at the University of Miami where he won a national title in 1983 as defensive coordinator, offers a semblance of that narrative.

"I'm concerned that overreaction will make it impossible for kids to want to play the game. Beyond that, with strict concussion protocols likely to cost at least a couple weeks of playing time, marginal players fighting for their jobs might do everything they can to avoid being diagnosed so they get to stay on the field. They'll take the risk and hide it, won't tell anybody including their teammates because they're afraid of losing their spot."

Olivadotti, author of several books on coaching himself as well as several instructional videos, points to a study conducted by *Coach* magazine ranking sports most likely to result in paralysis, something else football knows all too well from the perceived number of players ambulanced from the field on spinal boards. The study placed swimming and diving in the top slot, followed by gymnastics and, only then, by football.

"And there's something else," says my former assistant coach at Princeton, who began his collegiate career with me in 1976. "In many ways, it's more dangerous not to play a sport as inclusive as football. Because that boy who's not playing football is going to find something else to fill that gap, which is likely to be unsupervised, opening him up to greater risk than anything he'd face on the football field. Beyond that, this country is confronting a health crisis due to the epidemic of obesity that stems from a sedentary lifestyle that increasingly begins in childhood. So I ask you, what's more dangerous in the long term—playing football or video games?"

* * *

One coach who would have no trouble answering that question is Hall of Famer Vince Dooley, who spent 25 years as coach of the Georgia Bulldogs, highlighted by a national championship in 1980, six SEC titles, and twenty bowl games. He was named SEC Coach of the Year five times and has won the Walter Camp Coach of the Year as well as Bobby Dodd Coach of the Year honors.

"I think there is a crisis," he reflects, "but it's not the first time football has faced one. And I see this crisis as being addressed at all levels from the professional all the way down to Pop Warner, through colleges and high schools. Everybody's taking things seriously. They're coming forth with studies, looking at rules changes and techniques to address the problem. I think by going through all this the game is going to be even better."

Indeed, in many ways, Vince sees football in better shape than ever.

"Excitement has grown tremendously and with that the popularity of the game. Sure, some things have changed since I stepped away from coaching. But it's still a sport that has provided countless young people with an education and a profession. And the nature of what it means to be a coach hasn't changed much either. There's no one other than my parents who had more of an impact on me than my high school coach. When I think about it, that reminds me of all the young people, particularly at the high school level, who've had their lives positively influenced by football. And I am eternally grateful for the impact football has had on my life."

He began his storied career at Georgia so doubtful that he'd be able to keep his job that he famously told his wife Barbara not to bother unpacking the boxes. All you need to know about how things turned out is the title of Vince's book, *Dooley: My 40 Years at Georgia*. And what in those years, that began when he was only 31, did he enjoy the most?

"Well, all of the wins and the accolades, sure. But I'd say, most of all, being part of a team. Those memories and those great feelings never cease in their importance. And what becomes even more important is your relationship with your players as you watch them go on into their lives and do well and draw from their experience of playing the game and being part of a team. How they've applied all that into whatever profession they've gone into."

Vince speaks fondly of the frequent reunions held by his 1980 championship team, most recently early in the 2017 college season when a whole bunch of those players gathered to watch Georgia trounce Notre Dame in a rematch of their own title game from 37 years before. But he also gushes praise on a group of players you might not expect.

"The walk-ons. People don't realize four of our starters on that championship team were walk-ons. And one was a fella who came all the way from France, where he'd played rugby. His name was Richard Tardits, and he didn't even know how to put on a uniform. But he had the courage to come over here, to the University of Georgia, because he wanted to play football. And not only did he play, he became our all-time sack leader for a time. He went on to play in the pros for five years, and this was somebody who'd never played football for even a minute until he became a Bulldog."

Did you know the Georgia mascot wasn't always a bulldog? It was originally, briefly, a goat back in the very early days of college football when the University of Georgia was abuzz about their first-ever game against Auburn.

"They painted that goat in the school colors," Vince relates. "But after the team lost its first two games, at the first tailgate in Athens the boosters cooked the goat and ate him. That's how Georgia became the Bulldogs."

* * *

To make sure more young men get a chance to become Bulldogs, Steve Hatchell is committed to dispelling the myths that have roiled the sport.

"I've heard people equate letting kids play football with child abuse. That may sound crazy, but it's out there and there's an audience for that kind of talk. The counter-narrative has to come from the people speaking up whose football experiences contributed to all the success they've achieved. People like Jamie Foxx and LL Cool J, who both played high school football, as well as the actor Mark Harmon [of *NCIS* fame and an NFF scholar-athlete in 1973], recruited by Barry Switzer to be a wishbone quarterback and always talks about how important the game was to him. The list goes on and on."

Hatchell is quick to point out that the list of positive role models now playing the role of ambassadors for the game doesn't stop there. Toward that end he has spearheaded the first of its kind Football Matters campaign, for which the likes of Jeff Immelt have recorded commercial videos in support of the game. There's also Jim Hansen, a Rhodes Scholar from the University of Colorado who now runs a big operation for the Department of the Navy dealing with weather systems across the country. And NFL Hall of Famer and Super Bowl–winning linebacker Derrick Brooks, a 1994 National Football Foundation scholar-athlete whose name is synonymous with community service in the Tampa area through initiatives like Brooks' Bunch.

The one thing these former players and many more like them have in common is that they've all been inducted into the College Football Hall of Fame during Hatchell's tenure, which has been highlighted by his taking an already strong organization to the next level beginning in 2005.

"We moved our offices to Texas, the center of football, and we moved the College Football Hall of Fame to Atlanta, where it's drawn far more traffic. But what the National Football Foundation also needed to do," Hatchell explains, "was identify more great ambassadors for the game who had the kind of cachet that would make people listen to them, in contrast to all the negative stuff that's out there."

Toward that end, he's expanded the roles of NFL Hall of Fame members such as Archie Manning and Ronnie Lott, in addition to the likes of George Pyne, the former president of IMG Sports and Entertainment as well as NASCAR, toward promoting the good in the game.

"It's an easy task to take on," Pyne reflects, "because it's a cause I wholeheartedly believe in and want to do everything I can to contribute to. When you're playing football, you rally to the ball. Now, as a former player, myself and plenty of others are rallying in support of the game itself."

In 2013, Pyne was selected as one of the NCAA Silver Anniversary Award winners, recognizing distinguished individuals on the 25th anniversary of the conclusion of their college athletics careers. He was also the first inductee into the newly formed National Football Foundation's Leadership Hall of Fame a year later. Pyne, a two-year starter at offensive tackle and captain for Brown University's 1988 football team, was named to the All-Ivy League team in 1987 and the All-New England team in 1988.

"Football played an integral role in my life, and it changed my life forever," Pyne said in 2013. "My coaches and teammates taught me integrity, perseverance, dedication, and hard work. While these are the values I learned on the field, these are the necessary characteristics for finding success in business, school, and life."

"George has a true passion for everything that our organization represents, and as a former Ivy League star, he is a great example of our efforts to promote the scholar-athlete ideal," Hatchell noted in introducing him. "He is a truly gifted individual and the perfect inaugural inductee for the NFF Leadership Hall of Fame."

"I played the game, my brother played the game, and both my sons play the game," Pyne says. "So now I've gotten to see the game through their eyes as well and I'm seeing the same thing, the same benefits and positive experiences, that I saw through my own. And, in that respect, what amazes me the most about football is how the strategy of the game changes, the pace of the game changes, the Xs and Os of the game changes, but the experience of football never changes. What my sons are getting from the game is the same thing I got from it."

Steve Hatchell is effusive in his praise of Pyne and others who've joined together to fight the good fight in support of the game they love in the hope that young people will continue to have the opportunity to love it as well.

"What we're doing with Football Matters and beyond is like running a political campaign through social media, aimed at those we need to convince, to persuade. Moms want to talk to moms, and we want to give them something positive to talk about from the uplifting narratives of those who played the game."

CONCLUSION

"EACH OF YOU CAN BE A HERO..."

In July of 2017, the *New York Times* reported that "a neuropathologist has examined the brains of 111 NFL players—and 110 were found to have CTE, the degenerative disease linked to repeated blows to the head."

In the fall of 2016, ESPN reported that "the NCAA is now facing 43 class-action lawsuits related to the handling of concussions in Division I football programs after 18 more were filed this week."

In January of 2018, another *New York Times* article ran under the headline "New York Legislator Renews Effort to Ban Tackle Football in Youth Leagues," reporting that "[Michael] Benedetto's bill would ban the sport entirely for preteens, which would effectively shut down Pop Warner and other youth organizations in New York state. Lawmakers in other states, he said, are looking to introduce similar legislation."

Five years before that, the ESPN blog *Grantland* published an article entitled "What Would the End of Football Look Like?" based solely on CTE and the concussion crisis.

Football, you might say, is under siege, in a war of sorts. But a key point, as I've indicated, is that the war is not limited only to football, but to youth contact (or "collision") sports in general. That same January 2018 *New York Times* article notes that "in 2015 the United States Soccer Federation banned players age 10 and younger from heading the ball, and will reduce headers in practice for those from the ages of 11 to 13...National organizations governing youth hockey and lacrosse have also made rule changes to minimize potential head trauma."

Make no mistake about it, though: football finds itself under the most scrutiny and greatest threat of any sport. And what I've done in this book is strive to counter that attack by presenting the game through the experiences of some of those who played it and whose characters define the very essence of the game. What it was, what it is, and what it will be. The players and coaches you've met in these pages personify the values and benefits of the game. We've seen what football has done for them and what they've done for the game in return. We introduced you to them as football players, but they are first and foremost exceptional human beings who owe some portion of their success and character to football. Reading these pages is not intended to convince anyone they should play the game, only that they be given the opportunity to follow in the footsteps of the outstanding human beings you've met in these pages. They exemplify every definition of success, both on the field and off it.

Perhaps no one has ever better represented that, and the totality of coaching a student-athlete, than Yale's Hall of Fame coach, the late Carm Cozza, winner of 179 games during a 20-year career that saw him win ten Ivy League titles. Included among the most well-known names he coached are Dick Jauron, Brian Dowling, Doctor Rich Diana, Gary Fencik, Jack Ford, Calvin Hill, Kevin Czinger, John Spagnola, John Pagliaro, and Stone Phillips, along with seven National Football Foundation Scholar-Athletes.

"While academics was king," recalls Rich Diana, "Coach refused to let football take a back seat. And so he showed us how to be efficient, a quality which would serve me well throughout my professional life as a surgeon. He taught us how to juggle many things at one time and how to do it with poise and composure."

"Carm is a person who is, above all, a molder of character, a teacher, a person who deeply believes in what he does," the school's president Richard Levin said upon Cozza's 1996 retirement. "Carm cares deeply about his players—not just how they develop as athletes, but how they develop as human beings."

A human being like Alex Kroll, who followed up a stellar career at Rutgers and in the NFL by running Young & Rubicam, one of the nation's largest advertising firms.

"We're bonded, by a common experience so rich, it has helped us win outside the yard stripes," Alex said upon being inducted into the College Football Hall of Fame in 1997. "Think of it. When we were just kids, pubescent punks, the game taught us how to manage such trivia as heat, cold, rain, and mud—pressure, pain, strain, and even fame, all such impediments on the way to the great goal of winning—for the team.

"But the chance to be a football hero doesn't end when you strip off the pads for the last time. It doesn't matter whether you ever suited up. Each of you can be a hero now to a kid, or kids, who are out in the cold tonight, and might spend the rest of their lives there."

Thanks to men like Carm Cozza and Alex Kroll, who continue to populate the game in great numbers, the prospects for football aren't entirely gloomy. Far from it. Consider this statistic courtesy of Statistic Brain: over 36 million kids played organized sports in 2013–2014. Of that 36 million, 1.2 million played high school football, about the same number as soccer, basketball, and baseball combined. That may sound crazy, given the perceived dwindling of football's popularity. But overall the numbers are down, and the pressure from some quarters is increasing.

That said, the most ardent supporters and organizers of the game continue to expand their proactive measures aimed at securing football's safety and, thus, its future. For a prime example of this trend, look no further than football-mad Texas where, according to a March 28, 2018 article in Dallas-Fort Worth's *Star-Telegram*, "The University Interscholastic League's Legislative Council passed a rule in October that will require every Texas high school and junior high school football coach to become certified in teaching tackling as a part of the official UIL Coaches Certification Program."

"The UIL Legislative Council was overwhelmingly in favor of supporting this measure," said Dr. Charles Breithaupt, Executive Director, in a press release. "We view the addition of a mandatory tackling certification for football coaches as a positive educational extension that will ultimately improve the game and the welfare of our students."

"Texas," the article goes on to say, "is the first state to implement a mandatory statewide tackling certification program for all football coaches" to be overseen by "Atavus Sports, a Seattle-based organization that focuses on tackling techniques and data analytics."

Atavus is headed by Rex Norris, a noted coach in his own right, along with directors D. W. Rutledge and Joe Martin, all of whom are determined to see football not only survive, but thrive.

"If we lose football, we lose a lot in America," David Baker, the president of the Pro Football Hall of Fame, told a gathering at an Orlando, Florida conference, as reported by the *New York Times* on January 31, 2018. "I don't know if America can survive. That's why you're so important to what we're doing. That's why America needs to huddle up."

The way Deshaun Watson, the All-American quarterback, did when he led Clemson to a national title in 2016 and was drafted in the first round. He'd been the first person in his family to attend college and graduated with a degree in communications. The first thing he did with his money when he got out of school was buy his mother a car, because she'd never had one. And about that degree in communications he was so proud of?

"No one can ever take that away from me," he said with a smile.

Or All-American Jonathan Allen, who returned to Alabama and Nick Saban for his senior year because of, in Saban's words, "the importance of developing a career off the field."

"I've taken econ tests for years, sometimes brutal," Allen reflects, "but I'm leaving with a degree in financial planning that will empower me to take control of my future."

Following the senior season for which he returned, Allen was drafted in the first round by the Washington Redskins, meaning he'll likely have to put off his second career a bit longer.

Players like Jonathan Allen have made it easy for me to make the case here for the future of football, its contributions to our society, and how diminished that society would be without it. To illustrate that point, I've introduced you to plenty of greats whose stories are encompassed in these pages. They never lost their passion for the game that helped make them who they are, and now they join me in the fervent hope that countless more kids will be able to follow the same path they took to success on the field and off.

But that's the past. This book is also about the future, about young men continuing to have the opportunity to play a game that has enriched so many lives over multiple generations. Hopefully those young men will have their own stories to tell of their own experiences, how the game made a huge impact on their lives too, even as it continues to leave its indelible mark on the fabric of American life.

This isn't the end of football, in my mind, it's just the beginning. A metaphorical first down, with forever to go!

AFTERWORD

BY BOBBY BOWDEN

Even after a coaching career that spanned more than half a century, people ask me all the time why I became so interested in football. Football has always been a big part of my life. Almost from the day I was born, playing and coaching football were all I ever wanted to do. It just got into my blood.

Up until I was five, my family and I lived in the Woodlawn section of Birmingham, Alabama. Now, you have to understand: if you grew up in Alabama, you were a football fan. That's just the way it is in Alabama. In my case, the backyard of my family's home was adjacent to the east end zone of Woodlawn High School football field. At the time, Woodlawn was a perennial state champion. They were *the* football team to beat in the city of Birmingham in the early 1940s. As a kid I could step into our backyard and hear through the tall bushes growing across our fence the school band marching or the players practicing nearly every day. We had a garage that backed up to that fence, and I can remember my daddy getting a ladder so we could climb up on the roof of the garage and watch them practice. We would sit up there for hours every day. My father loved watching football, and I always loved watching it with him.

After I turned five, we moved three miles away, to a part of town called East Lake, into a small white-frame house that was half a block away from Berry Field, which was Howard College's football field. It was upon a hill, and I could see the Howard team practicing from my front lawn. During elementary school, I had to walk up that hill by the football field and the gymnasium, across campus, then two more blocks to get to school. I literally grew up on the Howard College campus.

Every autumn, I'd hear the sounds of boys playing football: kicking, tackling, grunting, things like that. Berry Field became my playground. I'd come home from school, load my pockets with unshelled peanuts and an apple, go meet my buddies, and we would play around with the tackling dummies or climb the fence. On Sundays, when Howard College wasn't practicing, the neighborhood kids would all go up there and play football. When I was ten, my dad brought me my first football uniform. It was practically cardboard with thin shoulder pads and a little helmet. But the shirt had "Howard College Bulldogs" across the chest, so it was a very big deal to me.

My father, Bob Bowden, was born in Clayton, Alabama. His father died when my daddy was very young. My father had thirteen brothers and sisters, but not all of them survived. Back in those days, a lot of babies died at birth. After my grandfather died, my daddy had to help his mother support their family. When my father was only seven years old, he sold newspapers at the street corner outside Nick's Drug Store in Woodlawn. He worked the rest of his life, and I like to think I learned a strong work ethic and determination from him. My father eventually became a teller at the First National Bank in Birmingham, and he worked there for seventeen years. During the Great Depression, he managed to keep his job while others lost theirs. He eventually was promoted and handled loans for a homebuilder named W.E. Bishop. My father and Mr. Bishop became very close and decided to go into business together. They bought an office building in Woodlawn, named their company "Bowden and Bishop," and did quite well. I worked every summer for Mr. Bishop and did all the things nobody else wanted to do—carrying lumber, bricks, cement, even digging foundations. Looking back, that was some of the hardest work of my life.

My mother, Sunset Cleckler Bowden, was born and raised in Anniston, Alabama. She was very small when she was born, probably premature. When she was a baby, they said you could sit her in a coffeepot. She grew to be only five feet tall. My mother was a very sweet lady, and, of course, she loved her boy. You know how mothers are. In January 1943, I was thirteen years old and was walking home after playing basketball at the local YMCA. It was winter and my knees were aching terribly the entire way. When I got home, I took off my shoes, and my feet were swollen. My mother was terrified when she saw them, and she immediately called our family doctor. Back in those days, doctors still made house calls. The doctor rushed to our house to see me. He diagnosed me with rheumatic fever, which was considered a very serious illness at the time. It killed people. Later we were told that I had an enlarged heart. I remember my mother crying when the doctor left our house.

The doctors told my mother to put me in bed and told me not to get up for anything. They wouldn't even let me go to the restroom. My mother had to help me use a bedpan. I hated it. When the doctor came back to see me a second time, a few weeks later, I started getting out of bed, and he yelled at me, "No, don't get up! Don't get up! Lay back down!" It made me think I was dying. But that is how scared they were about rheumatic fever back then. My parents must have thought it was pretty serious too, because over at Ruhama Baptist Church, every Sunday, the minister would say, "Pray for little Bobby Bowden."

Every Friday night during the fall of 1943, while I was still confined to my bed, I would listen to Woodlawn High School football games on the radio. Woodlawn won the Alabama state championship that season. Harry Gilmer, who grew up in my neighborhood, was the star tailback, and he led Woodlawn High to an undefeated record that season. I grew up idolizing Harry Gilmer. He went on to become an All-American at the University of Alabama, leading the Crimson Tide to a 1946 Rose Bowl win in Pasadena, California. He was one of the first players to throw a jump pass, and

I would go out in the backyard and run, jump, and throw a pass just like Harry Gilmer did. My father bought me an electric football game while I was sick. It had the players who would slide across the field while the game board vibrated. My friends and I would pretend we were Doc Blanchard and Glenn Davis, who were "Mr. Inside" and "Mr. Outside," respectively, the great backs at the U.S. Military Academy.

While I was sick, I missed playing football more than anything else. The doctors told me I would not be active anymore and that I'd be in bed for the rest of my life. My legs ached so badly at times that I would cry myself to sleep some nights. After I had been sick for about six months, I remember my mother walking through the doorway to leave my bedroom. Before she left, she turned to me and asked, "Bobby, do you believe in prayer?"

I told her, "Of course, I do, Mother."

"Well, why don't you ask Him to heal you? He will," she said.

My mother would hold me in her arms, praying to God to heal me. I prayed all the time, too. It was kind of a pledge. I told Him, "If you heal me, I will serve You. If you let me play football again, I will try to serve You through sports."

And He did heal me.

Finally, after nearly a year in bed, I got clearance from the doctors to go back to school. But my orders were clear: no lifting weights, no running, no exercise of any kind, and absolutely no football. They told me I could go to school and come home and that was it. I was devastated. In 1944, I finally finished elementary school. I was always older than most of my classmates and seemed even older after I fell behind in school because of my illness. I enrolled in Woodlawn High School in 1944. The doctors still would not let me exercise or play sports, so I joined the marching band. We would march at the football games and in parades. I played first trombone in the high school orchestra and even performed a solo at the University of Alabama summer band camp. For a while I also played in a jazz group called the Lee Jordan Band. I really loved music, but I still couldn't run or play sports, and I missed it dearly.

My mother knew how much I wanted to play football, so before my junior year she insisted on taking me to another specialist for a second opinion. It was there that I finally got the news I'd been praying for: the doctors pronounced me fit to play football again. I remember feeling like a heavy burden had just been lifted from me. I remember crying in that doctor's office, and my mother was crying, too. After waiting so long, I was finally getting the chance to do what I loved most. I went out for spring practice that year and was doing well. About two weeks before the first game in the fall of 1946, I went out for a pass in practice, fell down, and landed on my hand. When I got up, my thumb was bent backward. Kenny Morgan, my coach, looked at my thumb and started twisting it back into place, thinking it was only dislocated. He taped up my thumb and sent me back out to practice. My thumb was actually broken. It swelled up and hurt like mad, but I toughed it out. A few days later, I went to see the University of Alabama football team's doctor, who lived in Birmingham. He put my hand in a cast and told me my football season was over. After waiting so long to play again, I never even got into a game that first season at Wood-lawn High. I was heartbroken again.

That year, I weighed only about 130 pounds—not too small for running backs at the time, most of the big backs weighed about 150 to 155 pounds. You just didn't have really big players back then. You might have one player who weighed more than 200 pounds, and if you weighed 215 pounds, they'd say you were too fat to play. My coach called me to his office one day after I broke my thumb.

"Bobby, would you be interested in dropping out of school?" he asked me. "If you drop out for one semester, I think I can get you another year of eligibility. You can get bigger and might be able to get a scholarship to college."

I talked to my parents about it, and we decided that was what we would do. For the next few months, I worked around the house and didn't do much of anything else. But I would still go up to the high school and play football on the weekends with my friends. The next fall, I went back out for football again, this time weighing about 140 pounds. I was a backup halfback and played in some of the games. In my senior year, the coaches moved me to right halfback, and I was senior co-captain of the team, which was a big honor to me. During both of my football seasons at Woodlawn High School, we played eleven of our games at Legion Field in Birmingham. At times there were 18,000 fans in attendance. The high school games were always big in Birmingham because there were only five high school teams in the city. Nearly every season, Woodlawn High

School and Ramsay High School would rank number one and number two in the city, but my team never won a city championship.

Despite everything, I would not have traded my childhood for anything. I believe my illness as a child brought me closer to my family and to God. I believe it made me a better person, a better father, and a better coach. Looking back now, it's easy to see the lesson I learned at such a young age: if something bad has happened to you and you have faith, then something good is bound to happen. I've always believed that. I came to believe that faith, prayer, and a willingness to serve God will get you through everything.

Years and years later, my coaching career ended after Florida State defeated West Virginia, 33–21, in the Gator Bowl in Jacksonville, Florida on New Year's Day 2010. Winning the game was extra special because my boys came from behind to do it and I really enjoyed ending my career on a winning note. I told reporters after the game that I had prepared myself for retirement.

"I ain't got to set no alarm no more, I'll get up when I'm darn good and ready, then like I say, go out and look for a job," I told them.

After my postgame news conference, my wife Ann put her arms around me, smiled at me, and said, "Time to go home, baby."

It was time to go home, but my life's work is not finished. I continue to speak at churches and civic organizations around the country. I remain heavily involved in the Fellowship of Christian Athletes, trying to spread God's word to as many young people as possible. Even though I retired from coaching, I still believe that is my calling.

Because I'm eighty years old, I was more prepared for retirement. If I were fifty, it would have been terribly disappointing because I would have felt like most of my life was still in front of me. But now I can sit back and actually watch games on TV and enjoy them. I can spend more time with my family. Ann and I can go to the beach and take more trips together. We're planning our first trip to the Holy Land, which is something we've always wanted to do.

In a lot of ways, I'll always be a football coach. Shortly after I retired, Ann and I were visiting Rio de Janeiro, Brazil, where I spoke to a group of businessmen. While we were there, we visited the Christ the Redeemer statue, which overlooks the city at the top of Corcovado Mountain. While

Ann and I were preparing to make the long walk up the mountain, I overheard a group of people talking, and heard someone say "Bobby Bowden."

"Are you talking about me?" I asked them.

Sure enough, they were Florida State football fans.

"See you at the top," I told them.

I knew then that God still had a plan for me. It is up to me to follow His plan and stay the course.

Reprinted with permission from *Called to Coach: Reflections on Life, Faith, and Football* by Bobby Bowden with Mark Schlabach, Howard Books, 2010.

ACKNOWLEDGMENTS

In writing this book, I have benefitted from many sources from players to coaches to friends and, in particular, my daughter Jeanne Casciola, who first approached Jon Land about my stories which stirred his interest and began our dialogue. In that regard, a special "thank you" to Jon for his vision, direction, and masterful touch with the written word.

Special recognition goes to two great friends: Gary Golden, a high school teammate and coaching associate, and Tom Morris, my college roommate, teammate, and lifelong friend.

Through it all, how fortunate I was to share the love and support of my wife Janet and our four children, Jeanne, Don, Julie, and Lynn who have heard so many of these stories over the years. Oh, how patient they all have been!

In addition to the coaching associates I mentioned at Connecticut, a special thanks to the wonderful staffs at Princeton and Dartmouth for their support and loyalty.

- *Princeton: Ron Blackledge, John Brunner, Eddie Donovan, Gary Fallon, Warren Harris, Jake McCandless, "Pep" McCarthy, Tom Olivadotti, Walt Pierce, John Petercuskie, Bob Pflug, Len Rivers, Ferris Thomsen, Bill Whitton, Al Wilson and Artie Williams*
- *Dartmouth: Jake Crouthamel, John Anderson, Quintin Currie, John Curtis, George Darlington, Earl Hamilton, Charlie Harding.*

And, finally, a special thought goes out to three very special young men who played for me at Princeton, all quarterbacks, who left us too early: Ron Beible '76, Jack Flannery '77, and Kirby Lockhart '78.

PHOTO CREDITS

My Life in the Game: Property of subject, reproduced with permission.

Tom Cahill: Reproduced with permission of West Point Athletics

Ŝtas Maliszewski: Property of subject, reproduced with permission.

Cosmo Iacavazzi: Property of subject, reproduced with permission.

The Gogolaks: Reproduced with permission of the National Football Foundation

Grant Teaff: Reproduced with permission of the National Football Foundation

Jack Lengyel: Reproduced with permission of the National Football Foundation

Frank Cignetti: Reproduced with permission of the National Football Foundation

Bob Hall: Reproduced with permission of the Office of Sports Information, Brown University

Paul Savidge: Reproduced with permission of Princeton University Department of Athletics

Murry Bowden: Reproduced with permission of Dartmouth Sports Information

Steve Jordan: Property of subject, reproduced with permission.

Reggie Williams: Reproduced with permission of Dartmouth Sports Information

Mark Whipple: Reproduced with permission of Jon Crispin, UMass Athletics

Don McPherson: Reproduced with permission of the National Football Foundation

Bob Ehrlich: Property of subject, reproduced with permission.

Chad Hennings: Property of subject, reproduced with permission.

Tom Catena: Property of subject, reproduced with permission.

Gus White: Reproduced with permission of the Office of Sports Information, Brown University

Danny Wuerffel: Reproduced with permission of the National Football Foundation

Buff Donelli: Reproduced with permission of Columbia Athletics

Bill Campbell: Reproduced with permission of Columbia Athletics

Steve Hatchell and the National Football Foundation: Reproduced with permission of the National Football Foundation

ABOUT THE AUTHORS

Bob Casciola is the former president of the National Football Foundation and College Hall of Fame, a 14-year tenure in which he oversaw the Play It Smart program and the implementation of the NFL/NFF Coaching Academy, which annually educates more than 10,000 youth coaches. A member of that Hall of Fame himself, Bob had previously served as head coach both of Princeton University and the University of Connecticut, and served for three years as assistant coach to Hall of Fame head coach Bob Blackman at Dartmouth, in addition to a stint broadcasting college football games. In 2004, the NFF honored Bob with its Distinguished American Award, previously given to Vince Lombardi and Pete Rozelle. In presenting the award, noted sports artist Ted Watts looked at Bob and said, "I think your most admirable trait is to have faith and vision beyond the chalk marks of a football sideline." Bob Casciola currently lives in Scottsdale, Arizona.

Jon Land is the *USA Today* bestselling author of 43 books, including eight titles in the critically acclaimed Caitlin Strong series: *Strong Enough to Die, Strong Justice, Strong at the Break, Strong Vengeance, Strong Rain Falling* (winner of the 2014 International Book Award and 2013 USA Best Book Award for Mystery-Suspense), *Strong Darkness* (winner of the 2014 USA Books Best Book Award and the 2015 International Book Award for Thriller, and *Strong Light of Day* which won the 2016 International Book Award for Best Thriller-Adventure, the 2015 Books and Author Award for Best Mystery Thriller, and the 2016 Beverly Hills Book Award for Best Mystery. *Strong Cold Dead* became the fourth title in the series in a row to win the International Book Award in 2017 and about which *Booklist* said, "Thrillers don't get any better than this," in a starred review. It was followed by *Strong to the Bone,* winner of the 2017 American Book Fest Best Book Award for Mystery Suspense ahead of its December '17 publication Land has also teamed with multiple *New York Times* bestselling author Heather Graham on a new sci-fi series, the first of which, *The Rising,* was published by Forge in January of 2017. Jon's award-wining nonfiction titles include *Betrayal* (2011), winner of the 2011 International Book Award in True Crime and *Takedown* (2016) which won both 2016's USA Best Books Award and the International Book Award in True Crime. His latest nonfiction title, *No Surrender*, was published by Post Hill Press on July 4. And Jon has recently taken over the *Murder, She Wrote* book series based on the fabulously successful television show; his first effort writing as "Jessica Fletcher," *A Date With Murder*, was published in May of 2018. He is a 1979 graduate of Brown University, lives in Providence, Rhode Island and can be reached at jonlandbooks.com or on Twitter @jondland.